THE # 12

BOTTLE BAR

A DOZEN BOTTLES.
HUNDREDS OF COCKTAILS.
A NEW WAY TO DRINK.

David Solmonson & Lesley Jacobs Solmonson

WORKMAN PUBLISHING | NEW YORK

DEDICATION

To Raleigh, the greatest cocktail we've ever made.

COPYRIGHT © 2014 BY DAVID SOLMONSON & LESLEY JACOBS SOLMONSON

Library of Congress Cataloging-in-Publication Data is available.

ISBN 978-0-7611-7494-3

DESIGN BY JEAN-MARC TROADEC
PHOTOGRAPHY BY MELISSA LUCIER
DRINK STYLING BY CORY FITZSIMMONS
DIGITAL ILLUSTRATION BY JOHN PASSINEAU

Additional images: p. 14 (measuring cup), fotolia: Pavlo Sachek; p. 14 (measuring spoons), snyfer; pp. 11–12, karandaev; pp. 315–316, kornienko; pp. 325–326, Tim UR.

Workman books are available at special discounts when purchased in bulk for premiums and sales promotions as well as for fund-raising or educational use. Special editions or book excerpts can also be created to specification. For details, contact the Special Sales Director at the address below, or send an email to specialmarkets@workman.com.

WORKMAN PUBLISHING COMPANY, INC.
225 VARICK STREET
NEW YORK, NY 10014-4381
WORKMAN.COM

WORKMAN is a registered trademark of Workman Publishing Co., Inc.

Printed in the United States of America

First printing July 2014

10 9 8 7 6 5 4 3 2 1

Contents

INTRODUCTION

With the classic cocktail renaissance upon us, it has never been easier to enjoy a well-crafted drink. Bars across the country—and the world—are embracing old-school practices. Recipes from master mixologists appear regularly in magazines, and the new breed of cocktail book on the market extends far beyond the *Old Mr. Boston.* So why another cocktail book, particularly from two people who make no claims to being professional bartenders?

The road to the 12 Bottle Bar began, aptly enough, with a drink. A Penicillin, to be exact, which, at the time, no one knew would become a modern cocktail classic. It was the creation of bartender Sam Ross, but the man who made it for us was Chef David Myers. When we met Chef Myers more than ten years ago, we were utterly disillusioned with the lack of creativity in the Los Angeles food scene. Myers and his restaurant Sona changed all that. Not only did Sona quickly become the restaurant version of the Cheers bar for us, but it also became the platform upon which we expanded our culinary knowledge—and, as it turned out, our cocktail understanding and enthusiasm.

> The road to the 12 Bottle Bar began, aptly enough, with a drink. A Penicillin, to be exact.

One night, when the restaurant was getting quiet, Chef Myers snuck out of the kitchen, grinning like a kid at Christmas. "I've got to make something for you," he said, grabbing a shaker and assembling a bunch of ingredients—Scotch, honey syrup, ginger syrup, and a mist of a second, peaty Scotch. As he mixed up a drink, he told us he had just gotten back from a speakeasy bar in New York called Milk & Honey. That was where he met Sasha Petraske, Milk & Honey's owner, and tasted bartender Sam Ross's Penicillin, which rocked his (and soon after, our) world. Now he said, he was on a mission to kick-start the L.A. cocktail renaissance.

Sona eventually closed its doors, but David Myers's promise to get L.A. cocktail culture going held fast. His bistro, Comme Ça, was one of the first spots in the city to focus on pre-Prohibition cocktails and, to date, has launched more bartending careers than you can count. As we tasted more and more of these drinks, we quickly started to realize that there was an enormous gap—more like a chasm, really—in our spirits knowledge, and that the missing link just happened to be the golden age of cocktails. That was the era when a bartender and showman named Jerry Thomas—a name you will hear us reference time and time again—ruled the proverbial roost. That was the era when, not only because it tasted better but because you could do no differently, cocktail ingredients were made from scratch, ice was carved with a pick, and bartenders were serious career professionals.

> Suddenly, we felt a little cheated. After all, we had grown up in a world where ingredients like sour mix, "techniques" like topping off an Old Fashioned with club soda, and drinks like the Long Island Iced Tea were the standard.

Suddenly, we felt a little cheated. After all, we had grown up in a world where ingredients like sour mix, "techniques" like topping off an Old Fashioned with club soda, and drinks like the Long Island Iced Tea were the standard. We started to understand what cocktails could be and we were thirsty to learn more.

THE WHY AND WHAT OF 12 BOTTLES

Like most modern cocktail lovers, we went a little crazy in the beginning, grabbing whatever we could find to fill in the blanks—David Wondrich's *Imbibe!* was a game changer for us, as was David A. Embury's *The Fine Art of Mixing Drinks* (because Embury, like us, was not a professional but an enthusiast who saw cocktails as an art form in their own right). Much as home cooks enthusiastically try out recipes and experiment with flavors, we enjoyed tinkering in the liquor cabinet. After all, when the price of the average "classic" cocktail often starts around $15, going out becomes less about having fun and more of a financial investment. However, when we started trying to recreate the recipes we tasted in bars, read about in magazines, and found in modern mixology books, it turned out to be arduous, expensive, and sometimes downright impossible. Why was it that every new recipe demanded expensive ingredients that we didn't normally have on hand? As cocktail lovers, we admittedly have a pretty extensive liquor cabinet, but even we were amazed by how few drink recipes we could make without buying the newest bottle of Crème d'Esoterica, usually at $50 or more a pop (not exactly cost-effective when all you need is one teaspoon).

Of course, all of this just made us ask the question: How do we make the same classic cocktails at home that dot the pages of glossy magazines and are on offer in almost every forward-looking bar, as well (if not better), and without breaking the bank? And so, late into the night after long workdays, an idea was born.

We loved classic cocktails, but not the overly complicated or costly modern riffs on them. We believed that enough drinks could be made with a limited set of bottles to satisfy the majority of home bartenders. With that conceit, we launched 12bottlebar.com—built on the premise of "12 Bottles, Endless Tasty Concoctions"— in October of 2009. Through the site we were able to connect with the cocktail community at large—which was incredibly generous to two admitted neophytes like us. When the opportunity for this book came along, the relationships we had cultivated while writing on the site bloomed into friendships that produced many lovely cocktails, bits of advice, and stories for the book. For those contributions we are, corny as it sounds, eternally grateful.

> **We loved classic cocktails, but not the overly complicated or costly modern riffs on them. We believed that enough drinks could be made with a limited set of bottles to satisfy the majority of home bartenders.**

But back to the basic idea: Why 12 Bottles? When we first started studying recipes, we quickly realized two very important things. First, most contemporary cocktail books don't cater specifically to the home bartender, that is, those of us with limited space and a limited budget. Not to be defeated, we started seeking out old-school cocktail books from the formative days of drinking (the late 1800s mainly), a time when the selection of spirits was much more limited. Which brings us to point number two.

It turns out that a vast number of classic cocktails—both historic and modern—can be made with a pretty obtainable and maintainable collection of hooch. This made perfect sense to us. Every home cook keeps a well-stocked pantry from which to draw ingredients. Why shouldn't home bartenders have a similar arsenal, a sort of spirits pantry? The answer is simple—they should.

HOW THIS WORKS

The 12 Bottle Bar is the home bartender's arsenal, pantry, tool kit—the answer to entertaining confidently. With only twelve bottles (seven spirits, one liqueur, two vermouths, and two bitters) you can make literally hundreds of classic cocktail recipes—more than you ever will, or at least, ever should, drink. Add to that a little basic knowledge of fresh fruit juices and simple-to-make syrups (on pages 369 to 381; good-bye, sour mix!), and you have everything you need to produce freshly made, old-school, budget-minded cocktails at home.

> It turns out that a vast number of classic cocktails—both historic and modern—can be made with a pretty obtainable and maintainable collection of hooch.

By now you are probably asking, why twelve bottles and why these particular twelve bottles? While you can certainly go with fewer bottles if, for example, you dislike rum or whiskey or gin, these twelve bottles cover the vast spectrum of drink profiles and styles. (That said, if you want to trim the list, see page 9.) And rather than just go with a predictable list, we've thrown in genever, one of the oldest spirits known to man. So, here are our essential bottles.

BRANDY, DRY GIN, AMBER RUM, WHISKEY These are the "big four," the cornerstones of any good bar. Based on the recipes in existence, there are simply some spirits that you must have in your tool kit.

WHITE RUM, VODKA Because summer isn't the same without Daiquiris or Mojitos, we added white rum. (If you feel the same way about Margaritas, don't despair—we've got you covered on page 7.) And while vodka is the red-headed stepchild of most classically minded bars, it remains the bestselling spirit in North America. (Plus, we think it's a great base for personal expression.)

GENEVER Not quite gin, not quite whiskey, genever was one of the most important spirits of the nineteenth century, and it's making a comeback. Plus, having a bottle that you'll have to explain to your guests will make you deep and mysterious. If you fancy yourself fit company for drinking alongside William of Orange, Doc Holliday, or Papa Hemingway, genever is the drink for you.

ORANGE LIQUEUR Used in more cocktails than any other liqueur, the sweet-tart profile of a good orange liqueur can also help define more cocktails than any other ingredient.

SWEET VERMOUTH & DRY VERMOUTH You can't make the two most important cocktails around—the Manhattan and the Martini—or any proper martini-style drink for that matter, without vermouth.

AROMATIC BITTERS & ORANGE BITTERS Bitters are the spices of the cocktail world. Our choices, aromatic and orange, are like any good seasoning—you simply can't mix without them.

(A note about bitters and vermouth: While they are rarely the central element in a cocktail, a number of significant drinks are made with one or the other, or both. For this reason, we have condensed the pairings—sweet and dry vermouth, aromatic and orange bitters—into two chapters. And for the same reason, those chapters offer scant recipes specific to these ingredients; rather, the cocktails offered are the most vivid illustrations of the bottles' use.)

With these basic bottles and some well-chosen mixers at your disposal, we promise you can make hundreds of classic and classic-inspired recipes. And rather than hitting you for the tens of thousands of dollars it costs to stock a typical high-end bar, the full 12 Bottle Bar will set you back as little as $200.

Speaking of saving money, did we mention how much cheaper it is to mix individual drinks at home (see sidebar, page 6)? If you take that $15 cocktail and add in the cost of gas, parking, or a taxi, we think you'll see the wisdom of inviting a few friends over, throwing on some Kings of Convenience, and mastering the art of the cocktail party (we'll show you how). Not only is it much more economical to

The 12 Bottle Bar
DEFINED AND TALLIED

"A DOZEN BOTTLES.
HUNDREDS OF COCKTAILS."

THAT IS THE basic motto we live by, but you might also add "within a budget." Here is our master list, not including mixers or garnishes. The prices are for 750-milliliter bottles (except small bottles such as bitters, or where indicated), and being overly cautious, we've tried to capture the *highest* average price for each item—you're likely to find many of these items at lower prices.

	LOW	HIGH
BRANDY	$15	$40
DRY GIN	$11	$40
GENEVER	$35	$50
AMBER RUM	$20	$30
WHITE RUM	$16	$30
RYE WHISKEY	$18	$55
VODKA	$20	$26
ORANGE LIQUEUR	$32	$34
DRY VERMOUTH	$11	$17
SWEET VERMOUTH	$8	$35 (1L)
AROMATIC BITTERS	$10	$13
ORANGE BITTERS	$6	$9
TOTALS:	$202	$379

AT A BASIC level, the full 12 Bottle Bar will set you back about $200, before tax. How many drinks will it make? Figuring just the main seven bottles of spirits (we use the liqueur, vermouth, and bitters sparingly), at 1½ ounces of alcohol per drink, we get a figure of 116 drinks. Again, with a little rough, back-of-the-napkin math, we come up with a cost of about $1.70 per drink. Factor in the cost of mixers, syrups, juices, etc., and $2.50 per drink is a safe round number. Not too bad.

make your own ingredients—syrups, garnishes, infusions, and what-not—it's tastier (and very easy) to boot. And you'll find yourself in good company: The original nineteenth-century bartenders used only freshly made ingredients in their drinks and it made all the difference.

WHERE'S THE TEQUILA?

When our friends see our 12 Bottle list, the first thing they often ask is: Where's the tequila? Well, aside from the Margarita, the Paloma, and the Tequila Sunrise, tequila just isn't called for in that many old-school cocktails. Granted, bartenders today are finding ever more inventive ways to use tequila (and mezcal). But since efficiency is our goal, tequila just didn't make the cut.

If you are a tequila stalwart, by all means hang on to your bottle. And just so there are no hard feelings, here's a hard-to-beat Margarita recipe from the Too Hot Tamales, because even though we are 12 Bottle Bar, we do enjoy a tasty Margarita.

TOO HOT TAMALES MARGARITA

GLASS: MARTINI | ICE: CUBED | MAKES: 1 DRINK

Margarita salt or kosher salt

Lime wedge

2 ounces añejo tequila

1 ounce orange liqueur

½ ounce strained, freshly squeezed lime juice

½ ounce strained, freshly squeezed lemon juice

Lime slice, for garnish

1 Cover a small plate with salt to a depth of ¼ inch. Halve the lime wedge widthwise and run a cut edge around the outer rim of a martini glass to dampen it. Roll the glass in the salt to coat the outer rim.

2 Combine the tequila, orange liqueur, lime juice, and lemon juice in a mixing glass. Fill the glass three-quarters full with ice cubes, cover with a Boston shaker tin, and shake vigorously until thoroughly chilled, 15 seconds.

3 Strain into the prepared glass and garnish with the lime slice.

Jerry Thomas
THE BABE RUTH OF BARTENDERS

BEFORE WE JUMP in, we need to tell you about a fellow whose name will flow freely through this book. Let us introduce you to Jerry Thomas (1830–1885). Perhaps we are leaning toward hyperbole, but without Jerry Thomas, modern cocktail culture wouldn't exist. Jerry Thomas— bartender, showman, advocate for fresh, house-made ingredients—was America's first real bartender, and his showmanship, coupled with his infinitely tasty concoctions, helped popularize cocktails across America. He was, for all intents, Tom Cruise in the movie *Cocktail*, albeit nineteenth-century style.

When you see bartenders sporting vests, bow ties, and crisp white shirts, it's because of Jerry Thomas. The man was quite the dandy, using his generous salary (more than the Vice President of the United States earned at the time) to deck himself out in natty finery. No T-shirts need apply.

When the best modern bartenders loudly champion the freshness of ingredients, hand chip their own ice, and geek out over increasingly esoteric syrups, shrubs, and liqueurs, it's because of Jerry Thomas. In the gilded age of the cocktail, which started in the latter half of the 1800s and ended just prior to Prohibition in 1920, everything was prepared in house; there was no such thing as imitation sour mix or the ersatz cocktail cherries we know today.

When you see bartenders doing flashy tricks like lighting orange peels on fire, it's because of Jerry Thomas. Indeed, his signature drink, the Blue Blazer, required the bartender to ignite a measure of whiskey and pour it back and forth through the air, creating a free-flowing flame as it cascaded from one mixing glass to the other.

When you see the proliferation of cocktail books on the market, yes ours included, it's because of Jerry Thomas. His book, *Jerry Thomas' Bar-Tenders Guide*, also known as *How to Mix Drinks, or The Bon-Vivant's Companion*, was the first collection of drink recipes published in the United States, thus codifying what had, until then, been an oral tradition. It not only demystified cocktail making, but also spread the tradition to others, allowing it to evolve.

Let's just summarize this way: Jerry Thomas was one rockin' dude, and 12 Bottle Bar wouldn't even exist if it weren't for him. Cheers to you, J. T. May your memory ever live on.

IT'S OKAY TO START SMALL

Should the prospect of amassing twelve bottles seem overwhelming, we've given you the tools to customize your own one- (page 29), three- (page 41), or four-bottle (page 49) bar with drinks to match. Have just one lonely bottle of booze on your shelf? Add water, citrus, and sugar, and *presto*, you have some real options. Do you drink only gin? Then go for a three-bottle setup of gin, dry vermouth, and orange bitters to open your eyes to the wonders of the juniper spirit. Want to add a bit more pizzazz? Add orange liqueur, and you're done. You'll be surprised by the myriad drink possibilities. The bottom line is: No need to fear—it's your bar.

> Just as people have food preferences, they have liquor preferences (flavors are flavors, wherever you find them), but they don't always know it.

FANCY A DRINK?

To make mixing (and consuming) drinks even easier, we've taken a somewhat unorthodox approach to classifying our cocktails. When we have friends over, particularly those who don't drink a lot or drink only one thing, we always start by asking them a few simple questions.

- Do you have a favorite spirit?
- What are you in the mood for?
- Are you into sweet or tangy?
- How strong do you like your drinks?

Just as people have food preferences, they have liquor preferences (flavors are flavors, wherever you find them), but they don't always know it. Each chapter focuses on one spirit (gin, rum, and so on), while the cocktails in each chapter fall into three basic categories organized by flavor profile. In classifying our drinks by taste and sensation, not style of drink, we hope to give you a better way to understand your own palate and to figure out what your friends like, too. Here are our categories—certainly not the traditional cocktail classifications, to be sure—and how we define them.

SWEET & FRUITY These drinks depend on a high proportion of fruit or fruit juice and/or some form of sugar, making them easy to drink. Tiki drinks and anything with fruit in the name tend to fall into this category. We put the Cuba Libre (Rum and Coke) here, too.

TANGY & CITRUSY Many of these drinks sport the official label "the sour," defined mostly by the inclusion of fresh citrus juice. The Whiskey Sour and the Daiquiri are classic examples.

STRONG These are for people who really like to taste the character of the booze. It's worth noting that drinks of this ilk are often perceptually, if not actually, stronger in terms of alcohol content. The truth is that a shot of rye (approximately 1½ ounces) may have exactly the same amount of alcohol as a Whiskey Sour made with that same rye, but because, in the sour, the whiskey shares the stage with other elements, the drink is perceived to be lighter in taste. Thus, in our terms, a "strong" drink could be old-school or modern, but what defines it is the fact that the liquor takes center stage.

EASIER THAN YOU THINK

Now, if you find the idea of mixing drinks to be a little bit daunting, not to worry. Here's the big secret of 12 Bottle Bar: With the information in this book, you can make the best cocktails on the planet, hands down. How do we know this? Because the best cocktails can be made by anyone. If you can measure liquid into little tiny cups and shake things really well, then you too can make the greatest cocktails invented by mankind (as well as the original ones we've snuck in with them).

But bear in mind that this is not a cocktail book—it's a road map. Our goal is not simply to offer you hundreds of recipes to practice by rote; our goal is to put you in command of your home drink making. It's our hope that the 12 Bottle Bar will not only let you enjoy the process, but also return the cocktail to its roots as a drink for relaxing, alone or with friends.

CHAPTER 1

Tools of the Trade

Any craft requires tools. Baking calls for a pan; sautéing needs a skillet. Making drinks is no different. So, before you get started shaking and stirring, you will need to assemble some basic items.

A quick glance around your kitchen may reveal that you already have a good number of these tools. The suggestions below reflect our own experiences whittling down tools to the bare minimum. As to brands, choose what works for you. You won't mix drinks if you don't enjoy the process.

HARDWARE

If there's one thing that makes the head-first dive into mixology much less intimidating than, say, the culinary arts, it's the cost of the equipment. Whereas a sous-vide water oven can set you back $300 plus (and, if that's sticker shock, don't bother to Google "La Cornue"), everything you need to shake and stir like a pro can be had for about $50. As hobbies go, that's tough to beat. After a while, you may want to invest in a vintage shaker (our friend Mike uses a vintage bullet shell casing) or a set of Erlenmeyer flasks (those conical, long-necked beakers prized by mad scientists) to store your juices and syrups, but to get started, here's all you need.

> If there's one thing that makes the head-first dive into mixology much less intimidating than, say, the culinary arts, it's the cost of the equipment.

BOSTON SHAKER There are two basic kinds of shakers on the market. The first is the cobbler shaker, which typically comprises three metal pieces: a large cup, a strainer/spout that fits into the cup, and a cap. This is the kind of cocktail tool you find at department stores or boutiques. Skip it. While cobbler shakers can be pretty, they're 90 percent show and provide very little practicality. Plus, they tend to jam shut after a vigorous shake, making the process of churning out drinks much more arduous than it should be.

The better way (the only way, if you ask us) to go is a Boston shaker. Here, the only parts are a metal cup and a mixing glass—the best being a standard pint glass—that wedges in snugly at the top. The advantages of the Boston shaker are myriad. If you're making multiple drinks, you can have a collection of mixing glasses lined up. The transparency of the glass also lets you see what drinks you have in front of you, an often-useful reminder. Unlike their cobbler cousins, Boston shakers don't tend to jam, and a quick thump with the heel of your hand is typically all that's needed to separate the halves. If you have any concerns about the fragility of a pint glass, leave them behind. These are barroom workhorses; they can hold their own.

Tip:
BEND THE SPOON

Bending your bar spoon about 30 degrees at a point 4 to 5 inches above the bowl will make your stirring more ergonomic. Should you be able to bend the spoon with your mind, certainly wait until an audience has been assembled.

BAR SPOON While buying a special spoon for stirring cocktails may seem like an extravagance to some, the lowly bar spoon falls squarely in the category of "having the right tool for the job." A couple of key design elements separate it from its flatware friends. The length of the spoon allows you to keep your fingers out of the mixing glass, and the spiral design of the handle facilitates the quick twirling motion you'll need to properly stir at a steady, rapid pace.

JIGGERS / MEASURING CUPS / SPOONS Here are the basic measurements you're going to need to make cocktails quickly and often:

2 ounces, 1½ ounces, 1 ounce, ¾ ounce, ½ ounce, and ¼ ounce, as well as a range of tablespoons and teaspoons for smaller measures. These are made easy with two tools: a collection of variously sized stainless steel jiggers or a set of accurate measuring spoons and cups (we really like Oxo brand). What's the difference? Jiggers look a little cooler, whereas standard size measuring cups allow you to compound larger measurements of ingredients (especially helpful if you are mixing

more than one drink at a time) before you add them to your mixing glass. Measuring spoons are the choice for very small amounts that don't have corresponding jigger or cup measures. Depending on what equipment you have or choose to purchase, you can use the conversions noted below.

STRAINER If you ever use only one strainer, make it a Hawthorne. Like the bar spoon, the Hawthorne strainer is a tool that does one job and does it extremely well. You'll recognize it as the metal ping-pong-paddle-looking thing with the large spring running around three quarters of its circumference. It's the spring that not only makes it a Hawthorne, but also allows it to accommodate a wide variety of glass sizes. There's no need to spend good money here; the simplest models do the trick.

Should you feel limited by just one strainer, give the julep strainer a look. While it's designed to fit only certain glass sizes and requires a fraction more skill to use than a Hawthorne, the julep strainer is not only retro, but quite elegant in the hand. Use it on your stirred drinks and the Hawthorne on your shaken drinks, and your friends will admire your technique.

Jiggers to Kitchen MEASUREMENT

SHOULD YOU NOT have a collection of jiggers handy, here are useful conversions.

½ ounce = 1 tablespoon = 3 teaspoons

¾ ounce = 4½ teaspoons

1 ounce = 2 tablespoons = 6 teaspoons

1½ ounces = 3 tablespoons

2 ounces = ¼ cup = 4 tablespoons

MUDDLER Really, you don't need a muddler—you could just as easily use the peaceful end of a hammer, but we think you care more about your drinks than that. As with many of the tools on this list, there's no great mystery to the muddler. It muddles. More to the point, it's heavy enough to mash fruit and whatnot and typically contains spiked "teeth" that tear ingredients. How you use a muddler (gently) is much more important than what kind you buy—just make sure it's relatively heavy and comfortable to use.

Tip:
HOW TO MUDDLE

IT'S SAID THAT to a hammer, everything looks like a nail. Following that logic, the unfortunate police-baton shape of a muddler leads most people to wield it as if attempting to pacify their ingredients. We don't beat our cocktail components into submission, however. No, we massage and gently coerce them to release their magical goodness.

FOR DELICATE HERBS, such as mint, the muddler is used to release the inherent oils. Herbs will typically give these up easily and only a gentle "nudge" of leaves around the glass by the muddler is required to facilitate the surrender.

CITRUS REQUIRES a bit more muscle, but only just so. Using the flat or ribbed end of the muddler, simply press on the citrus repeatedly. There is no need to smash it with the power of Thor.

RESPECT YOUR ingredients, and you'll get the best from them.

OTHER HANDY ITEMS

CHEF'S KNIFE A low-priced but well-regarded brand is Victorinox

CHEESECLOTH Useful for straining spices or muddled solids from drinks or as an alternative to a fine-mesh sieve

CUTTING BOARD(S)

FINE-MESH SIEVE For removing pits, pulp, and other large undrinkables

FOOD PROCESSOR OR BLENDER

MANUAL CITRUS JUICE PRESS One for lemons and another for limes comes in handy

MICROPLANE ZESTER For zesting citrus and grating whole nutmeg

MISTER A small, usually metal bottle of about 2 to 4 ounces, with a spray nozzle; used for delivering a controlled mist of spirit or other liquid (such as Tincture of Clove, page 389) over the top of a cocktail

PARING KNIFE For slicing fruit and more

TOOTHPICKS OR COCKTAIL SKEWERS For holding olives, berries, and other small garnishes

VARIOUS BOTTLES AND JARS For infusions and liqueurs

VEGETABLE PEELER A swivel-head variety is the easiest to use

ICE

Treatises could be written—and most likely have been—about ice. Author Paul Theroux thought ice was so magical that he built an entire book, *The Mosquito Coast*, around it. In it, a man named Allie Fox packs up his family and leads them into the jungles of South America to bring ice to the natives, crying "Ice is civilization!"

The cocktail community would certainly agree, albeit for different reasons, of course. Indeed, when easily accessible ice made its first appearance in the early 1800s, thanks to the visionary Frederic "Ice King" Tudor, the world—and eventually cocktails along with it—was irrevocably changed. Back then, Tudor "harvested" his ice in 300-pound blocks from local Boston ponds. Nowadays, the average soul

MY KINGDOM FOR A STRAW

AS AMERICA EXPANDED its borders west, and technology advanced, ice production became cheaper and more localized, allowing ice to be used in such whimsical fashions as for chilling beverages. What better way to celebrate the conquest of the West than to enjoy an iced drink thousands of miles away from the nearest metropolis?

Of course, those cold, cold libations were all fine and dandy until ice met tooth. Cavity-stricken, decayed nineteenth-century tooth, that is. Fortunately one Marvin C. Stone, a college-educated fellow and Civil War veteran, solved this problem in 1888 by inventing the modern paper drinking straw. Paper replaced the hollow rye grass tube used until then, which tended to make drinks taste somewhat "grassy." Ice and tooth could now be kept safely apart (not to mention nixing those herbaceous flavors), while one's cooling elixir was sipped down.

can reach into his freezer and grab an ice cube whenever he wants it. The problem is that standard-issue freezer ice—clunky, often made from unfiltered water, and "flavored" with whatever scents float in the freezer—or, heaven have mercy, standard supermarket bagged ice with its often stale smell and inconsistent shapes—is, well, pretty horrible. Capitalizing on this fact, companies dedicated solely to cocktail ice have sprung up in the wake of the mixology renaissance.

THE RULES OF ICE

For our purposes, we're going to stick to the more practical aspects of cocktail ice, meaning how and why it's used and how to get the best out of it. Because, along with the dilution and chilling it provides, the proper application of ice to a mixed drink is as important as the proper application of heat to a sauté. That said, here are some basic rules to keep in mind.

RULE #1   Think of ice as an ingredient. You wouldn't use bottled sour mix or bruised fruit in your cocktails. Why compromise on your ice, which forms the foundation on which a drink is built?

RULE #2   When and if you make ice at home, use good neutral water (see "How to Make Ice at Home," opposite). You get out what you put in—it's as simple as that.

RULE #3   Consider how long you shake or stir your drinks. Shaking and stirring times vary markedly depending on the size, shape, and amount of ice you use. A slow stir with large ice cubes will result in a less diluted drink than an energetic shake with crushed ice. Which leads us to . . .

TO SHAKE OR STIR

COMMON WISDOM dictates that if your ingredients are particularly clear, you may prefer to stir in order to avoid a cloudy drink. Shaking causes aeration of the drink and may produce tiny ice crystals in the liquid. If you are using citrus or syrups, a healthy shake is called for, lest the ingredients fail to blend. Of course, there are a multitude of exceptions to every rule. Just ask James Bond.

> "It is no exaggeration to say that I would rather have garbage spirits and good ice than the reverse."
>
> —SASHA PETRASKE, BARTENDER AND BAR OWNER

RULE #4 Consider the size and function of your ice. Are you using a single large cube or spear? Several smaller cubes? A scoop of crushed ice? The bigger the ice, the slower it will melt. Crushed ice, used in drinks like juleps or brambles, melts quickly, so you get a quick chill as well as a controlled and constant dilution of liquor. In contrast, a chunk of ice—say a large cube in an Old Fashioned or a large block of ice in a bowl of punch—melts and dilutes more slowly, preserving the potency of the drink, but still softening it over time.

RULE #5 Consider the temperature of your ice. Is it truly frozen? Or did you—accidentally, misguidedly, foolishly—put it in an ice bucket for ease of use? Melty ice is watery ice, and that means the water on the surface of the ice will further dilute your drink. Not a good idea if you don't want a watery drink.

RULE #6 Add ice last, just before you are ready to mix, whether by shaking or stirring. This allows you to measure the liquid, should you suspect you may have forgotten something, and in the event you're distracted or called away midassembly, your drink will happily wait for you, undiluted.

RULE #7 Give your ice a helping hand. If you can, store your glassware in the freezer with the proper ice cube(s) alongside. This is particularly useful for parties. A cold glass means an even colder drink.

HOW TO MAKE ICE AT HOME

Now that we have covered the basics of protecting your cocktail MVP, let's get on with the game. The best way to control all the factors we have discussed—ice size, shape, and temperature—is to chip your own from large blocks (which is what many classic bars actually do). But let's be honest—for the home bartender, it's relatively impractical unless you are already skilled at carving ice sculptures for the Lido Deck buffet. So, what are the options?

CUBED OR SPEAR ICE   There is a panoply of readily available silicone mold ice trays on the market, in both small and large cube shapes, as well as rectangular, spear-shaped molds (see Resources, page 393). These yield uniform, fit-the-glass cubes for drinks served on the rocks or oblong shapes for those served in a collins glass.

To make molded ice: Fill a silicone ice mold with fresh, filtered, or bottled water and freeze. It is advisable to cover the mold with plastic wrap or carefully slide it into a ziplick storage bag to keep it from taking on any freezer odors.

ICE RINGS   An ice ring (essentially a mold) is key to properly chilling and diluting a bowl of punch for the duration of a party. The steps here are simple, but the result is stunning.

1   Pour water into a cake mold, preferably a Bundt or tube pan (one that is hollow in the center like a doughnut). If you like, float slices of lemon, lime, or other fruits, or edible flowers in the water.

2   Cover with plastic wrap and carefully place in the freezer until frozen solid, most likely overnight.

3   To unmold, place the pan in a shallow bowl of hot water, making sure the water doesn't reach the top of the pan, until the ice loosens. Turn the pan upside down to release the ice.

SPECIALTY SHAPES   There are a variety of silicone ice molds and trays in an array of wacky shapes—UFOs, vampire teeth, even capsule-shaped "chill pills"—on the market that have no particular use, but can be fun to play around with. For an Old Fashioned (page 229), we sometimes use large round plastic ice molds (see page 393) that add a bit of visual excitement—along with the requisite chilling and slow dilution. If you choose to dabble in novelty ice, just bear in mind that the size and shape of the ice will affect the rate of dilution of your drink and its drinkability.

CRUSHED ICE   A mound of crushed ice is the crowning touch in drinks like the Mint Julep (page 238), the Bramble (page 106), and many a tiki drink. Why crushed? These are strong drinks—spirits heavy—that require the slow, even dilution made possible by small pieces of ice. There are various methods for making crushed ice.

- Use a Lewis ice bag (see page 395). It is a loud but dramatic way to crush your ice and, as it was originally designed to be a coin bag for a bank, it's just plain cool.
- Put small ice chunks or cubes in a heavy-duty ziplock bag and crush with a rolling pin or meat mallet.
- If you are lucky enough to have an in-fridge crushed-ice maker that uses filtered water, it's a serviceable method that is welcome at the end of a long day when you want a julep stat.

ICE FOR SHAKING AND STIRRING If you keep only a small supply of "presentation ice" (such as molded cubes and spears) on hand, do not waste it on shaking and stirring—only use it for serving. Instead put ice-maker cubes or regular ice tray cubes to work; when made from filtered water, they are quite serviceable. High-quality store-bought ice is a good option, too (supermarkets typically sell different grades).

As you can see, how you apply ice can vastly change your drink. As the "starter pistol" in cocktail making, it can help win or lose the race. An underchilled drink is as bad as an overdiluted one. A cold, stirred martini is one of life's ultimate pleasures; hearing the clink of ice cubes in one's collins glass is part of the enjoyment of a Gin and Tonic. Punch calls for a large block that dissolves slowly over the course of an evening, preserving the punch's integrity with slow dilution but constant chill. And, of course, tiki drinks are lovely served in overflowing goblets of crushed ice. However you shake (or stir) it, be sure you do it with quality ice.

GLASSWARE

Bars and restaurants are in the business of entertaining, so they think nothing of having twenty different styles of glassware on hand. We will say this only once: You do not need twenty different styles of glassware in a home bar. You need about six, maybe seven, some of which you probably already own.

THE MARTINI GLASS This is our go-to glass for most drinks. Now, when we say martini, we do not mean those 6- to 8-ounce monstrosities sold in decor shops; 4½ ounces is about all you want. Along with the volume, consider the stem of the glass; something sturdy is in order. Pretty much any drink served "up," meaning without ice, calls for a martini-style glass because the stem allows you to hold your drink without warming it in your hand.

You can either purchase the traditional cone-shaped martini glass or opt for a more old-school coupe, whose shape was purportedly modeled after Marie Antoinette's breast. We use the 4½-ounce coupe from Libbey glassware (available through Amazon.com).

THE ROCKS GLASS At somewhere between 8 and 12 ounces, the rocks glass is roughly double to triple the volume of a martini glass. The hallmarks of the rocks glass are a sturdy bottom, as you sometimes muddle ingredients directly in the glass, and a wide mouth that allows you to swirl your drink to dilute it or breathe in the aroma. A glass with a little heft adds some gravitas to your cocktail experience.

> A glass with a little heft adds some gravitas to your cocktail experience.

The rocks glass is for a shot of spirit, any powerful drink (like an Old Fashioned), anything muddled (like a julep), and often for certain non-fizzy drinks that are served cold like Brandy Milk Punch or sangria because of the convenient size and feel in the hand.

THE COLLINS GLASS The collins glass is made for "long drinks," which are anything in the highball category—"tall" drinks that depend to a great extent on a mixer like tonic water, ginger beer, or cola for volume. Anytime a nonalcoholic mixer—in particular, something fizzy—takes up a large portion of a drink's volume, a collins glass is your ticket. Think a Gin and Tonic, a Buck, a Shrub, a Cuba Libre. A tall glass should never be clunky; it should feel light and sexy. Ten ounces should do it. Perfect for a summer afternoon.

THE CHAMPAGNE FLUTE An elegant, tulip-shaped Champagne flute is in order for classics like the French 75 or any tall, Champagne- or sparkling wine–based sipper.

THE HEATPROOF MUG OR GLASS If you serve hot drinks, you need a mug or glass (roughly 6 ounces) that keeps your hands from burning, and can also withstand the heat of the liquid. We're talking Toddies, Hot Buttered Rum, and the like here.

CHILLING GLASSES & SHAKERS

CHILLING GLASSES AND shakers doesn't take too much forethought. Simply pop them in the freezer about ten minutes before they are needed. When you remove them from the freezer, they will acquire a frosty sheen and will lend a chill to the drinks they contain. N.B.: If your shakers are chilled, your drinks will not dilute as much because the shaker will keep them cooler overall. If you need to dilute your drink further, add more ice to the shaker. And to keep your drink even colder, "frappe" it by filling the glass with ice (no water) for two to three minutes, then dumping it out.

PUNCH BOWL AND GLASSES Much as we don't want to advocate going out and buying ungainly additional items, if you're in the market for new glassware anyway, a punch bowl set is worth the investment, especially if you think you will be making a lot of party or holiday punch. A punch bowl is a lovely piece to display for a party, but it also serves the far more practical purpose of being a container in which to put a large ice ring, which will gradually dilute your punch all evening while keeping it cold.

There are cheap sets, there are expensive sets, there are vintage sets (including the classic Tom & Jerry set). You be the judge. You don't need to spend a lot of money as long as you buy a standard-size punch bowl (modern ones hold about 12 quarts, antique styles can hold as few as 5) with an accompanying set of glasses (usually six to eight). You will want a ladle as well, which sometimes comes with the set.

> If you're in the market for new glassware anyway, a punch bowl set is worth the investment.

KNOW YOUR SPIRITS

Should you happen to enjoy a recipe made with one particular brand of spirit and then decide to crack the seal on a bottle from another maker, you need to stop and consider the alcohol by volume (ABV). The balance of a drink is largely a numbers game, and changing up the central spirit—the gin in a sour, for example—can have a significant effect on the ultimate libation. Here's the breakdown of a sour using two gins with markedly different ABV levels.

SOUR #1

1½ ounces Plymouth gin (41.2% ABV)

¾ ounce strained, freshly squeezed lemon juice

¾ ounce Simple Syrup (page 369)

In the above recipe, 41.2 percent of the 1½ ounces of gin is pure alcohol. This translates to 0.618 ounces or 15.45 percent of the total drink (factoring in 1 ounce of water added from shaking with ice). Now here's the same drink made with Old Raj blue label.

SOUR #2

1½ ounces Old Raj blue label gin (55% ABV)

¾ ounce strained, freshly squeezed lemon juice

¾ ounce Simple Syrup (page 369)

Using the same proportions as before, we now have a drink with 0.825 ounces of pure alcohol or 20.63 percent of the total drink—a 30 percent increase in alcohol percentage over the Plymouth. We've used the sour as an example here because alcohol is but a small portion of the total volume. When you begin to look at drinks with much higher alcohol content—martinis and Manhattans—the differences become more marked.

MANHATTAN #1

· ·

2 ounces Rittenhouse rye
 whiskey (50% ABV)

1 ounce Carpano Antica
 Formula sweet vermouth
 (16.5% ABV)

MANHATTAN #2

· ·

2 ounces Old Overholt rye
 whiskey (40% ABV)

1 ounce Martini sweet
 vermouth (16% ABV)

To simplify the math, we've left out the bitters in both of the above, and both drinks assume the addition of an ounce of water after vigorous stirring. In Manhattan #1, we have 1.165 ounces of pure alcohol or 29.13 percent of the total drink. Manhattan #2, meanwhile, weighs in at 0.96 ounces or 24 percent. The difference is still about 5 percent, as with the sour, but the reality is a drink composed of one-third pure alcohol versus one-quarter alcohol. One way to compensate for this would be to cut back on the spirit in Manhattan #1 to a bit over 1¾ ounces. This, however, brings up a separate problem, as ABV isn't the only difference between these drinks. The flavor profile of the ingredients—namely the chosen sweet vermouths—creates two vastly different beasts.

In the Manhattan example, we've chosen to pit the spice-and-tobacco bomb that is Carpano Antica Formula against the serviceable but unremarkable supermarket stalwart Martini not to highlight their ABV differences, which are minimal, but to call attention to how different they smell and taste. Both are sweet vermouths, true, but in a blind taste test with an unfamiliar audience, they would never be classified as cousins. Coupling the Carpano with a higher-proof spirit only intensifies its characteristics, which, depending upon your proclivities, may or may not be such a bad thing.

Knowing the ABV and flavor profile of the spirits you are using is key when reaching for new or unfamiliar bottles. Don't be shy about tweaking the amount of any ingredient in your drinks to your liking, but keep in mind that reducing one element, such as the spirit in Manhattan #1, will emphasize the characteristics of the others. Unless a recipe is made with exactly the same ingredients and using exactly the same techniques every time, its taste is going to fluctuate from drink to drink. Ultimately, it's your drink, and you need to find the balance that is perfect for you.

MISCELLANEOUS TERMS AND TECHNIQUES DEFINED

Every trade has its terminology, and mixing drinks is no different. For easier reading, we've collected some definitions here for your reference. You may notice that some of them are not used in our recipes, but, as you are likely to see them crop up elsewhere, they are worth knowing.

CHILL To cool down a glass or spirit by placing it in the freezer ahead of time, fill with crushed ice (martini) or ice cubes (rocks/collins), allowing the glass to sit while you mix your drink. Dump the ice before using the glass.

DASH About ⅛ teaspoon

DOUBLE STRAIN To strain ingredients twice in order to remove all traces of solids, first through a Hawthorne strainer and then through a fine-mesh sieve placed over the glass. Used often for freshly squeezed citrus juice

FLOAT To gently place a small measurement of spirit or other liquid on the top of a cocktail, without mixing it in

FRAPPE A GLASS To put ice in a glass for 2 to 3 minutes to prechill it for a cocktail

FROST A GLASS To place a glass in the freezer so that when it is removed it frosts up (again, a quick way to chill a glass, especially for beer)

MIST A gentle spray, generally of a spirit, on top of an already made drink

NEAT When a measure of liquor is served at room temperature without ice (often served in a rocks glass, but not necessarily)

ON THE ROCKS Served with ice cubes or a single "chunk" cube of ice ("rocks") in the glass, usually in a rocks glass

RICH SIMPLE SYRUP A sugar solution with a 2:1 ratio of sugar to water, rather than the usual 1:1 ratio for standard simple syrup (see page 369 for a recipe)

RIM A GLASS To coat the outer rim of a glass with salt or other sugar/spice mixture

SHOOTER Often confused with a shot, but can contain more than one spirit component and, like a single shot, is meant to be drunk in one gulp

SHOT A single serving of roughly 1½ ounces, of a single spirit served neat; can be served alongside another drink or on its own (usually in a shot glass)

SIMPLE SYRUP A sugar solution with a 1:1 ratio of sugar to water (see page 369 for a recipe)

SPEAR A long, thin slice of fruit (like pineapple) or vegetable (such as cucumber) that usually fits loosely in a collins glass. Alternatively, a long rectangular chunk of ice

SPLASH A quick shake of a bottle of spirit into a cocktail glass, equivalent to roughly ¼ teaspoon

STRAIGHT UP A cocktail that is shaken or stirred, then strained (usually into a martini glass), and is thus without ice; also simply referred to as "up"

TWIST A thin, roughly bandage-shaped strip of citrus zest with as little pith as possible

WEDGE Roughly ⅛ of a lemon or lime, cut lengthwise through the central axis

WHEEL A thin slice of citrus, usually lemon or lime, cut crosswise through the fruit

CHAPTER 2

The 1 Bottle Bar

There's a story—apocryphal, we're sure—about why Hershey's Kisses are slightly sour compared to most other chocolates. The legend goes that Old Man Hershey—Milton to his friends—was too cheap to throw out a batch of spoiled milk for chocolate making, and the results were not only not offensive, but were actually embraced by the public. We imagine that the first alcoholic beverage found its way into circulation in a pretty similar fashion.

It's an interesting notion to ponder: What made one of our ancient ancestors look into the abyss of fermentation—fungus growing in and chemically altering some sugary soup to produce alcohol—and say, "I'll have a go at that"? We like to think the statement was more along the lines of "Here, try this . . ." and a new outlet for what would otherwise have been rubbish was found. When you stop to contemplate the very nature of alcoholic beverages and how they came into being—first beers and wines, then spirits—the process is at once ridiculously simple and staggeringly multilayered. Fortunately for all of us, this book is not meant to serve as a history of adult beverages through the ages, but if you have a passing interest in making cocktails, it's good to know a few key points.

AN INEXACT HISTORY OF WHY
WE DRINK WHAT WE DRINK

First, a bit about fermentation. As mentioned above, fermentation is the process of yeast turning sugars into alcohol and carbon dioxide (bubbles). This is how beer and wine are made, and up until the Middle Ages, if you wanted to get your buzz on, fermented beverages were the only way to go. And because the public could get weary of the same old taste pretty quickly (not to mention the off-flavors that can develop), flavoring agents such as spices and hops worked their way into the mix. Still, after centuries of recreational drinks with alcohol by volume hovering in the teens or lower, the people most likely craved something with a bit more kick—and medical science was finding that higher proof alcohol was just what the doctor ordered for fighting infection.

Leave it to the noble men and women of medicine to unleash the Lost Weekend.

Leave it to the noble men and women of medicine to unleash the Lost Weekend. Around the twelfth century, something close to pure alcohol was being distilled. Straight from the still, this new "water of life" proved miraculous when it came to fighting bacteria externally, such as when cleaning a wound. Given the nature of man, it probably wasn't much later that someone thought to himself, *If it fights disease outside, it must do wonders inside,* and promptly became history's first fatality from alcohol poisoning.

Our guess is that it wasn't long after that (or maybe it was decades, depending on your faith in humanity's ability to learn from its mistakes) that another enterprising guy first said, "Why don't we cut this nasty stuff with some water?" and second said, "That still tastes bloody awful." So man did what man does best; he went with what he knew and added sugar and spice—both hot commodities during the Age of Sail—and even a bit of citrus from the garden. And thus punch, the grandfather of the modern cocktail, was born.

The term *punch* is said to come from the Hindi word for "five," referring to the drink's five chief ingredients: alcohol, water, sugar, spice, and citrus. For the purposes of this chapter and cocktail making in general, punch is the cornerstone one-bottle drink chiefly because punch solves the core problem of alcohol: how to make it quaffable.

PICK YOUR POISON . . .

The first rule of any home bar is a hard and fast "drink what you like." No matter how much we or anyone else tries to sell you on, say, gin, if you don't like gin (sigh), skip the gin. Drink what you like—that's all that matters. Granted, you won't be able to make every classic drink (a martini is only made with gin, a Cuba Libre only made with rum), but if you don't care for that spirit, why worry? The question is, of course, what *do* you like? For the sake of this exercise, pick your favorite from among the following 12 Bottle Bar components: Cognac-style brandy, dry gin, genever, rum (either amber or white), or rye whiskey.

Whether your choice is light or dark, full of botanicals or funky from time in wood, some basic principles apply. Got your bottle in front of you? Good. Let's get mixing.

ADD SOME SUGAR . . .

f all your cupboard contains is one of the above bottles and a lump of sugar—congratulations, you're on your way to a mixed drink. Provided your faucet works, of course—or, better yet, you have some bottled or filtered water handy. Near the top of the Adult Beverage Periodic Table are two rudimentary drinks that require nothing more than a bit of booze, sugar of some sort, and some water: the sling and the toddy.

For all intents and purposes, the sling and the toddy are the same drink, the chief difference being that the sling is served cold while the toddy is hot. The amount of each ingredient may vary widely from drink to drink—you might have a scant teaspoon of water in a sling and several ounces in a hot toddy—but the goal of the drinks is the same: to make alcohol taste better.

THE SLING

GLASS: ROCKS | ICE: LARGE CUBE (OPTIONAL) | MAKES: 1 DRINK

1 teaspoon granulated sugar
or 1 cube sugar

1 teaspoon to 1 ounce
of water, to taste

2 ounces Cognac-style
brandy, dry gin, genever,
amber or white rum, or
rye whiskey

1 Combine the sugar and water to taste in a rocks glass. Stir to dissolve the sugar in the water, or muddle if using a sugar cube.

2 Add the spirit and stir to combine. Add a large ice cube if you wish.

In its most spartan form, employing a teaspoon of water—just enough to dissolve the sugar—the sling performs a bit of Mike Mulligan magic on the accompanying booze, lowering the hills and straightening the curves. This, however, does not rank the sling among the best things you can do with your hooch. Truth be told, we're not fans of the sling in its most raw form, but its place as a fundamental building block for mixed drinks cannot be denied.

The hot toddy, on the other hand, does possess certain simple charms. On a cold winter's night or when a scratchy throat nags at you, a toddy is just the thing.

THE TODDY

GLASS: HEATPROOF MUG | MAKES: 1 DRINK

1 teaspoon granulated sugar

4 ounces boiling water

2 ounces Cognac-style brandy, dry gin, genever, amber or white rum, or rye whiskey

1 Place the sugar in a heatproof mug and pour about 1 ounce of the boiling water into the glass. Stir to dissolve the sugar.

2 Add the spirit and the remaining boiling water and stir to combine.

You'll notice that in the toddy recipe we've added the water in two parts. Because sugar dissolves poorly in alcohol but fabulously in hot water—something you may have learned in high school chemistry class—we use a little boiling H_2O up front.

Having learned the basic foundations of the sling and the toddy, you are now free to run wild. You could add a dash of freshly grated nutmeg, replace the sugar with honey, or start with muddled mint, which with a glass of crushed ice gives you a Mint Julep (page 238). It's your drink, so feel free to experiment in any way that strikes you as potentially delicious.

. . . AND THEN ADD SOME CITRUS

The next step in this equation is the simple sour, wherein a sling meets some citrus. Citrus is often the magic component that turns a basic drink recipe into something truly divine. In fact, if you ask us to name our favorite type of cocktail, we'll quickly respond with the sour, a drink characterized by its citrus zing. The Whiskey Sour, Daiquiri, and Margarita all fall into this category, and in our book—which is this book—you'll find more variations on the simple sour than any other type of drink. Here's the basic formula: 2 parts spirit to 1 part sour to 1 part sweet.

Provided that you have your simple syrup premade and your citrus already juiced, with the sour you're always about thirty seconds away from liquid heaven. What separates the sour from the sling is, of course, the citrus, and alcohol likes citrus like superheroes like spandex. Not every combination works, but when it does, it's clobbering time.

With citrus, there are a few general maxims to keep in mind:

- The more perceived acidic/sour the citrus, typically the better it will work for a drink;
- the more perceived acidic/sour the citrus, the more sugar you'll potentially need to add—adjust to taste;
- and, oranges will generally disappoint.

THE SIMPLE SOUR

GLASS: MARTINI | ICE: CUBED | MAKES: 1 DRINK

• •

1½ ounces Cognac-style brandy, dry gin, amber or white rum, genever, or rye whiskey

¾ ounce strained, freshly squeezed citrus juice, typically lemon or lime

¾ ounce Simple Syrup (page 369)

• •

1 Combine all of the ingredients in a mixing glass. Fill the glass three-quarters full with ice cubes, cover with a Boston shaker tin, and shake vigorously until thoroughly chilled, 15 seconds.

2 Strain into a martini glass.

What's even more exciting is that the combination of spirit + sugar + citrus isn't limited to short drinks. Add some fizzy club soda and you expand your horizons to include collinses, rickeys, and lots, lots more. Add flat water and spices and you've got punch. And, if the spirit in question is rum, you get "pirate punch," aka grog.

GROG

GLASS: COLLINS OR ROCKS | ICE: CUBED | MAKES: 1 DRINK

½ ounce strained, freshly squeezed lime juice

2 teaspoons light brown or raw sugar, such as Demerara

4 ounces water

2 ounces rum (we like amber, but the pirate in you need not be picky)

Lime wheel, for garnish

1 Combine the lime juice and sugar in a collins or rocks glass. Add the water and stir to dissolve the sugar.

2 Add the rum and a few large ice cubes and stir to chill. Garnish with the lime wheel.

At first blush, most will decry grog as being a bit thin and uninspired. The naysayers will find it tasty enough, however, to indulge in a second round, and once plied thusly, will curse the demon rum for its surreptitious strategem. Like all good children of punch, grog arrives in full Trojan horse splendor—inviting to a fault and never to be underestimated.

> Like all good children of punch, grog arrives in full Trojan horse splendor—inviting to a fault and never to be underestimated.

As noted above, the only real difference between grog and something like a collins is that soda or fizzy water is exchanged for flat. Although Tom Collins is the most famous member of the family—sorry, Barnabas and Bootsy—and cousin John likely came first, there's a general promiscuity to the clan: They cozy up well to just about any spirit. If you fancy the idea of fizzy tart lemonade (or limeade, or pomelo-ade, or even tamarind-ade) with a shot of booze thrown in for good measure, you owe it to yourself to take up with the collinses.

THE COLLINS

GLASS: COLLINS | ICE: CUBED | MAKES: 1 DRINK

1 teaspoon confectioners' sugar, or to taste

1 ounce strained, freshly squeezed citrus juice (traditionally lemon)

3 ounces club soda, or to taste

2 ounces Cognac-style brandy, dry gin, genever, amber or white rum, or rye whiskey

Lemon wheel, for garnish

1 Combine the sugar and lemon juice in a collins glass. Add ½ ounce of the club soda and stir to dissolve the sugar.

2 Add the spirit and a few large ice cubes and stir to chill.

3 Top with remaining club soda, and garnish with the lemon wheel.

THE GOODNESS OF GROG

THERE'S A SHORT but delicious, practical, and inebriating history to grog (which is specifically rum-centric) that we'll get to later in the book (page 166), but for our purposes here, we'll simply advise that grog—and all drinks that combine spirit, sugar, and citrus with a tall measure of water—are the essence of enjoyable alcoholic perfection. Though they may not pack the perceived wallop of martini-class bombs, two ounces of booze is still two ounces of booze, whether you swig it down straight or sip it leisurely on the bow of the HMS *Bounty*.

THE HIGHBALL

SOMEONE WILL READ this book and promptly reprimand us that the Highball, much like the Cocktail or the Martini, is a specific drink and not a class of drinks. We won't argue with them, but we will kindly point out that when referring to a specific drink we capitalize the name, while for a class or category we employ the lowercase. That said, we're going to talk about the highball, not the Highball.

By definition and practicality, the highball is a shot of liquor mixed with a large measure of a carbonated beverage. Collinses fit that bill, so you'll get no argument from us if you call them highballs. Gin and Tonic (page 115) and our beloved Bucks (pages 116 and 241) also fall under the highball umbrella, as does what may be the perfect highball—the rum and Coke.

What's so special about the rum and Coke? First, it is a specific highball, using rum and only rum as its spirit. But it's the cola—preferably made with sugar, not corn syrup—that really makes it perfect. When you break down cola into its composite elements—sugar, water, citrus, spice, a bittering agent—what you have are all the components of punch. If you can find it, the real sugar Coca-Cola imported from Mexico is a great bet. You can also try Boylan or even Trader Joe's Cola, both made with sugar. Also, be sure to take the extra step of adding a lime wedge and turning your rum and Coke into a Cuba Libre.

CUBA LIBRE

GLASS: COLLINS OR ROCKS | ICE: CUBED | MAKES: 1 DRINK

1½ ounces rum
  (amber or white,
  take your pick)

6 ounces cola, preferably
  sugar-based (such as
  Boylan Cane Cola)

Lime wedge, for serving

1 Fill a collins or rocks glass with ice cubes, add the rum, and top with the cola. Stir gently to combine (you don't want to de-fizz the soda).

2 Squeeze the lime wedge into the glass and drop it in.

3 Smile.

Throughout this book, you'll find plenty of additional one-bottle recipes. If one bottle is all you need, simply flip to the appropriate chapter and start mixing. A few basic recipes like the sour, the collins, and a simple highball will elicit plenty of flexibility in that one bottle, and you'll be able to work your way through it without ever making the same drink twice.

Should you at some point, however, crave a bit more variety, let's crack the cap on the 3 Bottle Bar.

> "The desire to improve oneself is the essential quality to learning how to make better drinks."
>
> —CHRIS MCMILLIAN, BARTENDER

CHAPTER 3

The 3 Bottle Bar

CHAPTER 3

The 3 Bottle Bar

I f you've made it this far, we'll assume you've picked at least one base spirit, are comfortable with the general concepts of the sour, collins, and highball, and are looking to expand your repertoire. Excellent. It's time to make the acquaintance of the salt and pepper of cocktails: vermouth and bitters. Let's begin with the spicy stuff. . . .

A DASH OF PEPPER

I n the previous chapter, we introduced the sling. Important drink, the sling, but as mentioned, it lacks a certain pizzazz. Fortunately, we're not the first ones to feel this way, because sometime around the dawn of the nineteenth century, some right-thinking gentleman or lady of our kind of disposition mixed a few dashes of the local snake oil into their morning constitutional and created the king of all mixed drinks: the Cocktail (notice if you will the capital "C," denoting a distinct and singular drink, not a style of drink). Surely, you've heard of it—and of all the many bastardizations that have since carried its name—but there's a good chance you don't know that in the capital "C" variety, bitters play a central role.

Our first response when anyone asks, "What are bitters?" is to reply with the following question: "Remember, in Western films, those cure-all elixir and tonic peddlers who were always filtering into town uninvited and riling up the good townsfolk?" The miracle panaceas they were selling—bottles of compounded herbs, roots, and other bittering agents, like cinchona bark—were no different (save a lethal ingredient or two) from the little bottles of handmade tinctures lining the shelves of today's hoity-toity liquor shops.

> Sometime around the dawn of the nineteenth century, some right-thinking gentleman or lady of our kind of disposition mixed a few dashes of the local snake oil into their morning constitutional and created the king of all mixed drinks.

You guessed it—chief among them were bitters.

Much like spices in the kitchen, bitters provide layers of flavor, and a sort of bridge to other ingredients in a mixed drink. Where rye is spicy, and sweet vermouth herbal and viscous, the right bitters bridge the gaps between them. Think of a lead guitar and drums, and then imagine bitters providing the bass.

Along with the recent cocktail renaissance, an unprecedented variety of bitters is now on the market. Where once Angostura stood relatively alone, now dozens of bitters, from standard aromatic (like Angostura) to esoteric (chocolate mole and dandelion burdock) are as close as a click on a "Buy Now" button. They are well worth trying (and for deeper insight, see the Bitters chapter, page 301).

As for the Cocktail, we recommend you try the following experiment: First, take a sip of a sling (page 33). Then make the simple addition of aromatic bitters. You'll see the difference.

THE COCKTAIL

GLASS: ROCKS | ICE: 1 LARGE CUBE (OPTIONAL) | MAKES: 1 DRINK

1 teaspoon or cube light brown or raw sugar, such as Demerara

1 to 2 dashes aromatic bitters

1 teaspoon water

1½ ounces Cognac-style brandy, dry gin, genever, amber or white rum, or rye whiskey

1 Place the sugar in a rocks glass. Dash the bitters directly onto the sugar and muddle them together.

2 Add the water and stir to dissolve the sugar as much as possible.

3 Add a large ice cube, if you like, then the spirit, and stir gently to combine.

While the steps to make a proper Cocktail may seem somewhat laborious and arcane, the magic lies in the very process. Making a Cocktail instantaneously turns you into a compounding pharmacist. All in, the process takes no more than a minute, but in that time you have handcrafted one of the most important, delicious, and flexible potions known to mankind. Plus, your guests will dig watching you.

The application of bitters, of course, doesn't stop there. Take Dale DeGroff's Fitzgerald, a staple around our house, and one of the prime examples of how a dash of bitters can turn an average drink on its head and provide layers of flavor that are otherwise unimaginable. For those of you who have chosen gin as your spirit, rejoice. The Fitzgerald is one of the loveliest examples of a gin sour we have ever tasted.

THE FITZGERALD

GLASS: MARTINI | ICE: CUBED | MAKES: 1 DRINK

1½ ounces dry gin

¾ ounce strained, freshly squeezed lemon juice

¾ ounce Simple Syrup (page 369)

2 dashes aromatic bitters (here, we like Dale DeGroff's Pimento Aromatic Bitters)

1 Combine all of the ingredients in a mixing glass. Fill the glass three-quarters full with ice cubes, cover with a Boston shaker tin, and shake vigorously until thoroughly chilled, 15 seconds.

2 Strain into a martini glass.

A PINCH OF SALT

If bitters is our pepper, then vermouth is our—well, salt really doesn't capture it right, does it? Still, much like salt, vermouth provides a palette—an herbal, wine-based one—against which other flavors can shine. More important, if bitters made the Cocktail possible, then vermouth gave birth to the only drink mightier than the Cocktail: the Martini.

As with bitters, we have a whole chapter about vermouth later (page 291), so here we'll stick to the basics. While there are a handful of styles of this aromatized (flavored with botanicals) and fortified (usually with brandy) wine, we're concerned with the two major types: sweet and dry. In booze terms, sweet typically means a lower alcohol content, and you'll see that if you compare Dolin dry (17.5% ABV) and the sweet Dolin rouge (16% ABV). The botanicals can also vary between brands, giving each vermouth its own distinct character.

While there is no hard-and-fast rule about how to apply vermouth, you'll typically see dry (clear) paired with white spirits and sweet (reddish brown) with brown spirits. We even like the latter with beer (see Blue Harvest, page 329). As for classic examples of how vermouth creates an entirely new class of mixed drinks, look no further than the gin-based Martini and the whiskey-based Manhattan.

MARTINI

GLASS: MARTINI, CHILLED | ICE: CUBED | MAKES: 1 DRINK

2½ ounces dry gin

½ ounce dry vermouth

Dash orange bitters (optional)

Lemon twist or olives,
   for garnish

1 Combine the gin, vermouth, and bitters in a mixing glass and place it in the freezer to chill, 10 minutes.

2 Fill the mixing glass three-quarters full with ice cubes and stir rapidly to chill the drink further, 30 seconds.

3 Strain into a chilled martini glass and garnish with the lemon twist, or serve olives in a dish along side.

If You Don't Know the Bartender,
WHAT DO YOU ORDER?

"A Manhattan if I can see him make it—you learn a lot about someone from the way they make a Manhattan—but if I can't, then Maker's [Mark] on the rocks. He can't screw it up, and Maker's isn't fancy enough for him to try and substitute something cheaper."

—DANIEL HANDLER, AUTHOR

MANHATTAN

GLASS: MARTINI, CHILLED | ICE: CUBED | MAKES: 1 DRINK

2 ounces rye whiskey

1 ounce sweet vermouth

Dash aromatic bitters

Orange twist, for garnish

1 Combine the rye, vermouth, and bitters in a mixing glass and place it in the freezer to chill, 10 minutes.

2 Fill the mixing glass three-quarters full with ice cubes and stir rapidly to chill the drink further, 30 seconds.

3 Strain into the chilled martini glass and garnish with the orange twist.

What you'll notice between these two drinks is the vast difference in the amount of vermouth employed. Part of this is due to the desired flavor profile of each drink. Another part is due, however, to the relative difference in the alcohol content of the vermouths. It's always important to consider the strength of your ingredients when making a drink. Should you go with a much higher-proof base spirit (such as overproof navy-strength gin, at 57% ABV), you may need to cut back the spirit and up the vermouth. Choose an intensely flavored vermouth like Carpano Antica (see page 296), and the opposite is true.

Once you have a base spirit chosen, begin to explore bitters and vermouth. Fine examples of each cost as little as $5 or surpass $35—with the price having less to do with outright quality than the size of the producer and the demand. Some bitters are made by large corporations, others by craftspeople in their home kitchen. As with wine and spirits, each has a unique flavor profile, and a bottle of either vermouth or bitters (especially bitters) tends to go a long way.

CHAPTER 4

The 4 Bottle Bar

Imagine you could replace the sugar you normally add to your drinks with sugar-infused booze. Sound tempting? Then say hello to liqueur, a pleasing potion of sugar, spirit, and flavoring. While there are hundreds of liqueurs on the market, we've chosen only one basic class for inclusion in this book: orange liqueur, in which the sweet stuff gets cozy with bitter oranges or tangerines to offer a distinct tanginess. This introduces both a measure of sweetness and a hint of bitterness (you may still need to add sugar to your drink)—but also an additional citrus-and-spice depth.

> While there are hundreds of liqueurs on the market, we've chosen only one basic class for inclusion in this book: orange liqueur.

While we go into greater depth on the distinct styles of orange liqueur—and offer our bottle picks on page 285—here all you need to know is that orange liqueur is a workhouse that plays nicely with any of our spirits. It is as at home in an Old Fashioned or a Manhattan as it is in a sour. And, speaking of sours . . . What happens if you replace part of the sugar with orange liqueur in a drink like the sour? If your base sour is made with Cognac-style brandy and lemon, you get the stalwart Sidecar, a founding member of Cocktail Olympus.

THE SIDECAR

GLASS: MARTINI | ICE: CUBED | MAKES: 1 DRINK

Superfine sugar

Lemon wedge

2 ounces Cognac-style brandy

1 ounce orange liqueur

¾ ounce strained, freshly squeezed lemon juice

Lemon wheel, for garnish

1 Cover a small plate with superfine sugar to a depth of ¼ inch. Halve the lemon wedge widthwise and run a cut edge around the outer rim of a martini glass to dampen it. Roll the glass in the sugar to coat the outer rim.

2 Combine the brandy, orange liqueur, and lemon juice in a mixing glass, fill the glass three-quarters full with ice cubes, cover with a Boston shaker tin, and shake vigorously until thoroughly chilled, 15 seconds.

3 Strain into the prepared martini glass and garnish with the lemon wheel.

If the rimming of the glass for a Sidecar reminds you a bit of a Margarita, you're spot-on. The Sidecar and the Margarita are close cousins, especially if you opt for a bit of orange liqueur in the latter. And don't forget, it's the orange liqueur that turns an everyday Margarita into a Cadillac Margarita.

Elsewhere, the addition of a little orange liqueur can provide additional layers to a traditional recipe. Take, for example, the basic Manhattan recipe on page 47. Before making our Manhattans at home, we like to rinse the glass with a dash of well-chilled orange liqueur. The result (recipe follows) is a drink that's only infinitesimally sweeter, but suddenly has bright citrus notes that are missing from the standard Manhattan.

Our primary reason for choosing orange liqueur over all other liqueurs is its flexibility. Not only does it marry well with all of the primary spirits recommended in this book, it can provide the base drink ingredient all on its own (see Curaçao Punch, page 287) or be applied elsewhere in the kitchen with equal aplomb (think Crêpes Suzette).

MANHATTAN, 12 BOTTLE BAR STYLE

GLASS: MARTINI | ICE: CUBED | MAKES: 1 DRINK

1 teaspoon orange liqueur

2 ounces rye whiskey

1 ounce sweet vermouth

Dash aromatic bitters

Orange twist, for garnish

1 Place the orange liqueur in a martini glass. In a separate mixing glass, combine the rye, vermouth, and bitters. Place both glasses in the freezer to chill, about 10 minutes.

2 Remove the chilled martini glass from the freezer and gently swirl the glass to evenly coat the inside with the liqueur. Shake out any excess liquid.

3 Remove the mixing glass from the freezer and fill it three-quarters full with ice cubes. Stir rapidly to chill the drink further, 30 seconds, then strain into the chilled martini glass and garnish with the orange twist.

Tip:
HOW TO RIM A GLASS

MANY COCKTAILS have the additional flash of a rimmed glass edge, which contributes a sweet, salty, or sometimes spicy component when the drink is sipped. The salted margarita glass is the gold standard, but the technique is also used for drinks as diverse as the Sidecar (opposite page) and the Limoncello Drop (page 266) or Cosmopolitan (page 271).

1. Cover a small plate with your rimming agent (salt, celery salt, chili powder, sugar, and so on) to a depth of ¼ inch.

2. Halve a citrus wedge and run a cut edge along the outer rim of the glass to dampen it.

3. Hold the stem or bottom of the glass (depending on whether it's a martini, collins, or rocks) at a slight angle to the plate and roll the rim into the salt or what-have-you, slowly and carefully turning the glass to coat only the outer edge.

BRANDY / COGNAC
Page 57

DRY GIN
Page 89

GENEVER
Page 135

THE 12 B

VODKA
Page 257

ORANGE LIQUEUR
Page 281

DRY VERMOUTH
Page 291

AMBER RUM
Page 163

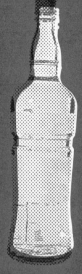

WHITE RUM
Page 207

RYE WHISKEY
Page 231

OTTLES

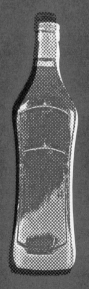

SWEET VERMOUTH
Page 291

AROMATIC BITTERS
Page 301

ORANGE BITTERS
Page 301

CHAPTER 5
Brands

B randy is made everywhere, and can be distilled using any kind of fruit, from apples to grapes, from peaches to pears. For the purposes of stocking a 12 Bottle Bar, though, we are talking about Cognac-style brandy, which is made from grapes, rather than fruit brandies like Calvados (made from apples). And while brandy may have its roots in the alchemy of the Arab world, we can say *Proost* to the Dutch—those intrepid adventuring traders—who sealed the fortunes of a spirit they called *brandewijn*, or burned wine, which they had discovered in their travels and brought home.

T o make Cognac-style brandy requires several rudimentary steps. After fermenting your fruit of choice, you distill the "wine" to create spirits. Then you age the spirit in wood barrels, a process that alters the final style and quality of the brandy. Finally, as with nonvintage Champagne, you blend the spirit to create a consistent flavor profile.

The supreme expression of brandy is Cognac, from the Charente region of western France, where distinct conditions—the maritime climate and chalky soil, in particular—create a soaring evocation of the spirit. In the nearby southwest,

> The supreme expression of brandy is Cognac, from the Charente region of western France.

you will find Armagnac, also known as "France's other brandy," with its own distinct style and fan base (Armagnac, whose single continuous distillation makes it more aggressive and in-your-face than double-distilled Cognac, has an intensely strong flavor).

For the uninitiated, brandy, whether cheap or fine, can seem rather harsh. Once you move past the "burn," the flavor is slightly sweet, sometimes caramelly, a bit orangey even, with notes of oak

Brandy
IN A NUTSHELL

DEFINING FEATURES: A sweet, slightly alcoholic burn

FLAVOR PROFILE: Vanilla, butterscotch, apple, orange, even floral qualities and spices

WHY WE CHOSE IT: It makes some of the most elegant cocktails out there, thanks to its smooth mouthfeel and slightly sweet, fruity character.

EMBLEMATIC DRINKS: Sidecar (page 52), Brandy Milk Punch (page 69)

and tannic dryness. And even if it isn't your tipple of choice, brandy is far more versatile in drinks than you might imagine, lending itself admirably to every category and style, from punch to cocktail, sweet to strong. A Buck (page 241) made with brandy has just enough boozy sweetness to refresh; Brandy Milk Punch (page 69) is the ultimate holiday libation; the Sidecar (page 52) is simply a classic. In fact, brandy can be substituted for pretty much every other spirit in a cocktail, easily making the drink its own. Include brandy in your bottle choices and it won't disappoint you.

COGNAC OR BRANDY?

JUST AS CHAMPAGNE is a sparkling wine made in the Champagne region of France, Cognac is a brandy made only in the Cognac region of the country.

Less than 100 miles north of Bordeaux, which produces some of the most expensive and complex wines in the world, Cognac has always been in the shadow of its Southern brother. Grapes from Cognac—Ugni Blanc, mostly—simply don't produce fine wines, but by a happy accident, they do produce the world's greatest brandy.

Why? Three words: chalk, ocean, and aging. The combination of the region's chalky soils and marine climate married with the technique of oak barrel aging make for modern alchemy.

Peasant Brandy

BRANDY MAY BE called the poor man's Cognac, but every country has a poor man's brandy. Italy has grappa, Spain has aguardiente, even France has its own, called *marc*. Such "peasant brandy," as it's sometimes known, is made not from the grapes themselves, but from the leftovers—pips, skin, pulp—after the grapes are pressed for wine or brandy.

THE BOTTLES TO BUY

There's a middle ground to everything, but here we offer only the high and low roads. The high: a Cognac, for those who don't mind doling out a few more dollars to elevate their cocktails. The low: an inexpensive brandy, for those who wish to count their pennies but still want full, satisfying flavor.

Budget
($20 or less/750 ml)

Artisan/ Premium
($30–$50/750 ml)

PAUL MASSON GRANDE AMBER VSOP BRANDY There are several reasons we like this. First, it's made from a blend of American brandy and French Cognac, which happily makes it taste more like Cognac. Further, it's dry, spicy, and coffee-like; for the price, hard to beat.

REMY MARTIN VSOP COGNAC Vintage Cognacs that specify a year of bottling can set you back thousands of dollars, which is certainly not the aim of 12 Bottle Bar. However, if you are keen to showcase a bottle of Cognac instead of the more generic brandy, then Remy is a solid bet. The price isn't so terribly steep, but the flavors are spot on, especially for cocktails.

All Remy Cognacs are made solely with grapes from the Grande Champagne and Petite Champagne regions, then aged in oak barrels to intensify their flavor.

BRANDY LABEL DESIGNATIONS

You will often see the following initialisms and terms commonly used on bottles. These terms have no "legal" standing, but rather are used by Cognac shippers based on their own conditions. The number of stars can vary from producer to producer. Still, there is a general consensus as to the basic meanings, essentially those having to do with age.

V.S. "Very special," aged four and a half years, also known as "three star"

V.S.O.P. "Very superior (or special) old pale," aged a minimum of four and a half to six years, also known as "five star"

X.O. "Extra old," aged a minimum of six years, up to twenty or more, also called "reserve" or "luxury"; this designation can include "Napoleon" style.

NAPOLEON BRANDY At least six years old but usually older, this term signifies an aged brandy of high quality, in a style that Napoleon was said to have prized.

HORS D'AGE Beyond age. Buy it if you can and savor it.

CHAMPAGNE COGNAC Not to be confused with Champagne itself or the Champagne region. This Cognac is made from grapes specifically produced in the region's two finest zones: Petite Champagne and Grande Champagne.

Theoretically, any of these brandies could be used for mixing—we find that the V.S.O.P. designation works admirably and for a reasonable price.

BRANDY BRETHREN

FRUIT BRANDY CAN be made from any distilled fruit "essence," the pure juice of the fruit, and can be found in countries around the globe, including the good ole U. S. of A. Fruit brandies are often quite nationalistic, so to speak, reflecting a country's or region's favorite or most prolific fruit. Unlike Cognac, these so-called eaux-de-vie are generally colorless because they are rarely aged in wood.

Below are some of the most familiar versions and the fruits from which they are made.

CHILE/PERU—Pisco (grape; the spirit is used in the famed Pisco Sour)

FRANCE—Calvados (apple), Framboise (raspberry), Kirsch (cherry, also made in Germany, Switzerland, and Austria), Poire William (pear)

GERMANY—Schnapps (a generic term for various fruit brandies)

UNITED STATES—Apple Jack, also known as American apple brandy (one of the country's first spirits due to the plethora of apple trees)

CROATIA, SERBIA, AND OTHER COUNTRIES IN FORMER YUGOSLAVIA—Slivovitz (plum)

THE DRINKS

Sweet & Fruity

FEDORA

GLASS: ROCKS | ICE: CUBED, CRUSHED | MAKES: 1 DRINK

There's a longstanding history of naming drinks after anything that's in fashion at the time. We've even committed the crime with our nerdgasm Blue Harvest (see page 329), and back in the golden age of drinks, the practice was even more pronounced. Whether the Fedora cocktail was named after Victorien Sardou's play *Fédora* we can't say, but the late 1800s timing of both sure works in favor of the theory. The play did popularize the hat of the same name.

Flavorwise, this one is strong, sweet, and best consumed in a rocks glass filled with crushed ice.

- 1 tablespoon confectioners' sugar
- 1 teaspoon water
- 1 ounce Cognac-style brandy
- ½ ounce amber rum
- ½ ounce rye whiskey
- 1 ounce orange liqueur
- Lemon wheel, for garnish

1 Combine the sugar and water in a mixing glass and stir until the sugar is mostly dissolved. Add the spirits and liqueur.

2 Fill the mixing glass three-quarters full with ice cubes, cover with a Boston shaker tin, and shake vigorously until thoroughly chilled, 15 seconds.

3 Fill a rocks glass to the brim with crushed ice. Strain the drink into the glass and garnish with the lemon wheel.

JAPANESE COCKTAIL

GLASS: MARTINI | ICE: CUBED | MAKES: 1 DRINK

n 1860 the first Japanese diplomatic mission arrived on U.S. shores. The visit was quite a sensation, and as such, a bit of Japan mania swept America, particularly New York. It should be of little surprise, then, that when Jerry Thomas, then located in NYC, published his pioneering *Bar-Tender's Guide* two years later, a Japanese Cocktail was included within its pages.

Orgeat is a sweet, almond-flavored syrup most commonly used in tiki drinks, and here it provides a beautiful balance between the spirit and the bitters. For the best effect, we recommend you make your own (page 379), though a store-bought variety such as Torani will do. However, if you don't love a sweet, marzipan-y almond flavor, steer clear of the drink altogether, as it does wholly embrace the almond element.

There's nothing particulary Japanese about this drink, except the possible connection to that 19th-century Japanese mission. It is interesting to note, however, that it is the first recorded cocktail named for the sake of cleverness, rather than for its defining spirit. The seemingly simple combination of brandy, orgeat, and bitters is deceiving; they create a sum greater than their parts, with the orgeat adding a creaminess and smoothing out the brandy. All in all, the flavor combination is reminiscent of an intense cocktail cherry.

MOLDY ROOFS

IN COGNAC, BLACK mold grows everywhere, even on the rooftops of the houses and Cognac distilleries. As the alcohol evaporates from the barrels where the Cognac lies aging, the fumes, known as "the Angel's Share," feed—and literally create—the mold. In a fascinating twist of ecosystems, this mold, which also covers the Cognac cellars, is host to thousands of spiders (Cognac producers love the web-spinning beasties) that dine on a very specific type of worm that feeds only on the oak barrels of Cognac.

2 ounces Cognac-style brandy	½ ounce Orgeat Syrup, homemade (page 379) or store-bought
2 dashes aromatic bitters	Lemon twist, for garnish

1 Combine the brandy, bitters, and orgeat syrup in a mixing glass. Fill the glass three-quarters full with ice cubes and stir rapidly until thoroughly chilled, 30 seconds.

2 Strain into a martini glass, rub the lemon twist around the rim of the glass, and place it on top of the drink.

LAWN TENNIS COOLER

GLASS: COLLINS | ICE: CUBED | MAKES: 1 DRINK

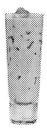

The 1870s saw a new fad—the game of lawn tennis—sweep the western world like wildfire. This meant, of course, that it wasn't long before somebody invented a drink to go along with it. By 1891, William "Cocktail" Boothby's *American Bar-Tender* declared the Lawn Tennis Cooler "a new and popular beverage." If on paper the drink sounds a bit strange, we'll offer that, like the Snowball (page 72), the Lawn

Tip: EGGS IN DRINKS

THE FIRST RULE in using raw eggs in drinks is to make sure that none of your guests has an allergy to them. After that, freshness is key. Always buy the freshest eggs possible from a reputable vendor. Buy pasteurized eggs, in which any bacteria have been killed. Store eggs in the coldest part of your fridge and toss any that are cracked or smell spoiled.

Should you have trouble getting your eggs to froth, first, try shaking harder (you might try the hard shake described on page 98). If that consistently fails, try another brand and you may have better luck—different egg producers have different quality eggs.

Tennis Cooler—which includes a whole egg and ginger beer among its ingredients—immediately evokes an Orange Julius; it's trapped somewhere between lemonade and an ice-cream parlor treat. In other words, it's the perfect quencher to sip while enjoying a lawn tennis match.

• •

2 teaspoons granulated sugar

1½ ounces strained, freshly squeezed lemon juice

1½ ounces Cognac-style brandy

1 large egg (see box, page 98)

Ginger beer (see Note)

Ground cinnamon or fresh whole nutmeg, for garnish (see Note, page 70)

• •

1 Combine the sugar and lemon juice in a mixing glass and stir to dissolve the sugar. Add the brandy and egg, then shake without ice (this is a "dry shake") to emulsify, 15 seconds.

2 Fill the mixing glass three-quarters full with cubed ice and shake again vigorously until thoroughly chilled, 15 seconds.

3 Fill a collins glass with cubed ice (or a spear) and strain the drink into the glass.

Top with ginger beer, stirring gently to combine.

4 Garnish with a dusting of cinnamon or a grating of nutmeg over the top.

NOTE: Ginger beer is a frequent addition to many cocktails, one that is available at most natural foods supermarkets and liquor stores. We especially like Reed's Premium Ginger Brew. Whichever brand you choose, note that we are not talking about ginger ale here.

• •

STINGER

GLASS: MARTINI | ICE: CUBED | MAKES: 1 DRINK

For many a year, the Stinger was last on the list of cocktails we were anxious to try. Maybe it's just us, but the combination of brandy and crème de menthe sounded as far from appetizing as a drink could get. Then, as luck would have it, we tried one. And everything changed.

Ostensibly, the Stinger is an Andes candy in a glass, and like its confectionery cousin, it does the after-dinner thing just right. Should you find yourself loosening your belt a notch post-meal, the digestif Stinger may be just what you need to help ease your overindulgence.

On another front, if you're invited to a '50s- or '60s-themed dinner party, we suggest bringing a bottle of homemade Stingers (see Variations), which makes for a lovely, theme-appropriate contribution to the festivities.

• •

1½ ounces Cognac-style brandy

1½ ounces Crème de Menthe Liqueur (page 384)

• •

1 Combine the brandy and crème de menthe in a mixing glass, fill the glass three-quarters full with ice cubes, cover with a Boston shaker tin, and shake vigorously until thoroughly chilled, 15 seconds.

2 Strain into a martini glass.

VARIATIONS

STORE-BOUGHT STINGERS Our recipe is based on homemade crème de menthe. If you'd rather use a ready-made bottle, start with the following proportions: 2¼ ounces brandy, ¾ ounce crème de menthe. The results will be noticeably less subtle, probably more cloyingly sweet. Err on the side of clear, not green, crème de menthe.

STINGERS FOR A CROWD To make a bunch of Stingers for a party, combine equal parts brandy and homemade Crème de Menthe Liqueur in a bottle or other tightly sealed container. Shake or stir to combine. When it comes time to make the drinks, shake or stir again and measure 3 ounces per drink into the mixing glass, then shake each drink as directed in the recipe. The bottled Stinger mix will keep almost indefinitely when stored, closed, in the fridge.

Great Bars
THEN & NOW

21 CLUB | 21 WEST 52ND STREET
NEW YORK, NY 10019 | 212-582-7200 | 21CLUB.COM

THERE ARE FEW Prohibition-era speakeasies more famous than the 21 Club, whose reputation has been earned as much for the elaborate system used to hide the booze from raiding boys in blue as for the row of jockeys adorning the entrance (and, of course, for its celebrity clientele). Over the years, the famous 21 wine cellar—actually located in the basement of the building next door—has played host to the private wine collections of presidents Ford and Nixon, Elizabeth Taylor, Aristotle Onassis, and many others.

Have a drink in the legendary Bar Room, its ceiling blanketed with toys donated over the years by notable guests. If you visit the 21's website beforehand, you can locate the tables favored by various celebrities. Which table James Bond and Tiffany Case chose when they enjoyed Stingers in *Diamonds Are Forever* isn't indicated, but we'd be happy sidling up to table 51, Bill Murray's favorite.

BRANDY MILK PUNCH

GLASS: ROCKS | ICE: CUBED | MAKES: 1 DRINK

I f you've ever pondered the purpose of brunch, here we'll offer that the long, leisurely Sunday nosh was invented solely as an excuse to consume copious Brandy Milk Punches. So perfect is the combination that, should you not yet have had the pleasure of meeting the Milk Punch, we insist that you immediately put this book down and—regardless of time of day—whip up a Dutch baby pancake, a side of bananas Foster, and as many Brandy Milk Punches as you can muster. After one glass of creamy sweetness and brandy warmth, you'll immediately want another. And probably another. Just don't plan on going anywhere for a while—and you won't have to, because it'll be brunch. You'll notice that we suggest vanilla extract as an optional addition; for us, it adds just a hint more sweetness and roundness, but since some folks are not fans of the flavor, it's in your court.

1½ ounces Cognac-style
   brandy

1 ounce Simple Syrup
   (page 369)

2 ounces half-and-half

Dash pure vanilla extract
   (optional)

Fresh whole nutmeg,
   for garnish (see Note)

1 Combine the brandy, Simple Syrup, half-and-half, and vanilla, if using, in a mixing glass. Fill the glass three-quarters full with the ice cubes, cover with a Boston shaker tin, and shake vigorously until thoroughly chilled, 15 seconds.

2 Place 4 or 5 ice cubes in a rocks glass. Strain the drink into the glass and garnish with a grating of nutmeg.

NOTE: We like to keep a whole nutmeg on hand for garnishing drinks, so that we can freshly grate a bit on top with a Microplane zester (see Tools of the Trade, page 16). Feel free to use a dash of ground nutmeg instead.

VARIATION

RUM MILK PUNCH Replace part or all of the brandy with amber rum.

BOMBARDINO-CALIMERO

GLASS: HEATPROOF MUG, WARMED | MAKES: 1 DRINK

When you find yourself desperate for a spur-of-the-moment getaway to a chalet in the Italian Alps, then the Bombardino-Calimero is your ticket to paradise. Egg-based drinks are immensely popular in the alpine resorts; advocaat, a Dutch egg-based liqueur, is easier to find in stores than its Italian cousins, hence the reason we use it in the recipe. If you are feeling ambitious, do make your own advocaat (page 382); it is vastly superior to the bottled version and is so lusciously eggy, you may be tempted to eat it with a spoon. Warning: advocaat already has brandy in it—it's potent stuff.

The Bombardino-Calimero varies subtly depending on where you order it. The basic Bombardino, also known as "the Bomb," is equal parts advocaat and brandy, sort of an Italian spin on boozy eggnog. The Calimero version includes an equal part of coffee. Call it what you will, it warms your cockles on a chilly day.

¼ cup heavy (whipping) cream (or store-bought whipped cream), for serving

Granulated sugar (optional)

Pure vanilla extract (optional)

1 ounce Advocaat (page 382)

1 ounce Cognac-style brandy

1 ounce brewed hot coffee or espresso

Cocoa powder, for garnish

1 If making homemade whipped cream, place the heavy cream in a medium bowl, add sugar and vanilla extract to taste, and whip until stiff. Set aside.

2 Combine the advocaat and brandy in a small saucepan over medium-low heat and bring to a simmer, stirring constantly.

3 Meanwhile, heat the mug by running it under very hot water; dry it thoroughly.

4 Remove the advocaat mixture from the heat and pour into the warmed mug. Top with the coffee and stir to combine.

5 Top with the whipped cream and garnish with a dusting of cocoa powder.

"When it comes to cocktails, the way that the senses are interconnected is often overlooked. To truly make something delicious you have to triumph over flavor—manipulate it, have a command over it. The scent of a drink, the way it looks in the glass, or the sounds that are emitted whilst making it are all part of our experience of that drink. Inspiration can come from many places."

—TONY CONIGLIARO, BARTENDER, CONSULTANT, AND BAR OWNER

SNOWBALL

GLASS: COLLINS | ICE: CUBED | MAKES: 1 DRINK

If Ron Burgundy had been in London during the swingin' '70s, he would have drunk a Snowball. While the drink appears to date back to the 1940s or 1950s, it hit its stride in the '70s and experienced a massive upsurge in popularity when British entertaining maven Nigella Lawson championed it in 2007. At first glance, the combination of flavors—egg liqueur and American-style lemonade—sounds positively repulsive. When blended together, however, the drink tastes like an orange Dreamsicle, that illogically wonderful ice-cream bar with vanilla ice milk inside and orange Popsicle outside. While you can opt for bottled advocaat and store-bought lemonade, do yourself a favor and make the whole thing from scratch. You will not be disappointed.

1 ounce Advocaat (page 382)

3 ounces freshly made
    Lemonade (recipe follows)

Lime wedge (optional)

Fill a collins glass with ice cubes and add the advocaat and lemonade to the glass. Stir to combine. A squeeze of lime is optional.

Lemonade

MAKES: 5 CUPS

1½ cups strained, freshly
    squeezed lemon juice
    (about 8 medium-size
    lemons), plus extra as
    needed

1 cup Simple Syrup
    (page 369), plus extra
    as needed

2½ cups water

1 In a pitcher or large airtight container, stir together the lemon juice and simple syrup to combine.

2 Add the water and stir to combine. Adjust the sweetness or tartness by adding more syrup or lemon juice to taste.

TOM AND JERRY

GLASS: HEATPROOF MUGS, WARMED | MAKES: ABOUT 8 DRINKS

I n the 19th century, London sports writer Pierce Egan chronicled the fictional misadventures of one Jerry Hawthorn, Esq., and his dapper friend Corinthian Tom. Egan surely created the characters, but he lays no claim to the drink itself. For that, we look to golden-age barman Jerry Thomas, who says he invented the drink himself in 1847, but a reference in the 1835 *Rambler in North America* by Charles Joseph La Trobe debunks Thomas's claim. Let's just say that the Tom and Jerry, perhaps not yet named as such, seems to have appeared sometime between 1821, when Egan wrote his tale, and 1835.

Those rambles aside, it's clear that during the nineteenth and early twentieth centuries, Christmas simply wasn't Christmas without a punch bowl of Tom and Jerry in the mix. In the past fifty years, the drink has sadly gone out of fashion, but it remains a winning eggnoglike dance of spirits and batter that will liven up any party.

This is a drink that requires a bit of patience to acquire the right technique, so if your version seems a little out of balance, practice! As writer Damon Runyon said, "Making Tom and Jerry is by no means child's play. In fact, it takes quite an expert. . . . a good hot Tom and Jerry maker commands good wages and many friends."

As holding with tradition, you would do best to keep the batter in a bowl of its own and mix each drink individually as requested. And make sure you stir the batter between each use, lest the ingredients separate, then stir the drink thoroughly as you add spirits and water.

• •

4 large eggs, separated

Pinch cream of tartar

¾ cup confectioners' sugar

Pinch ground allspice

Pinch ground cinnamon

Pinch ground cloves

4 ounces Cognac-style brandy

4 ounces amber rum

Boiling water or hot milk
 (about 1½ cups per drink)

Fresh whole nutmeg,
 for garnish (see Note,
 page 70)

• •

1 Combine the egg whites and cream of tartar in a large, clean bowl and beat them with an electric mixer until stiff.

The Devil Made Him Do It
AN APOCRYPHAL TALE OF COGNAC

IN THE SIXTEENTH century, a knight by the name of Jacques de la Croix-Maron came home from the Crusades and found his wife in bed with another man. Overwhelmed with rage, Jacques killed both of them, only to be plagued by a recurring dream in which the Devil boiled him twice over in Hell. Jacques woke up thinking he needed to burn something he loved, so he chose his favored wine, thus inventing double distillation, the process that produces smoother Cognac.

2 In a separate large bowl, beat the egg yolks until thin and blended. Add the confectioners' sugar and beat to combine. Add the allspice, cinnamon, and cloves and beat to combine.

3 Fold the egg whites into the egg yolk mixture and beat until light and frothy.

4 Heat the mugs by running them under very hot water; dry them thoroughly.

5 Fill half of a warmed mug with batter. Add ½ ounce each of the brandy and rum and stir to combine. Top with the boiling water or hot milk and stir to combine. Garnish with a fresh grating of nutmeg.

6 Repeat step 5 with the remaining batter, spirits, and boiling water, garnishing each drink with a grating of nutmeg.

HORCHATA CON COÑAC

GLASS: ROCKS OR PUNCH | MAKES: 2½ QUARTS

Horchata is a milk-based drink made most commonly from ground rice, as well as seeds or nuts, and flavorings like cinnamon and vanilla. Its origins most likely date back to milks made from barley. As to Coñac, aka Cognac, well, funny you should ask. That part goes back to Napoleon

III, *the* Napoleon's nephew, who got a bit overly ambitious and decided to invade Mexico, in what culminated in the Battle of Puebla, on May 5, 1862. Mexico versus France, thus horchata and Cognac. (We swear this is how we got the idea.) The story may be a stretch, but we think this drink is a nice alternative to the usual Cinco de Mayo cerveza.

Horchata is one of those drinks that gets better over time, so be sure to allow it a few hours in the fridge for the flavors to meld. Tradition says to serve it over ice. As this dilutes the drink, skip the ice and just keep it cold in the refrigerator.

1 cup uncooked long-grain rice

8 cups warm water

½ teaspoon ground cinnamon

1¼ cups whole milk

1 can (14 ounces) sweetened condensed milk

1 teaspoon pure vanilla extract

¼ cup Cognac-style brandy, or to taste

1 Combine the rice and warm water in a large bowl and let it stand, covered, at room temperature, for 30 minutes.

2 Drain the rice, reserving the water, and place the rice in the bowl of a food processor. Add the cinnamon and process until the rice is the consistency of a fine meal.

3 Return the rice to the reserved water and let the mixture stand, covered, at room temperature, stirring occasionally, until the water turns milky white, at least 2 hours.

4 Strain the rice mixture through a fine-mesh sieve into a bowl or pitcher. Add the milk, condensed milk, vanilla, and brandy and stir to combine. Refrigerate at least 2 hours and up to several days. Stir before serving.

Tangy & Citrusy

BETWEEN THE SHEETS

GLASS: MARTINI | ICE: CUBED | MAKES: 1 DRINK

I f cocktails hadn't provided a little social lubrication between the sexes, they probably wouldn't still be with us today. In any case, the subtle—or, at least, less adolescent—seductions of adult beverages seem to have been lost somewhere across the decades. Whereas today we might ply the future mother or father of our children with a Wyoming Legspreader—yes, it's a real drink—or a Three-legged Monkey (both drinks we have apologetically neglected to include herein), there was a time when a drink could have both an instigating moniker *and* quality ingredients. The Between the Sheets, which originated during the Prohibition era, offers a lovely balance of sweet and sour to appeal to both sexes. The first drink breaks the ice; the second comes with complimentary turndown service.

¾ ounce Cognac-style brandy

¾ ounce dry gin

¾ ounce orange liqueur

¾ ounce strained, freshly squeezed lemon juice

1 Combine all the ingredients in a mixing glass. Fill the glass three-quarters full with ice cubes, cover with a Boston shaker tin, and shake vigorously until thoroughly chilled, 15 seconds.

2 Strain into a martini glass.

BRANDY DAISY

GLASS: ROCKS | ICE: CUBED, CRUSHED | MAKES: 1 DRINK

T he Daisy is an old drink, coming to us from the early days of portable potable potions. Pick at its petals and you'll find a sour lurking within; in fact, it's the soda that separates a Daisy from your garden variety sour.

Recipes for a proper Daisy abound, and here we've cobbled together a few of our favorites to create a drink that is not so far removed from San Pellegrino brand's orangey Aranciata soda.

If you're inclined to believe that the orange liqueur here provides enough sweetness and that the grenadine can be skipped, we're inclined to disagree. Just a small touch of the pomegranate syrup not only provides additional depth but also acts as a binder that pulls everything else together.

1½ ounces Cognac-style brandy

¾ ounce strained, freshly squeezed lemon juice

¾ ounce orange liqueur

¼ teaspoon Grenadine, homemade (page 376) or store-bought

Club soda

1 Combine the brandy, lemon juice, orange liqueur, and grenadine in a mixing glass. Fill the glass three-quarters full with ice cubes, cover with a Boston shaker tin, and shake vigorously until thoroughly chilled, 15 seconds.

2 Fill a rocks glass one-third full with crushed ice. Strain the drink into the rocks glass and top with club soda.

Tip:
STRAIN YOUR CITRUS JUICE

ALL CITRUS FRUITS have pulp in them and, when they are juiced, some of the pulp makes its way into the juice. In order to have a perfectly smooth, unpulpy drink, *always double-strain your citrus juice.*

To do this, squeeze your citrus fruit through a hand juicer (see Tools of the Trade, page 16) to catch the seeds, thus "straining" it, and then pass the juice through a fine-mesh sieve to remove any excess pulp before adding the juice to your drink ingredients.

EMBASSY

Should you have ranked among the rich and famous of Prohibition-era Hollywood, odds were that you would have spent your nights out at a club run by Adolph "Eddie" Brandstatter. Back in the day of Clark Gable, Brandstatter owned the nightlife about town—Sardi's, Café Montmartre, and the Embassy Club, the namesake of this 1930s tipple.

While the Embassy's combination of brandy and amber rum may seem counterintuitive, the two are perfect bedfellows, and when rounded out by very traditional sour ingredients, the result is a nice light sour with a good amount of depth.

1 ounce Cognac-style brandy

1 ounce amber rum

1 ounce orange liqueur

½ ounce strained, freshly squeezed lime juice

1 teaspoon Simple Syrup (page 369)

1 Combine all of the ingredients in a mixing glass. Fill the glass three-quarters full with ice cubes, cover with a Boston shaker tin, and shake vigorously until thoroughly chilled, 15 seconds.

2 Strain into a martini glass.

HORSE'S NECK

If you're wondering how a drink consisting of brandy, ginger beer, and bitters became known as Horse's Neck, it's due to the garnish that traditionally adorns the glass—a curvaceous peel of lemon that dangles over the rim much like, well, a horse's neck. Mixed drinks containing ginger beer became popular toward the latter half of the nineteenth century, a time when mass-produced sodas began to hit the market.

There's little mystery to the Horse's Neck. If you like the ingredients, you'll like the drink. It's a classic "highball" in the most basic sense, and any of the parts can be tweaked as your heart desires, with the style of ginger beer you choose—spicy, sweet, or dry—having perhaps the greatest impact.

··

1 lemon

2 ounces Cognac-style brandy

3 dashes aromatic bitters

Ginger beer

··

1 Peel the lemon in a single, long strip using a vegetable peeler, removing as little of the white pith as possible. Insert the peel in a collins glass, leaving one end hanging over the rim.

2 Add a few ice cubes to the glass, then the brandy and bitters. Top with ginger beer.

··

KNICKERBOCKER CLUB

GLASS: COLLINS | ICE: CUBED | MAKES: 1 DRINK

I n 1809, missing person advertisements appeared in New York newspapers for one Diedrich Knickerbocker, historian. The notices were apparently placed by a hotelier who threatened to publish a manuscript belonging to Mr. Knickerbocker, should the latter not return and pay his outstanding debt. The citizens followed the story anxiously and were rewarded when *Knickerbocker's History of New York* soon landed on bookstore shelves. The book was a hit, and it made a name for its true author—the man behind the missing person/hotelier hoax, a viral marketing stunt if ever there was one—Washington Irving. Irving wrote the book under the pseudonym Knickerbocker, the actual surname of a friend, which he borrowed to describe New York's upper class. Soon, everyone and everything wanted to be a Knickerbocker (and the name eventually became synonymous with "New Yorker").

It should come as no surprise that a Gilded Age gentleman's club should appropriate the moniker and, subsequently, lend its name to the drink. In The *Old Waldorf-Astoria Bar Book* of 1935, the cocktail is simply "Knickerbocker," and we are told that it was purportedly created for the members of the club, which would one day include Franklin D. Roosevelt. For the purposes of this book, we've changed its name to avoid confusion with the better-known rum-based Knickerbocker (rum, raspberry syrup, orange liqueur, lime) but the original Waldorf-Astoria recipe remains intact. Tip: Don't overdo it on the club soda.

• •

1½ ounces Cognac-style brandy

¾ ounce strained, freshly squeezed lemon juice

1 teaspoon Simple Syrup (page 369), preferably made with raw sugar, such as Demerara

2 dashes aromatic bitters

Club soda

• •

Place 3 or 4 ice cubes in a collins glass. Add the brandy, lemon juice, Simple Syrup, and bitters, top with club soda, and stir gently to combine.

Great Bars
THEN & NOW

**LE HARRY'S NEW YORK BAR | 5 RUE DAUNOU
75002 PARIS | (33) 1-42-61 71-14 | HARRYSBAR.FR**

HARRY'S BAR AMERICAINE, as it was originally called, was an oasis in the sea of American Prohibition, playing host to everyone from Hemingway to Knute Rockne. When the U.S. dried out in 1920, American bartender Harry MacElhone set his sights on the alcohol-friendly Parisian landscape, opening his bar to cater to American expats and tourists desperate for a bit of booze and camaraderie.

Harry is as famous as his namesake bar, laying claim to inventing some of the cocktail world's most famous drinks, including the White Lady (1919), the Bloody Mary (1921), the Scoff-law (1924), and the Sidecar (1931).

SIDECAR

GLASS: MARTINI | ICE: CUBED | MAKES: 1 DRINK

There are a number of stories about how the Sidecar got its name. Some say it comes from the famed Harry's Bar in Paris, the drink apparently being named in honor of a patron who always arrived on his sidecar-clad motorcycle. Harry's Bar owner Harry MacElhone gave credit for the drink to Pat MacGarry, the bartender at Buck's Club in London. (Later, MacElhone would claim he invented it himself.) On the other hand, master mixologist Dale DeGroff likes the simple answer that, in barman's terms, a sidecar is a small glass of "extra from the shaker" served alongside a cocktail. However the name came to be, there's little debate that the Sidecar, scion of the more antiquated bitter-spiked Brandy Crusta, owns a place in the Classic Cocktail Hall of Fame. Look at the ingredients and you'll see that you have a Margarita of a different stripe—a strong, tangy, and refreshing quaff.

Superfine sugar

Lemon wedge

2 ounces Cognac-style brandy

1 ounce orange liqueur

¾ ounce strained, freshly squeezed lemon juice

Lemon wheel, for garnish

1 Cover a small plate with superfine sugar to a depth of ¼ inch. Halve the lemon wedge widthwise and run a cut edge around the outer rim of the glass to dampen it. Roll the glass in the sugar to coat the outer rim.

2 Combine the brandy, orange liqueur, and lemon juice in a mixing glass. Fill the glass three-quarters full with ice cubes and shake vigorously until thoroughly chilled, 15 seconds.

3 Strain into the prepared martini glass and garnish with the lemon wheel.

SOOTHER

GLASS: MARTINI | ICE: CUBED | MAKES: 1 DRINK

T he Soother is one of those drinks that just screams autumn. Warming, sweet, a bit tart—this cocktail is a cozy sweater and a crisp evening stroll through crunchy leaves. The apple note is heightened by the lemon juice and conjures orchards and fresh pressed cider, which would be a brilliant substitution for the apple juice should you have it. If you find yourself wondering which liquid companion should join you fireside or on a hayride, look no further. (In which case, you may wish to warm the concoction: Heat it in a small saucepan over medium-low heat and pour it into a heat-resistant glass.)

1 ounce Cognac-style brandy

1 ounce amber rum

½ ounce orange liqueur

1 teaspoon apple juice

½ ounce strained, freshly squeezed lemon juice

½ teaspoon Simple Syrup (page 369)

1 Combine all of the ingredients in a mixing glass. Fill the glass three-quarters full with ice cubes, cover with a Boston shaker tin, and shake vigorously until thoroughly chilled, 15 seconds.

2 Strain into a martini glass.

CORPSE REVIVER SHOT

GLASS: SYRINGE | ICE: CUBED, CRUSHED | MAKES: 8 DRINKS
(15CC EACH—A GOOD-SIZE DOSE)

T he Corpse Reviver is a classic. Historically, the name was given to a collection of drinks, all numbered to denote the spirit used in the drink and all offering ways to riff on the basic format. Ours comes from the *Café Royal Cocktail Book* (1937), but we have substituted orange liqueur for the standard orange juice to give the drink a shooter quality.

Our Halloween version is served in syringes (see Resources, page 393) and any size from 5cc to 50cc—we find 15cc works well—can be used; one recipe makes 120cc.

BAR CONS

"SAY, THIS might interest you..."

That's how so many cons and scams start—everything from the grand thievery of Bernard Madoff to the small stings used to win a free drink have begun with some variation on this phrase. And these words have more often than not been uttered while the predator and victim have shared a frosty beverage.

The essence of con artistry lies in the first part of that name: con. It is short for confidence, and there is no better place to gain the confidence of another than in a drinking establishment. It was while having a drink that "Count" Victor Lustig sold the Eiffel Tower to a sucker. And it was while imbibing a cocktail that Titanic Thompson took Al Capone for several hundred bucks.

There is something about communal drinking that fosters camaraderie and good will, the very things con artists use to their advantage. It is a scientific fact that people lower their guard when they raise a glass to their lips. And there is an element of art to it all. The object of con artistry is to separate a mark from their money. The challenge is to do it not with brute force, but with finesse. Beguiling subterfuge is the tool. It makes the mark think one thing when the reality is something very different. What is ideal is not to steal the mark's money, but to have him simply hand it over— to make it so that giving you the money was his idea. The ultimate goal is to achieve such a level of refinement that the crime is not even detected. To this end, alcohol greatly helps.

—TODD ROBBINS, AUTHOR,
THE MODERN CON MAN

---

1 ounce Cognac-style brandy

1 ounce orange liqueur

1 ounce freshly squeezed lemon juice

Dash Grenadine, homemade (page 376) or store-bought

1 Combine all of the ingredients in a mixing glass, fill the glass three-quarters full with ice cubes, cover with a Boston shaker tin, and shake until thoroughly combined, 15 seconds.

2 Strain into a small bowl or glass and load the syringes. Serve the syringes on a bed of crushed ice.

Strong

BRANDY PUNCH

GLASS: ROCKS | ICE: CUBED, CRUSHED | MAKES: 1 DRINK

We're suckers for tropical drinks that are more than just rum layered upon more rum. Brandy Punch comes to us via *Dr. Siegert's Angostura Bitters Drinks Guide* of 1908, and we've translated the proportions solely to make the drink easier to assemble. Much like the Mint Julep (page 238) this is a strong drink that insists on a glass chock full of crushed ice, which not only chills things but also provides a gradual and much needed dilution.

Given its booze-forward profile, we debated whether this was a strong drink or a sweet one, as it's too much of one to really be the other. In the end, however, there's no denying that this is first and foremost a cocktail and not a confection. Having said that, its middle note is sweetness—feel free to up the sugar to your liking.

• •

2 ounces Cognac-style brandy

¼ teaspoon amber rum

½ teaspoon strained, freshly squeezed lemon juice

¼ teaspoon Raspberry Syrup (page 372) or Grenadine, homemade (page 376) or store-bought

2 dashes aromatic bitters

½ ounce Simple Syrup (page 369)

Seasonal fresh fruit such as berries, pineapple, or citrus, sliced and/or skewered, for garnish

• •

1 Combine all the liquid ingredients in a mixing glass. Fill the glass three-quarters full with ice cubes, cover with a Boston shaker tin, and shake vigorously until thoroughly chilled, 15 seconds.

2 Fill a rocks glass with crushed ice. Strain the drink into the glass and garnish with the fruit.

FROM CRIME TO COGNAC

ONE OF COGNAC'S first spirited opportunists was Jean Martell, who left behind a life of smuggling to found the House of Martell in 1715. When Martell died in 1753, his wife, Rachel, took over the family business.

In 1775, the House of Martell shipped its first barrels of Cognac to America; two centuries later, it was the Cognac of choice aboard the inaugural launch of the *Queen Mary*.

HAPPY ACCIDENT

GLASS: MARTINI | ICE: CUBED | MAKES: 1 DRINK

There's that old candy bar jingle, "Sometimes you feel like a nut, sometimes . . ." well, you know. When it comes to strong cocktails, sometimes you feel like a Manhattan or a Martini, and sometimes you feel like something a little less jaw-tightening. Enter the Happy Accident, which came to be via its very namesake. One day, while making a drink called the Augui from the *Sloppy Joe's Bar* book of 1932–33, we mistakenly left out the juice of a whole lemon. We enjoyed the resulting drink so much that it wasn't until a subsequent attempt that we finally caught our mistake and made the drink as written. As happy accidents are prone to go, we preferred the mistake.

Present here is all the bold varnish you'd expect from the composite ingredients—woodsy vermouth, herbal gin, and oaky brandy—tempered by just enough sweetness to keep the occasion from turning too serious.

1 ounce Cognac-style brandy

1 ounce dry vermouth

1 ounce dry gin

¼ teaspoon orange liqueur

¼ teaspoon Grenadine, homemade (page 376) or store-bought

Lemon twist, for garnish

Brandied Cherry (page 367) or high-quality maraschino cherry (we like Luxardo brand), for garnish

1 Combine all of the liquid ingredients in a mixing glass. Fill the glass three-quarters full with ice cubes, cover with a Boston shaker tin, and shake vigorously until thoroughly chilled, 15 seconds.

2 Strain into a martini glass and garnish with the lemon twist and cherry.

METROPOLITAN

GLASS: MARTINI, CHILLED | ICE: CUBED | MAKES: 1 DRINK

As gin has its Martini and whiskey (rye, thank you very much) has its Manhattan, brandy has its Metropolitan. More akin to the Manhattan than the Martini, this is an equally old drink, stemming from the late nineteenth century, when vermouth exploded on the American cocktail scene. You might find riffs on the Cosmopolitan out there that are also called Metropolitans. Those drinks would be wrong.

If you're a brandy fan looking for your own "serious" cocktail, the Metropolitan will provide what you need.

2 ounces Cognac-style brandy

1 ounce sweet vermouth

½ teaspoon orange liqueur

Dash aromatic bitters

Lemon twist, for garnish

Brandied Cherry (page 367) or high-quality maraschino cherry (we like Luxardo brand), for garnish

1 Combine the Cognac, vermouth, liqueur, and bitters in a mixing glass. Fill the glass three-quarters full with ice cubes, cover with a Boston shaker tin, and shake vigorously until thoroughly chilled, 15 seconds.

2 Strain into a chilled martini glass and garnish with the lemon twist and cherry.

SARATOGA

GLASS: MARTINI, CHILLED | ICE: CUBED | MAKES: 1 DRINK

During the late nineteenth century, what happened in Saratoga Springs stayed in Saratoga Springs. Not long after the end of the Revolutionary War, this New York town renowned for its healing waters began to grow into the Las Vegas of its day. First came the luxury hotels, then came the ponies and the gambling. Of particular note was the Saratoga Clubhouse. The proprietor of the Saratoga Clubhouse was one John Morrissey, champion bare-knuckle fighter turned U.S. Congressman with links to Manhattan's Dead Rabbits gang, and enemy of William "Bill the Butcher" Poole of that city's Bowery Boys gang. That should give you some idea of what kind of place the Saratoga Clubhouse was. The *New York Times* proclaimed it to be "the finest hell on earth," where, as one reporter noted, "fast young men" lost their money gambling with "a strange, unvarying regularity." The drink—which may or may not have been named for the Clubhouse, or even the town itself—offers not only a fine variation on the classic Manhattan but also a liquid trip to a grand, elegant, and undeniably brutish age now forever lost in time.

1 ounce Cognac-style brandy

1 ounce rye whiskey

1 ounce sweet vermouth

2 dashes aromatic bitters

½ lemon wheel, for garnish

WISCONSIN LOVES BRANDY!

NO ONE KNOWS why or when it started, but Wisconsinites adore the fruit-based spirit. Order an Old Fashioned and it's likely to be made with brandy. As of 2012, the state drank one-third of all the brandy that Korbel, a California-based megaproducer, makes. Why this mysterious affection for brandy? Some historians speculate that it's rooted in the state's German/Polish heritage, which is steeped in the tradition of drinking schnapps. Regardless, these folks like their Old Fashioned cocktails so much that in 2013 a couple of entrepreneurs started producing and bottling the stuff as Arty's Brandy Old Fashioned Sweet.

1 Combine the brandy, rye, vermouth, and bitters in a mixing glass. Fill the glass three-quarters full with ice cubes and stir rapidly until thoroughly chilled, 30 seconds.

2 Strain into a chilled martini glass and garnish with the lemon.

Great Bars
THEN & NOW

**THE AMERICAN BAR | SAVOY HOTEL | STRAND
LONDON, UNITED KINGDOM WC 2R 0EU | (44) 20-7836-4343
FAIRMONT.COM/SAVOY-LONDON/DINING/AMERICANBAR/**

TWO OF THE greatest bartenders in history—Harry Craddock and Ada Coleman—worked there. One of the most comprehensive early twentieth-century cocktail books comes from there. Sir Winston Churchill and Frank Sinatra stayed there. The Savoy Hotel, which opened in 1889, is one of the world's great hotels, and the Savoy Hotel bar is a part of history.

We like to call the Savoy "the house that Gilbert & Sullivan built." More correctly, though, it's the hotel that Richard D'Oyly Carte built. Carte was Gilbert & Sullivan's manager, a brilliant promoter whose success with his clients led him to build a theater just to stage their shows. The Savoy Theater, which opened in 1891, staged every G&S operetta from then on. The Savoy Hotel, which swung wide its doors eight years later, housed every tourist and aficionado who came to see the Savoy operas.

The American Bar at the Savoy has been a part of the hotel's history since the beginning, launching the careers of hundreds of bartenders then and now. If you go to only one bar while you are visiting London, make it the American Bar.

CHAPTER 6

Dry Gin

CHAPTER 6

Dry Gin

We love gin. It's one of the most versatile and malleable of all spirits, making it the darling of bartenders the world over. It's also refreshing and invigorating, a winning combination when it is used as a cocktail base. The Martini, the Gimlet, the Rickey, the Fizz—they all demand dry gin.

If you happen to be one of many people who think gin tastes like Pine-Sol, we understand. Gin can start more "love it—hate it" arguments than jazz. Yes, we admit that some (not all) gin tastes like you are drinking a Christmas tree. But, the simple fact is, if you are going to make real drinks, especially classic cocktails, you need to show gin some love.

For all intents and purposes, gin—the anglicized name of the word *genever* ("juniper" in Dutch), the spirit that is gin's precursor—starts its life as vodka. This grain-neutral spirit (usually a combination of corn, barley, rye, and wheat) or grape-neutral spirit is then distilled with a wide variety of botanicals, particularly berries from the coniferous juniper shrub, which are generally what gives gin its distinctive, sometimes unpopular, flavor. The predominant use of juniper over other botanicals, as well as a lack of additional sugars, is what classifies a gin as dry. And the more juniper, the more perceived dryness. The bottom line is that with dry gin, there's really no way to get around the presence of the juniper; after all, that's how gin got its name.

Gin
IN A NUTSHELL

DEFINING FEATURES: Botanicals, botanicals, and more botanicals

FLAVOR PROFILE: Juniper is most often key, along with floral, citrus, and herbal notes.

WHY WE CHOSE IT: It is the most versatile cocktail spirit there is.

EMBLEMATIC DRINKS: Martini, Gin and Tonic, Tom Collins, Gin Fizz

A Dry Gin

1688

DUTCH-BORN William of Orange becomes king of England and brings with him his love of the malt-based, juniper-flavored genever, the original Dutch gin.

1720

THE POOR want to drink like kings, so they start making their own genever. Distilled from low-quality grain and cut with nasty additives like lime, oil of vitriol—that's sulfuric acid, folks—and turpentine, this rotgut made moonshine seem downright healthy.

1736

LONDON PROPER has more than twenty thousand gin shops, which include everything from back alley sellers to bars and general stores. Welcome to the Gin Craze era.

1750

LONDON ALONE, with its population of only 600,000, consumes roughly 11 million gallons of gin a year—at 160 proof! In comparison, modern gin is generally 80 to 90 proof.

1751 & 1756

THE FINAL Gin Act drastically raises gin prices in 1751. Then a lousy grain harvest in '56, coupled with a change in tastes (rum and porter are the new drinks of choice), signal the death knell to rotgut gin.

1761

THE ARRIVAL of the first of the new breed of distillers, G & J Greenall's. Dry gin does not yet exist. The improved recipes are in the "Old Tom" style (possibly so named because of the "tom cat" sign used by the first Old Tom gin seller), sweetened and lightly flavored with botanicals.

Time Line

1778

HELLO, GORDON'S Gin. (Not yet a "dry" gin, but more : in the Old Tom style)

1793

PLYMOUTH GIN, made only in Plymouth, with a sweeter, more : citrusy profile than the future London Dry, arrives on the scene.

1830

THE YEAR *that changed everything.* The Coffey, or continuous, still is patented, allowing alcohol to be : continuously distilled, rather than distilled in parts. Continuous distillation results in smoother taste and no impurities.

1830

THE OPENING of the first gin palace, or "respectable" : drinking establishment.

1830s – Late 1800s

LONDON DRY gin emerges, catering to the new taste for "nonsweet," more refreshing : alcohol. In America, the gin martini is the new "it" drink.

1920 – 1933

DURING PROHIBITION in the United States, "bathtub" gin—essentially moonshine : mixed with artificial flavors— substitutes for the real thing.

1950s – 1980s

VODKA OVERSHADOWS gin with its flavorless profile.

2000 & Beyond

NEW ARTISANAL gins, dry and otherwise, which often use old-fashioned pot stills to : intensify flavors, continue to emerge, catering to the cocktail renaissance.

THE BOTTLES TO BUY

If you already have a gin you love, we hope we can convince you to try something new. And if you're yet to be convinced that gin is an essential cocktail spirit, we promise you that there are plenty of new gins out there with flavors that run the gamut from citrus to herbs and spices to garden flowers. Instead of spending a chunk of change on a bunch of full-size bottles that you may or may not like, go to the liquor store and buy up every mini you can find; they'll set you back anywhere from $2 to $5 per 50-milliliter bottle, but you'll be able to try a bunch of gins side by side, figure out what works for you, and maybe even discover something new.

One of the great things about gin is that even the cheapest brand—as long as it's labeled "London Dry"—is going to be a quality product. That means that you can spend as little as $10 a bottle and still get your drink on. When you start looking at the "artisan" gins with higher price points, it becomes a bit more difficult to differentiate what's what. Just remember, more expensive doesn't necessarily mean better (some ingredients and distilling techniques just cost more)—and it certainly doesn't mean that you'll like it. Still, there's a good, even great, gin at every price and for every palate.

Budget
($20 or less/750 ml)

GORDON'S LONDON DRY GIN Gordon's is one of the original post–Gin Craze London Dry gins. Even though it's now made in America, it retains its juniper character and makes for a good, solid mixer at a ridiculously low price point.

BEEFEATER LONDON DRY GIN This is what we reach for when we want a satisfying Gin and Tonic and don't feel like using the extra-special stuff. Beefeater is reliable and flavorful, and you won't be ashamed to have it on your shelf. Plus, its profile is classic London Dry.

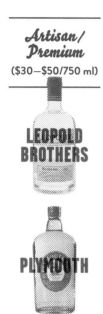

Artisan/ Premium

($30–$50/750 ml)

LEOPOLD BROTHERS AMERICAN SMALL BATCH GIN What happens when you distill cardamom, coriander, Valencia oranges, and pomelos in your gin? You get magic—big, citrusy magic. When we were trying to decide which gin to include in our 12 Bottle Bar repertoire, Leopold's won out only slightly over Plymouth. The citrus notes and the somewhat more esoteric nature of this American brand really get our engines revving.

PLYMOUTH GIN Along with Gordon's, this is the gin that the British Royal Navy took a cotton to. The navy had good taste; Plymouth is unlike any other gin. (Today, it comes in both standard—our choice here—and navy strength.) It's not officially dry, being more aromatic and less juniper-centric (perhaps even somewhat sweet), but it still uses juniper and citrus in the mix. The result is full-bodied and perfect in any cocktail where the gin takes center stage.

FROM PLYMOUTH GIN TO PLYMOUTH ROCK

TODAY, PLYMOUTH GIN features a ship on its bottle—one that any school kid will recognize. Before the Pilgrims left for the New World, they spent their last night in England at the Black Friars monastery in the town of Plymouth. Many years later, the monastery would become a distillery—one where Plymouth Gin is made to this day. You guessed it: the ship featured on the label is the *Mayflower*.

Sometimes a Cucumber Isn't Just a Cucumber. . . .
AND A GRAPE ISN'T JUST A GRAPE

WANT TO TRY something really different? Crack a bottle of Hendrick's or G'Vine gin. The Hendrick's is all cucumber and rose petals and chamomile. The G'Vine offers a sweet, perfumed floral bouquet thanks to green grape flowers macerated in the grape spirit. Either of these nontraditional profiles shines in Gin and Tonics and Gimlets.

Will either of them make a traditional Martini? Not so much; there's nothing dry to the palate about these non juniper-centric gins, which tend to have a fruitier character and a perceived sweetness. On the other hand, if you are on the fence about gin in general, one of these—or any other artisan gin—might change your mind. Besides, you gotta love the irreverence of these upstarts. Hendricks's Monty Python–esque website offers instructions for making "cucumber balls," while G'Vine riffs on the G in its name with words like *g'infusion*, *g'inesis*, and *g'intensity*.

THE DRINKS

Sweet & Fruity

HONOLULU

GLASS: MARTINI | ICE: CUBED | MAKES: 1 DRINK

We like the Honolulu because it really wants to be a fruity rum drink, and you can't blame it for that. After all, this is a Prohibition treat from the golden age of Hollywood, when many a gin drink traveled west in search of Tinseltown stardom. As a friend once described the Honolulu, "it's kind of puzzling and enjoyable at the same time"—much like the private lives of many movie stars.

With lemon, orange, and pineapple juices plus simple syrup at play, fruitiness is central here, but the two ounces of gin and the addition of bitters keep any cloying sweetness in check.

2 ounces dry gin

¼ ounce strained, freshly
    squeezed lemon juice

¼ ounce strained, freshly
    squeezed orange juice

¼ ounce pineapple juice

1 teaspoon Simple Syrup
    (page 369)

Dash aromatic bitters

1 Combine all of the ingredients in a cocktail shaker. Fill the shaker three-quarters full with ice cubes and shake vigorously until thoroughly chilled, 15 seconds.

2 Strain into a martini glass.

HARD SHAKE

JAPANESE MASTER bartender Kazuo Uyeda invented the "hard shake" style of mixing a drink—a method endorsed by its disciples as the best way to blend and aerate a cocktail simultaneously. On paper, it's a bit difficult to explain the technique behind the hard shake, so we recommend you search the Web for videos or ask any friendly bartender who shakes his drinks as if they owe him money.

The technique may take some practice, but it's a valuable skill to have in your repertoire for drinks like the Ace Cocktail (page 98) or the Clover Club (page 108) where you want to emulsify ingredients such as egg whites. Plus, it looks damn cool.

ACE COCKTAIL

GLASS: MARTINI | ICE: CUBED | MAKES: 1 DRINK

The Ace is a funny little drink—one that really only has a place at brunch. But, oh what a brunch drink it is. Most likely dating back to Prohibition (the earliest version we have is from the 1934 recipe book *Boothby's World Drinks*), the Ace was a small drink—half the size we present here. If you find a more diminutive portion appealing, the best approach is to make a full recipe and share this creamy, rich, sweet-sour slice of heaven with a friend.

1½ ounces dry gin

½ ounce Grenadine, homemade (page 376) or store-bought

½ ounce heavy (whipping) cream

¼ teaspoon strained, freshly squeezed lemon juice

White from 1 large egg

Fresh whole nutmeg, for garnish (see Note, page 70)

1 Combine gin, grenadine, heavy cream, lemon juice, and egg white in a cocktail shaker. Shake the drink vigorously without ice to emulsify the egg white, 15 seconds.

2 Fill the shaker three-quarters full with ice cubes and shake again vigorously until thoroughly chilled, 15 seconds.

3 Strain into a martini glass and garnish with a grating of nutmeg.

OPAL

GLASS: MARTINI, CHILLED | ICE: CUBED | MAKES: 1 DRINK

One of the most familiar drinks to come out of Prohibition was the Orange Blossom, which is nothing more than gin and orange juice. It's horrible (apologies to Snoop Dogg, but we prefer a slightly more complex tipple). The Opal, on the other hand, is what the Orange Blossom should have been—light, delicate, delicious, and above all else, a great brunch drink that can easily be made in batches. It's almost a fizz (see page 100), but lacks the requisite egg white. Instead, the result is an explosion of mouthwateringly sweet orange with a gin kick on the back.

1½ ounces dry gin

1 ounce strained, freshly squeezed orange juice

½ ounce orange liqueur

½ teaspoon Simple Syrup (page 369)

Small dash food-grade orange flower water (see Note, page 100)

1 Combine all of the ingredients in a chilled cocktail shaker. Fill the shaker three-quarters full with ice cubes

Tip:
PLAY WITH THAT DRINK

DRINKS LIKE THE Opal are a great canvas for experimentation. Try substituting clementines or another more assertive citrus, like pomelos, for the orange juice. You'll like what you taste.

and shake vigorously until thoroughly chilled, 15 seconds.

2 Strain into a chilled martini glass.

NOTE: Orange flower water is distilled from bitter orange blossoms, which offer up an aromatic addition to cocktails. It is typically available at natural foods markets.

POM GIN FIZZ

GLASS: COLLINS | ICE: CUBED | MAKES: 1 DRINK

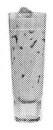

The fizz is a wonder of mixology, a stunning combination of ingredients including but not limited to egg white or yolk, club soda, sugar, and usually dry gin. The resulting drink is almost ethereal, with the flavors of sweet citrus (and in the case of the Pom Gin Fizz, vanilla and pomegranate juice) plus the smoothness of cream and egg, as well as the bubbles of club soda. Satisfying, comforting, and eye-opening all at once.

The Pom Gin Fizz is our variation on the classic Ramos Gin Fizz (see Variation), one of the finest drinks ever created by man. The change—due to the pomegranate juice—is subtle, but it brings a beautiful pink color to the drink. Unlike many Ramos recipes, this one employs a technique we picked up from a barman of the old school: Rather than adding the orange flower water to the shaker, simply dash it onto the top of the finished drink, which amplifies the lovely bouquet.

1½ ounces dry gin

1 ounce Simple Syrup (page 369)

½ ounce strained, freshly squeezed lemon juice

½ ounce pomegranate juice

2 drops pure vanilla extract

2 ounces heavy (whipping) cream

White from 1 large egg

Club soda

2 drops food-grade orange flower water (see Note, above)

1 Combine all of the ingredients except the club soda and orange flower water in a cocktail shaker. Shake the drink vigorously without ice to emulsify the egg white, 15 seconds.

2 Fill the shaker three-quarters full with ice cubes and shake vigorously again until your arm tires, about 30 seconds. The goal is to shake the drink in keeping with the tradition in which it has always been shaken—until it hurts.

3 Strain into a collins glass.

4 Insert a bar spoon into the glass and chop the spoon up and down as you top the drink with club soda, to create a thick head. Add the drops of orange flower water to the top of the drink.

VARIATION

RAMOS GIN FIZZ The original classic. Replace the pomegranate juice with lime juice.

If You Don't Know the Bartender
WHAT DO YOU ORDER?

"As a bartender, I always appreciate customers who express curiosity about drinks. Ask a question about a spirit or cocktail showing genuine interest, and odds are good I'll try to make you something off menu or give you something unusual."

—JACOB GRIER, BARTENDER AND DRINKS WRITER

THE SLOE STUFF

IF YOU EVER stumble across sloe gin, give it a try. This British liqueur is flavored with sloes, the berries of the blackthorn bush. In late October and early November, folks across Great Britain make their sloe berry pilgrimages, gathering fruit and infusing it in a good bottle of dry gin, along with some sugar. For a commercial version, Plymouth makes one of the best. Use it in place of dry gin in a Gin and Tonic (page 115).

SHERRY BERRY BRAMBLE

GLASS: COLLINS | ICE: CRUSHED | MAKES: 1 DRINK

This bramble recipe comes to us courtesy of Trevor Easter, English Gins brand ambassador, and is a more savory version of the classic, fruit-based Bramble cocktail (page 106). It calls for amontillado sherry, which is off-dry and fuller-bodied than fino, and offers a distinct nuttiness that tames the sweeter elements of this drink. If you tend to prefer your cocktails sweeter, up the proportion of the blackberry liqueur from ¼ ounce to ½ ounce.

A note about that amontillado sherry: While we typically don't advocate buying extra bottles for mixing, we do use this sherry in the Mo Chi Chi (page 264) as well, and you will find that it is a frequent ingredient in cocktails today (not to mention in cooking—you may have a bottle in your pantry already). Further, amontillado is a luscious addition to any home bar, perfect as a savory dessert accompaniment (paired with a nut tart or cheese plate) or as a solo after-dinner drink. Good bottles, such as Lustau, can be had for $15 to $20.

1½ ounces dry gin

¾ ounce amontillado sherry

¾ ounce strained, freshly squeezed lemon juice

¾ ounce Simple Syrup (page 369)

¼ ounce Blackberry Liqueur (page 379)

Blackberry, for garnish

Fresh mint sprig, for garnish

Confectioners' sugar, for garnish

1 Combine all of the liquid ingredients in a collins glass. Fill the glass three-quarters full with crushed ice and stir until diluted, 30 seconds. Refill the glass with crushed ice all the way to the top.

2 Garnish with the blackberry, the mint sprig, and a dusting of confectioners' sugar.

NO. 1 FRUIT CUP COCKTAIL

GLASS: COLLINS | ICE: CRUSHED | MAKES: 1 DRINK

Alas, many spirits are still available only overseas, and Plymouth's "Fruit Cup" is one of them. It is a lovely, deep, winey, red brew based on Plymouth's aromatic, citrus-forward gin with fruit liqueurs and a touch of bitters; it creates, as its name suggests, a superb fruit cup cocktail with the simple addition of 7-UP, sparkling lemonade (such as San Pellegrino's Limonata soda), or ginger beer.

The term "cup" refers both to a single drink and the bottled mixture to make that drink. If you ever make it to the U.K., bring a bottle (or a few) back with you. If you want to travel to the U.K. without leaving home, make this instead.

1 ounce Cheater's Cup (page 389)

5 ounces ginger beer or sparkling lemonade (see headnote)

Cucumber spear or orange slice, for garnish (optional)

1 Fill a collins glass with crushed ice and add the fruit cup and ginger beer.

2 Garnish with the cucumber spear or orange slice, or any herb or fruit you desire.

BIRD'S CUP

GLASS: COLLINS | ICE: CRUSHED | MAKES: 1 DRINK

C hef David Myers is one of our favorite people in the world, culinary or otherwise. Not only did we get our first taste of a Penicillin cocktail—a honey-ginger-Scotch marvel—from him (see page 1), but we watched as his Sam Ross–conceived cocktail program at his bistro, Comme Ça, quietly started the Los Angeles cocktail awakening. When Myers opened his restaurant Hinoki & the Bird, he continued the classic cocktail program, again expertly curated by Ross. The Bird's Cup is a wonderfully seasonal take on a Pimm's (a branded style of fruit cup) that can be changed up depending on what fruits and herbs you have on hand.

1 lemon wedge

1 lime wedge

1 cucumber wheel, plus extra for garnish

1 grape, plus extra for garnish

1 strawberry, plus extra for garnish

¼ orange

2 or 3 fresh mint leaves

2 ounces Cheater's Cup (page 389)

½ ounce Ginger Syrup (page 374)

3 ounces club soda

1 Combine all of the ingredients except the club soda and garnishes in a Boston shaker tin and muddle.

2 Pour the mixture into a collins glass, top with the club soda, then fill the glass with crushed ice. Garnish the glass with the cucumber. Skewer the strawberry and grape on a toothpick and garnish the drink.

THE BLOODBATH

GLASS: MARTINI | ICE: CUBED | MAKES: 1 DRINK

The original name of this drink was "Bloodbath in the Bronx," but we changed the name for thematic reasons because it was paired with the movie *The Texas Chainsaw Massacre* for our movie-themed Halloween.

This is a version of the classic Bronx/Income Tax cocktails—gin mixed with OJ and dry and sweet vermouths—that appeared in gaz regan's *The Bartender's Gin Compendium* by way of bartender/journalist Simon McGoram, who spent a good deal of time bartending at Mea Culpa restaurant in Auckland, New Zealand. In McGoram's drink, spiced sweet vermouth subs for regular sweet vermouth, while blood orange juice stands in for regular orange. Blood oranges aren't generally available in October in the States (their season tends toward December–March), so we tweaked the recipe to approximate the color and berrylike flavor by muddling raspberries in orange juice. If you would like a deeper red color and a bit more sweetness, you can add a touch of grenadine to taste.

6 raspberries

¾ ounce strained, freshly squeezed orange juice

1½ ounces dry gin

¾ ounce dry vermouth

¾ ounce Spiced Sweet Vermouth (page 388)

2 dashes orange bitters

1 Combine the raspberries and orange juice in a mixing glass and muddle to release the berry juices.

2 Add all of the remaining ingredients, fill the glass three-quarters full with ice cubes, cover with a Boston shaker tin, and shake until thoroughly combined, 15 seconds.

3 Strain through a fine-mesh sieve into a martini glass.

Tangy & Citrusy

BEE'S KNEES

GLASS: MARTINI | ICE: CUBED | MAKES: 1 DRINK

I n concept, the Bee's Knees just sounds delicious. It's a classic sour but made with honey—what's not to love? The key here is to find the perfect balance among all of the ingredients, so you can taste each of them without any one dominating. And while logic would say that this drink, with its fresh lemon juice, gets a lemon twist for a garnish, we prefer an orange twist. The sweet honey balances the tart lemon, and the gin—particularly a more citrus-forward style of gin, such as our recommended Plymouth (or others like Uncle Val's and Leopold)—makes for a refreshing but not-too-tart sipper.

1½ ounces dry gin

¾ ounce strained, freshly squeezed lemon juice

¾ ounce Honey Syrup (page 371)

Orange twist, for garnish

1 Combine the gin, lemon juice, and honey syrup in a cocktail shaker, fill the shaker three-quarters full with ice cubes, and shake vigorously until thoroughly chilled, 15 seconds.

2 Strain into a martini glass and garnish with the orange twist.

BRAMBLE

GLASS: ROCKS | ICE: CRUSHED | MAKES: 1 DRINK

C reated in the mid-1980s by Dick Bradsell at the innovative and trendy Fred's Club, in London, the Bramble is a true modern classic and a lovely ode to the way the fruit element can make a drink come together. The Bramble is all about the juiciness of the blackberry liqueur, which complements the aromatics of the gin (we like Plymouth for this).

We use Bradsell's original recipe here, but make our own blackberry liqueur. Of course, if you'd rather pop down to the local liquor store for your *crème de mûre,* the drink will be just as delicious.

1½ ounces dry gin

¾ ounce strained, freshly
   squeezed lemon juice

½ ounce Simple Syrup
   (page 369)

¾ ounce Blackberry Liqueur
   (page 383)

2 raspberries, for garnish

Lemon slice, for garnish

1 Fill a rocks glass halfway with crushed ice. Add the gin, lemon juice, and Simple Syrup to the glass, stirring gently to mix.

2 Pour the blackberry liqueur over the top of the drink. Do not stir. Garnish with two raspberries and a lemon slice.

BOX CAR

GLASS: MARTINI | ICE: CUBED | MAKES: 1 DRINK

If you look at this recipe closely, you'll see that it's a Sidecar (page 81) in sheep's clothing—gin instead of brandy, plus some grenadine to tame it—which is far from a bad thing. The original recipe we adapted is from 1945 and included a sugared rim for the glass, strengthening the Sidecar connection. We think the orange liqueur and grenadine add more than enough sweetness, so we skip the sugar here, allowing the sour quality to shine through.

1½ ounces dry gin

¾ ounce strained, freshly
   squeezed lime juice

½ ounce orange liqueur

1 teaspoon Grenadine,
   homemade (page 376)
   or store-bought

1 Combine all of the ingredients in a cocktail shaker, fill the shaker three-quarters full with ice cubes, and shake vigorously until thoroughly chilled, 15 seconds.

2 Strain into a martini glass.

CLOVER CLUB

GLASS: MARTINI | ICE: CUBED | MAKES: 1 DRINK

I n 1934, *Esquire* magazine named the ten worst drinks to come out of Prohibition (see box, page 115), and the Clover Club was among them. Part of the reason people tend to deride the Clover Club is that, despite its origins as the eponymous cocktail of an old-school men's club, this is a big, pink, frothy drink. We ask you: What's wrong with big, pink, and frothy, as long as the thing's tasty? The pink comes from raspberry syrup and the froth from an egg white. And while there are similarities to the Ace Cocktail on page 98, the lack of cream makes for a decidedly lighter, zingier beverage, making it perfect for a picnic, lawn party, or hot summer afternoon.

1½ ounces dry gin

¾ ounce strained, freshly squeezed lemon juice

¼ ounce Raspberry Syrup (page 372)

White from 1 large egg

1 Combine all of the ingredients in a cocktail shaker and shake vigorously without ice to emulsify the egg white, 15 seconds.

2 Fill the shaker three-quarters full with ice cubes and shake again vigorously until thoroughly chilled, 15 seconds.

3 Strain into a martini glass.

If You Don't Know the Bartender,
WHAT DO YOU ORDER?

"Simple drinks with muddled citrus are easy to ensure quality. When muddling a fresh lemon or lime, you are guaranteed freshness of juice. Try a Caipirinha, Caipiroska, or Bramble to make sure you get a nice drink. If it's 1:30 a.m. and the bar is packed, skip the cocktail and grab a beer."

—JUSTIN DARNES, BARTENDER

"The Gin and Tonic has always been the traditional 'Cocktail Hour' standard for summer gatherings. Several years ago, while [I was] working the Promenade Bar at the Rainbow Room, a customer challenged me to create a new summer drink, saying he was tired of the G and T, and asked me to do something more exciting with gin to get him through the summer. I made a Gin Sour, but I spiced it up by adding Angostura bitters, and called it the Gin Thing. Well it became quite the thing that summer, so I put it on my cocktail menu. One guest who enjoyed the drink was a fiction reader for *The New Yorker* named Valerie, who insisted I give the drink a classier name. Since the Hemingway Daiquiri was on the menu at the time, she thought F. Scott Fitzgerald should get some equal representation, so she suggested 'The Fitzgerald.'"

—DALE DEGROFF, *THE CRAFT OF THE COCKTAIL*

THE FITZGERALD

GLASS: MARTINI | ICE: CUBED | MAKES: 1 DRINK

You know that scene in *Good Will Hunting* where Matt Damon's character walks up to the chalkboard and easily solves the unsolvable equation? That's pretty much what Dale DeGroff, who started the modern American bartending revolution, did with the Fitzgerald. With the simple addition of a couple of dashes of bitters, he turned an ordinary gin sour into something much more textured and interesting. How do you like *them* apples?

Dale's original recipe simply called for aromatic bitters, but now that he's bottled his own, he always uses Dale DeGroff's Pimento Aromatic Bitters (see page 307). If you can't get DeGroff's, any aromatic bitters will work, and we have used Angostura countless times to superb effect.

1½ ounces dry gin

¾ ounce strained, freshly squeezed lemon juice

¾ ounce Simple Syrup (page 369)

2 dashes aromatic bitters

1 Combine all of the ingredients in a mixing glass. Fill the glass three-quarters full with ice cubes, cover with a Boston shaker tin, and shake vigorously until thoroughly chilled, 15 seconds.

2 Strain into a martini glass.

FRENCH 75

GLASS: FLUTE | ICE: CUBED | MAKES: 1 DRINK

Taking its name from the Soixante-Quinze, the French 75-millimeter field gun of World War I, the French 75 will hit you like cannon fire. Consider yourself warned. The quality and flavor profile of the Champagne you use here will have a great influence on the resulting drink. While we could have classified this as a "strong" cocktail, the use of Champagne puts it firmly in the festive camp. Still, remember that the combination of sugar and alcohol is heady, allowing the drink to go straight to your head.

2 teaspoons Simple Syrup (page 369)

¾ ounce strained, freshly squeezed lemon juice

1½ ounces dry gin

Champagne or sparkling wine, chilled

1 Combine the Simple Syrup, lemon juice, and gin in a mixing glass.

2 Fill the glass three-quarters full with cubes and shake vigorously until thoroughly chilled, 15 seconds.

3 Strain into a flute and top with chilled Champagne.

VARIATION

FRENCH 125 Substitute Cognac-style brandy for the gin.

EASTER SORBET PUNCH

GLASS: COUPE | MAKES: 1 DRINK

This is a real crowd pleaser in both appearance and flavor. The pineapple and mint in the sorbet offer bright flavors that complement the gin's citrus/herbal character. And while we originally created it for Easter, there's no reason to relegate it to just one holiday. It is a perfect springtime quencher. In fact, the sorbet is so refreshing you might be tempted to eat it on its own—and we say, why not?

Gin-Pineapple Sorbet
(recipe follows)

Champagne
Fresh mint sprig, for garnish

1 Add a scoop (or, if you're feeling fancy, a quenelle) of sorbet to a coupe glass.

2 Fill the coupe with Champagne.

3 Garnish with a sprig of mint.

NOTE: For a nonalcoholic version, replace the gin in the sorbet with lemonade or water and fill the drink with ginger ale or 7UP.

Gin-Pineapple Sorbet

MAKES: ABOUT 3½ CUPS

1 cup strained pineapple juice, chilled

1 cup Rich Mint Simple Syrup, chilled (page 370)

1 cup water

Yellow food coloring (optional)

6 ounces dry gin, chilled

1 Place all of the ingredients in an airtight container and stir to combine. Add 4 or more drops of food coloring, if desired, to brighten the color. Cover and freeze until the mixture becomes slushy, 3 to 4 hours.

2 Transfer the sorbet to a blender and blend until smooth. Return to the container, cover, and freeze overnight. The sorbet will keep, covered and frozen, for up to a week.

FRESH LIME GIMLET

GLASS: MARTINI | ICE: CUBED | MAKES: 1 DRINK

T hese days, it seems like you can't mention a gimlet recipe without upsetting someone. The classic version calls
for Rose's Lime Juice (opposite), but as bartenders have
increasingly returned to freshly squeezed juice, this
version has become very popular. You can debate the com-
position of a real gimlet all you want, but you can't debate
how delicious this one is.

The flavor of whatever gin you use will come through clearly here,
but the tart quality of the lime and the sweetness of the Simple Syrup
are equally present. The result: lip-puckering, energizing, and fresh.

· ·

1½ ounces dry gin

¾ ounce strained, freshly
   squeezed lime juice

½ ounce Simple Syrup
   (page 369)

Fresh mint sprig or cucumber
   slice, for garnish
   (see Note)

· ·

1 Combine all of the liquid
ingredients in a cocktail shaker,
fill the shaker three-quarters
full with ice cubes, and shake
vigorously until thoroughly
chilled, 15 seconds.

2 Strain into a martini glass
and garnish as desired.

NOTE: You may wish to tailor
the garnish to the gin you use:
a sprig of mint for a dry gin
like Beefeater, a cucumber with
the cucumber-rose-forward
Hendrick's.

THE CHRONICLES OF GIMLET

BACK WHEN THE British Navy commanded the high seas, navy men were faced with all sorts of nasty shipboard illnesses. One of these was scurvy, which came with various picturesque symptoms such as bleeding gums. Enter citrus fruits (officially required aboard ship from 1795 on) and, indirectly, a little mixed drink known as the Gimlet.

Like the story behind so many drinks, the history of the Gimlet is infuriatingly murky. First off, the Gimlet is forever linked to Rose's Lime Juice Cordial, a sweetened mixing syrup patented in 1867. It appears that soon after its first production, Rose's found its way aboard navy ships and, presto, some enterprising officer mixed it with his gin ration. Most books—and the British Navy itself—claim that the drink is named for naval surgeon General Sir Thomas D. Gimlette. Others say that it gets its title from a gimlet, a sharp corkscrew used to open kegs of spirits aboard ship.

The truth as we see it is that navy men had likely been mixing lime juice rations with gin for quite a while before Rose's came along. In fact, lime rations had been given with a dose of sugar, most probably mixed in, as far back as the 1740s; Rose's just figured out a way to preserve the sweetened syrup they created. And even though a lot of histories claim that Rose's was created to supply the navy, it's more likely that it was invented to cater to the newly emerging market for soft drinks.

So, which came first? Rose's or the Gimlet? You could probably go so far as to say that, without Rose's, there would be no Gimlet—at least not the Gimlet as defined by purists (equal parts gin and Rose's Lime Juice Cordial). Others add a squeeze of fresh lime along with the Rose's. Whatever the answer—and there is no one answer here—the Gimlet, along with the Gin and Tonic (page 115), is a shining example of the British discovering how best to "take their medicine."

THE REINVENTED GIMLET

GLASS: MARTINI | ICE: CUBED | MAKES: 1 DRINK

This subtle but complex version of the gimlet is the handiwork of Sebastian Hamilton-Mudge. As international brand ambassador for Beefeater and Plymouth gins, his enviable job has him jetting around the world to spread the gin gospel. While very much a traditionalist when it comes to his gin cocktails, Seb also likes to play with the classics, and his Reinvented Gimlet is a perfect example of how you can enrich a standard with some creativity. Here, he has added hints of spice to his homemade cordial recipe, bringing the gimlet into the twenty-first century.

You'll see that Seb recommends a navy-strength gin, with its higher ABV, for this cocktail. While we don't specifically recommend one in our list of preferred brands, this drink calls for it if ever a drink did. As Seb explains, "More alcohol carries more flavor, so with more flavor we need a little more dilution to unlock this drink. . . . I always use aroma to decide at what point to stop stirring a Martini or Gimlet. You can just tell the difference when you hit the perfect point of dilution as the aromas really flood the senses. When that citrus hits you, you know you are good to go!"

2 to 3 ounces dry gin (navy strength, if you have it)

1 ounce Lime Cordial (page 377)

Lime twist, for garnish

1 Combine the gin and the cordial in a mixing glass, fill three-quarters full with ice cubes, and stir the mixture rapidly until the aroma of the spirit is released, 30 seconds. You will smell it.

2 Strain into a martini glass and garnish with the lime twist.

Esquire Magazine's
TEN WORST DRINKS
of 1924–1934

WE CERTAINLY DON'T agree with all of *Esquire's* choices here—we would argue against the Pink Lady and the Clover Club in particular—but this list goes to the taste of the times, and we really could live without the Pousse-Café.

Alexander	Fluffy Ruffles	Pousse-Café
Bronx	Orange Blossom	Sweetheart
Clover Club	Pink Lady	
Cream Fizz	Pom Pom	

GIN AND TONIC

GLASS: COLLINS | ICE: CUBED | MAKES: 1 DRINK

As with the Gimlet (page 112), the gin you choose here will make the drink. Leopold's will make it citrusy; Tanqueray will be powerful and full of juniper. The tonic adds a refreshing tingle and subtle bitterness, and lime (or, as preferred by some, lemon) gives the necessary citrus zing.

Tonic water is a peculiar beast, with its fizzy, sweet-bitter quinine kick. For many decades, we had nothing but Schweppes and Canada Dry tonic waters, both serviceable but, with their reliance on high fructose corn syrup, a far cry from the more subtle original versions using cane sugar. Today, many artisan brands, including Fever Tree and Q—both personal favorites—are turning the tonic landscape back to more subtle, naturally sweetened recipes. If you believe the hype behind cocktails—and why wouldn't you?—the Gin and Tonic is the healthiest thing in a glass. Along with the "medicinal" kick of the juniper-based gin, there's tonic water, used to fight malaria, and a squeeze of lime to ward off scurvy. Even if you're not headed to the tropics, this British military classic is a mighty tasty way to keep cool during the summer.

2 ounces dry gin

Tonic water

Lime wedge, for serving

• •

1 Fill a collins glass with ice cubes and add the gin. Top with tonic water.

2 Squeeze the lime wedge into the glass, then drop it in.

• •

GIN RICKEY OR GIN BUCK

GLASS: COLLINS | ICE: CUBED | MAKES: 1 DRINK

As cooling drinks go, it's hard to beat gin Rickeys and Bucks. Although club soda was on the cocktail scene before ginger beer, both the Rickey (made with seltzer or club soda) and the Buck (made with ginger beer) are products of the tail end of the nineteenth century. The basic formula for both is given here, with more specifics and some popular variations listed below.

The Rickey is utter simplicity, but should things go wildly awry and you mess it up by using lemon instead of lime, leaving out the fruit shell, and adding a bit of sugar, you'll have yourself a Tom Collins. Not so bad. Shake everything but the soda, serve it in a small glass without ice, and add the soda at the end—it's a Gin Fizz. The variations are almost endless.

Bucks didn't become Bucks until Prohibition. Before that, the Scotch version was the Mamie Taylor, and over the years the drink has had so many names it's hard to keep track. The most recent popular moniker has been the "mule," perhaps because of the association with the vodka-based Moscow Mule, or bartender Audrey Saunders's modern riff on the latter, called the Gin-Gin Mule. If you ask us, though, a Buck sounds like a much tastier option.

• •

2 ounces dry gin

¾ ounce strained, freshly squeezed lime juice

Squeezed shell of ½ a lime

Club soda or ginger beer

1 Fill a collins glass with ice cubes. Add the gin, lime juice, and lime shell and stir gently.

2 Top with the club soda (for the Rickey) or ginger beer (for the Buck).

VARIATIONS

All of the following iterations make the basic Buck or Rickey fruitier or sweeter.

CIRCUS RICKEY Add 1 dash of Grenadine (page 376); top with club soda

FLORADORA Add ½ ounce Raspberry Syrup (page 372); top with ginger beer

FIN DE SIÈCLE Use lemon juice and lemon shell in place of the lime; add 1 teaspoon Raspberry Syrup (page 372); top with club soda

If You Don't Know the Bartender, WHAT DO YOU ORDER?

PHILIP DUFF, OWNER of Liquid Solutions Bar and Beverage Consulting, suggests a Gin and Tonic. We agree. Even the cheapest London Dry gin is decent stuff. Add a little tonic and a twist of lime—refreshing, and it won't break the bank. And you could just as easily request a Buck or Rickey—with ginger beer or club soda, respectively, standing in for the tonic.

GREEN SNAPPER

GLASS: COLLINS | ICE: CUBED | MAKES: 1 DRINK

Bartender and consultant Dre Masso, who calls London home, created this gin-based spin on the Bloody Mary using a zingy fruit-herb blend that replaces the typical tomato mixer and works wonderfully with gin's botanicals. The sugar measurement will depend on the sweetness of the pineapple juice you choose (we tend to like the familiar and consistent Dole brand). This drink is easily scaled up for parties (see page 321), allowing you to mix it ahead of time based on your number of guests and thus free yourself up for entertaining.

• •

2 ounces dry gin

6 ounces Green Snapper Mix (recipe follows)

• •

Fill a collins glass two-thirds full with ice cubes, add the gin and the snapper mix, and stir gently to chill and combine.

Green Snapper Mix

MAKES: ENOUGH FOR 4 DRINKS

20 ounces pineapple juice

2 ounces strained, freshly squeezed lime juice

Granulated sugar

2 tablespoons chopped fresh mint

2 tablespoons chopped fresh cilantro

½ teaspoon sea salt

• •

Combine the ingredients in a blender and pulse to combine. Strain into a pitcher or nonreactive airtight container. The mixture will keep, covered, in the refrigerator, for up to 2 days.

MONTFORD SNAPPER

GLASS: COLLINS | ICE: CUBED | MAKES: 1 DRINK

Beefeater brand ambassadors Sebastian Hamilton-Mudge (now also representing Plymouth gin) and Tim Stones created this veggie-rich twist on the tomato elements in the Bloody Mary. The gorgeous deep beet-red color is a true showstopper. Like the Green Snapper (page 118), it can easily be expanded for a bigger group merely by tinkering with measurements to size up the mixture (see page 321). The "Montford" in the name refers to the Montford Place address of the Beefeater Distillery in London. As to the amount of gin, you be the judge—a little or a lot.

1½ to 2 ounces dry gin

6 ounces Montford Snapper Mix (recipe follows)

Tabasco Sauce

Salt and freshly ground black pepper

Fresh parsley sprig, for garnish

Lemon wheel, for garnish

1 Fill a collins glass two-thirds full with ice cubes and add the gin as desired and the snapper mix.

2 Season with the Tabasco, salt, and pepper, to taste.

3 Stir gently to chill and combine. Garnish with the parsley sprig and lemon wheel.

Montford Snapper Mix

MAKES: ENOUGH FOR 4 DRINKS

9 ounces tomato juice

6 ounces beet juice (see Notes)

6 ounces strained, freshly squeezed blood orange juice (see Notes)

3 ounces carrot juice (we like Odwalla or Naked brands)

¾ ounce strained, freshly squeezed lemon juice

¾ ounce Simple Syrup (page 369)

½ teaspoon sea salt

⅛ teaspoon freshly ground black pepper

Place all of the ingredients in a blender and pulse to combine. Strain into a pitcher or nonreactive airtight container. The mixture will keep, covered, in the refrigerator, for up to 2 days.

NOTES: To make "beet juice," puree 1 can (15.5 ounces)

beets with their liquid in a food processor or blender, then strain through a fine-mesh sieve, pushing on the solids to extract the juice.

If you can't find blood oranges, you can tint 4 ounces of orange juice with 1 ounce of raspberry juice (muddle 4 ounces of raspberries, then strain).

VARIATIONS ON A THEME

IN ADDITION TO the Green and Montford Snappers on pages 118 and 119, the Bloody Mary has been reincarnated with every booze there is, as well as a few other goodies. Behold:

BLOODY BULL: Beef bouillon is added.

BLOODY CAESAR: Clamato juice instead of tomato (this is popular in Canada)

BLOODY FAIRY, RED FAIRY: Absinthe instead of vodka

BLOODY GEISHA: Sake instead of vodka

BLOODY MARIA: Use tequila instead of vodka.

BLOODY MAUREEN: Guinness instead of vodka

BLOODY MOLLY: Replace vodka with Irish whiskey.

CHELADA (see page 334): Mexican beer instead of vodka

CUBANITO: White rum instead of vodka (found frequently in Havana)

DANISH MARY: Substitute Aquavit for the vodka.

HIGHLAND MARY, OR THE BLOODY SCOTSMAN: Scotch replaces the vodka.

RED SNAPPER with gin instead of vodka

GUNPOWDER AND SMOKE

GLASS: MARTINI | ICE: CUBED | YIELD: 1 DRINK

Want to really impress your guests? Insurance up to date? Nothing adds flair to cocktail assembly quite like fire. Here, bartender Jamie Boudreau, co-owner of Canon in Seattle, offers up a visually dramatic and distinctly tasty variation on the classic Egg Sour (see page 252). This drink is a perfect example of how to take an existing classic and add additional levels of depth and excitement, namely the Gunpowder Liqueur, a heady balance of sweet and smoky with an alcoholic bite. Misting the rye over the drink and igniting it in quick succession takes some practice but it's worth the show (note that you'll need a cocktail mister for this purpose).

White from 1 large egg

2 ounces dry gin

½ ounce strained, freshly squeezed lemon juice

½ ounce Gunpowder Liqueur (page 385)

100-proof rye whiskey in a cocktail mister

1 Combine the egg white, gin, lemon juice, and liqueur in a mixing glass. Cover with a Boston shaker tin and shake vigorously to emulsify the egg white, 15 seconds.

2 Fill the mixing glass three-quarters full with ice cubes and shake again vigorously

until thoroughly chilled, 15 seconds.

3 Strain into a martini glass.

4 Holding the mister almost vertically, mist the rye over the surface of the drink, and ignite it with a lighter. Repeat the misting and lighting three times.

PEGU CLUB

GLASS: MARTINI | ICE: CUBED | MAKES: 1 DRINK

T his is a drink that was invented to battle a tropical swelter; if the pucker of lime, smoothness of orange liqueur, and coolness of gin can't quench your thirst, nothing can.

Rudyard Kipling once wrote: "In the Pegu Club I found a friend . . . upon whose broad bosom I threw myself and demanded food and entertainment." He was talking, of course, about the famed British gentlemen's club the Pegu Club, in what was then Burma. He could, however, just as easily have been talking about the club's signature drink.

1½ ounces dry gin

½ ounce orange liqueur

¾ ounce strained, freshly squeezed lime juice

2 dashes aromatic bitters

1 Combine all of the ingredients in a cocktail shaker, fill the shaker three-quarters full with ice cubes, and shake vigorously until thoroughly chilled, 15 seconds.

2 Strain into a martini glass.

SOUTHSIDE

GLASS: MARTINI | ICE: CUBED | MAKES: 1 DRINK

W e love mint and, so it goes to reason, we love cocktails that feature mint. Although most people think of mint in the classic Mint Julep or Mojito, we really enjoy the energizing herbal twist it brings to the lemon and gin in the Southside.

The Southside has many potential origin stories, which typically place its provenance on the South Side of Chicago. We're inclined to agree with the *Wall Street Journal*'s Eric Felton, however, who places its birth at the Southside Sportsmen's Club on Long Island. After all, the Southside remains a favorite summer tipple of New York's country club set, a group that knows a good drink when they taste it.

2 ounces dry gin

¾ ounce strained, freshly squeezed lemon juice

2 teaspoons Simple Syrup (page 369)

6 fresh mint leaves, plus extra for garnish

1 Combine the gin, lemon juice, Simple Syrup, and mint leaves in a cocktail shaker, fill the shaker three-quarters full with ice cubes, and shake vigorously until thoroughly chilled, 15 seconds.

2 Strain into a martini glass and garnish with the mint.

Bar Con:
THE UNIQUE EXPERIENCE

"The con artist sidles up to the mark (the con artist's target) and says: 'People spend so much money to find a *unique experience*. I can give you a unique experience; I will show you something that no one has seen before or will see again.' The mark is curious and accepts the bet. Then, the con artist brings a peanut shell out of his pocket, cracks it open, shows the mark one of the peanuts inside ('something no one has ever seen') and then pops it in his mouth, eating it all until it is gone (i.e., never to be seen again). Technically, the claims of this con aren't 'true,' but that's hard to prove and, if it wins the con artist a drink, the job has been done."

—TODD ROBBINS, AUTHOR, *THE MODERN CON MAN*

TEA'S KNEES

GLASS: ROCKS | ICE: CUBED, BLOCK (OPTIONAL) | MAKES: 1 DRINK

One of the seminal drinks in the modern cocktail repertoire is the Scotch-based riff on a Whiskey Sour called the Penicillin. Created in 2005 by Sam Ross, while he was bartending at the now-legendary Milk & Honey in New York, the cocktail literally swept across the country and has become emblematic of the cocktail renaissance. Scotch was not often seen in cocktails when Ross created the drink. To add the smoky top note that has become the drink's hallmark, he topped it with a little Islay Scotch to add an element of surprise.

As we don't have Scotch in the 12 Bottle Bar, a real Penicillin isn't possible. However Trevor Easter, former English Gins Brand Ambassador, has his own gin version, which we have officially dubbed the Tea's Knees as a play on the well-known classic Bee's Knees (page 106) (both drinks use gin and honey). The Lapsang Souchong–Infused Gin stands in admirably for the float of smoky, peaty Scotch on the original.

* * *

¾ ounce strained, freshly squeezed lemon juice

½ ounce Honey Syrup (page 371)

½ ounce Ginger Syrup (page 374)

1½ ounces dry gin

½ ounce Lapsang Souchong–Infused Gin (page 387)

Candied ginger, for garnish

* * *

1 Combine the lemon juice, Honey Syrup, Ginger Syrup, and gin (reserve the infused gin) in a mixing glass, fill the glass three-quarters full with ice cubes, cover with a Boston shaker tin, and shake vigorously until thoroughly chilled, 15 seconds.

2 Place large ice cubes in a rocks glass and strain the drink into the glass.

3 Hold a bar spoon against the inside wall of the glass, just below the rim and not touching the surface of the liquid. Slowly pour the infused gin into the bowl of the spoon and down the inside of the glass so that it floats on the surface of the drink. Garnish with the candied ginger.

WHITE LADY

GLASS: MARTINI | ICE: CUBED | MAKES: 1 DRINK

As visually spectral as it is simple, the White Lady is another kissing cousin to the Sidecar (page 81). This is a classic "sour" cocktail, with the orange liqueur adding just the right amount of sweetness. Both Harry MacElhone and Harry Craddock lay claim to the drink. Either way, the White Lady is certainly a case of less being more.

1½ ounces dry gin

¾ ounce orange liqueur

¾ ounce strained, freshly squeezed lemon juice

1 Combine all of the ingredients in a cocktail shaker, fill the shaker three-quarters full with ice cubes, and shake vigorously until thoroughly chilled, 15 seconds.

2 Strain into a martini glass.

ZELLI'S SPECIAL

GLASS: MARTINI | ICE: CUBED | MAKES: 1 DRINK

The original Zelli's, a swinging 1920s Paris cabaret, called for two limes cut up into very small pieces and added to the shake—something we've tried to approximate here in a slightly simpler manner. However you make it, the Zelli's Special is a nice little hybrid of martini and sour.

2 ounces dry gin

½ ounce dry vermouth

½ ounce strained, freshly squeezed lime juice

Shells of the squeezed lime(s)

1 teaspoon Grenadine, homemade (page 376) or store-bought

1 Combine all of the ingredients in a cocktail shaker, fill the shaker three-quarters full with ice cubes, and shake vigorously until thoroughly chilled, 15 seconds.

2 Strain into a martini glass.

Strong

BLOODHOUND

GLASS: MARTINI | ICE: CUBED | MAKES: 1 DRINK

I n cocktail parlance, equal parts of sweet and dry vermouth is known as "perfect," which makes the Bloodhound a perfect strawberry martini. As with any drink using fresh fruit straight off the vine, the quality of your final product is going to rely heavily on the quality and ripeness of the strawberries. Wait until they are in season, and then don't wait to whip up a round of Bloodhounds. What you'll get is the power of a martini softened by the sweetness of the berries and vermouth.

3 to 4 sweet, ripe strawberries, hulled

1½ ounces dry gin

¾ ounce dry vermouth

¾ ounce sweet vermouth

1 Set one strawberry aside; place the remaining strawberries in a cocktail shaker and muddle them to crush the fruit.

2 Add the gin and both vermouths, fill the shaker three-quarters full with ice cubes, and shake vigorously until thoroughly chilled, 15 seconds.

3 Strain into a martini glass and garnish with the reserved strawberry.

SATAN'S WHISKERS

GLASS: MARTINI | ICE: CUBED | MAKES: 1 DRINK

H ow can you not love a drink called Satan's Whiskers? This variation on the Bronx (see page 105) can be ordered in two varieties: straight, with Grand Marnier, and curled, with Curaçao. How you enjoy your sin is, of course, up to you. Satan's Whiskers is a powerful but remarkably well-balanced drink and, if you like some additional flavor (in this case, orange) on top of the basic spirit profile, these whiskers will tickle your fancy. Needless to say, we're always fond of drinks that use as many of the 12 bottles as possible; Satan's Whiskers is a fine example.

1 ounce dry gin

½ ounce dry vermouth

½ ounce sweet vermouth

½ ounce orange liqueur

1 ounce strained, freshly squeezed orange juice

Dash orange bitters

1 Combine all of the ingredients in a cocktail shaker, fill the shaker three-quarters full with ice cubes, and shake vigorously until thoroughly chilled, 15 seconds.

2 Strain into a martini glass.

WEST INDIAN COCKTAIL

GLASS: ROCKS | ICE: CUBED | MAKES: 1 DRINK

I f you've ever wondered what all those Gold Rush forty-niners were spending their hard-earned gains on, it was something close to the West Indian Cocktail—if they were spending their gold dust on booze, that is. This basic recipe—simplicity itself, with the sugar smoothing out the potent gin–bitters one-two punch—dates back to the early nineteenth century, and we can attest that it's just as tasty and invigorating today as it was then.

1 cube sugar

4 dashes aromatic bitters

1 teaspoon strained, freshly squeezed lemon juice

2 ounces dry gin

1 Place the sugar cube in a rocks glass and dash the bitters over it, to saturate the sugar. Then muddle the sugar and bitters.

2 Add the lemon juice and stir to dissolve sugar.

3 Add the gin and 1 ice cube, stirring again to chill, 15 seconds.

BIJOU (RITZ VERSION)

GLASS: MARTINI, CHILLED | ICE: CUBED | MAKES: 1 DRINK

The most popular version of the Bijou calls for green Chartreuse and sweet vermouth, but the 1936 version from the Ritz Hotel in Paris is a lovely little drink that fits nicely within our bar's 12-bottle parameters, instead using dry vermouth and orange liqueur. We've modernized the proportions here, reducing the liqueur and vermouth by half, but if you're feeling nostalgic, try the original, which called for equal parts gin, vermouth, and orange liqueur. Take out the orange liqueur and you have an old-school Martini. Here, the orange liqueur softens the perception of the drink, but does nothing to take away its power.

· ·

2 ounces dry gin

½ ounce orange liqueur

½ ounce dry vermouth

Dash orange bitters

Brandied Cherry (page 367) or high-quality maraschino cherry (we like Luxardo brand), for garnish

· ·

1 Combine all of the liquid ingredients in a chilled mixing glass, fill the glass three-quarters full with ice cubes, and stir rapidly until thoroughly chilled, 30 seconds.

2 Strain into a chilled martini glass and garnish with the cherry.

· ·

DELMONICO NO. 1

GLASS: MARTINI, CHILLED | ICE: CUBED | MAKES: 1 DRINK

For the better part of a hundred years, beginning in the 1830s, society's upper crust flocked to Delmonico's restaurant in New York. A veritable chef's bounty of high-end dishes, like Lobster Newberg, Eggs Benedict, and Baked Alaska, were invented there, as were a number of cocktails. This one, which straddles the fence between a Martini and something close to a Manhattan, is our favorite. This is not for beginners—it's boozy, relatively dry, and packs a wallop.

1 ounce dry gin

½ ounce Cognac-style brandy

½ ounce dry vermouth

½ ounce sweet vermouth

2 dashes aromatic bitters

Lemon twist, for serving

1 Combine all of the liquid ingredients in a chilled mixing glass, fill the glass three-quarters full with ice cubes, and stir rapidly until thoroughly chilled, 30 seconds.

2 Strain into a chilled martini glass and squeeze the lemon twist over the surface to express the oils (discard the lemon twist).

GIN-BLIND

GLASS: MARTINI, CHILLED | ICE: CUBED | MAKES: 1 DRINK

I n 1939, Charles H. Baker published *The Gentleman's Companion, Vol. II*, a compendium of drinks he had collected during his voyages around the world. He had the opportunity to taste the Gin-Blind while voyaging with Commander Livesey of the British Navy, a man whose head butler was also "a wizard with the shaker." As Livesey said of the drink: "We don't prescribe this just before target practice, gentlemen." Sage advice, indeed.

2 ounces dry gin

¼ ounce orange liqueur

½ ounce Cognac-style brandy

2 dashes orange bitters

1 Combine all of the ingredients in a chilled mixing glass, fill the glass three-quarters full with ice cubes, and stir rapidly until thoroughly chilled, 30 seconds.

2 Strain into a chilled martini glass.

"You can no more keep a martini in the refrigerator than you can keep a kiss there. The proper union of gin and vermouth is a great and sudden glory; it is one of the happiest marriages on earth and one of the shortest-lived."

—BERNARD DE VOTO, AUTHOR, *THE HOUR: A COCKTAIL MANIFESTO*

THE MARTINI

GLASS: MARTINI, CHILLED | ICE: CUBED | MAKES: 1 DRINK

The Martini is the undisputed king of cocktails. This version takes the early twentieth-century ingredients—gin, dry vermouth, orange bitters—and brings them to more modern proportions. Dry vermouth is key to a proper Martini, so ignore all the hokum about waving the vermouth cap over the glass or using a spray atomizer and enjoy yours the way it was intended. This is a serious cocktail for serious drinking—it is, simply, all about the gin.

The best way to finish this drink is with a lemon twist, but we won't begrudge you a few beautiful olives served on the side. Reach for a cocktail onion instead, and you've got yourself a Gibson.

• •

2½ ounces dry gin

½ ounce dry vermouth

Dash orange bitters (optional)

Lemon twist or olives,
    for garnish

• •

1 Combine the gin, vermouth, and bitters in a mixing glass and place it in the freezer to chill, 10 minutes.

2 Fill the mixing glass three-quarters full with ice cubes and

stir rapidly to chill further, 30 seconds.

3 Strain into a chilled martini glass and garnish with the lemon twist, or serve olives alongside.

Great Bars
THEN & NOW

**ALGONQUIN HOTEL | 59 WEST 44TH STREET
NEW YORK, NEW YORK 10036
212-840-6800 | ALGONQUINHOTEL.COM**

IN JUNE OF 1919, a group of about twenty-five New York literati met for lunch at the Algonquin Hotel. Over the next ten years, this cozy crew—which included critic and writer Dorothy Parker, playwright Noel Coward, *Vanity Fair* editor Robert Benchley, and others—exchanged barbs and booze at a lightning pace. The world of words and wit has never been the same. This group has probably been quoted more than any other in history, and much of what they said revolved around booze—especially martinis. A few choice examples:

. . . .

"I like to have a martini, two at the very most. After three I'm under the table, after four I'm under my host."

—**DOROTHY PARKER**
(how we love her)

. . . .

"One martini is too much, two is too little, three is not enough."

—**JAMES THURBER**

And perhaps this one, of arguable lineage:

"I must get out of these wet clothes and into a dry martini."

—**ROBERT BENCHLEY**

. . . .

As the clique grew to include more members (there was something of a revolving-door policy), it relocated to the Rose Room and took up a round table, which led to the moniker "the Vicious Circle." The so-called VCs reigned supreme for ten years until 1929.

Today, "the Gonk" Hotel is a literary landmark, albeit one that's a bit mired in the lure of tourism (the hotel's gift shop sells "Round Table" mugs and other souvenirs). However, for the literarily curious, walking tours are available; for the more alcoholically inclined, you can still have lunch in the Round Table Restaurant, formerly the infamous Rose Room, and drinks are served in the Blue Bar.

THUNDERBOLT

GLASS: MARTINI, CHILLED | ICE: CUBED | MAKES: 1 DRINK

O ur friend Mike—a filmmaker and a home mixology enthusiast like us—makes some of the best martinis on the planet. His house martini is called the P-47, after the plane his father flew in the military. We fiddled with Mike's recipe slightly and called our version the Thunderbolt, after the nickname for the P-47 fighter. The drink tastes even better if it's mixed, as Mike does it, in a World War II shell casing. It is, on every level, a classic martini—strong, potent, and stimulating.

• •

1 teaspoon orange liqueur

3 ounces dry gin

¼ teaspoon dry vermouth

2 to 3 drops strained, freshly squeezed lime juice

Lemon twist, for serving

• •

1 Place the orange liqueur in the martini glass and place it and a mixing glass in the freezer to chill, 10 minutes.

2 Remove the mixing glass from the freezer, and in it combine the gin and vermouth. Fill the glass three-quarters full with ice cubes, and stir rapidly until thoroughly chilled, 30 seconds.

3 Remove the chilled martini glass from the freezer and gently swirl the glass to evenly coat the inside with the liqueur. Discard the excess orange liqueur.

4 Strain into the prepared martini glass and add the drops of lime juice. Squeeze the lemon twist over the surface to express the oils (discard the twist).

WILD ROSE

GLASS: MARTINI | ICE: CUBED | MAKES: 1 DRINK

We wish we could tell you that the Wild Rose was named for poor, dear Elisa Day of Nick Cave's "Where the Wild Roses Grow," but the drink is much older than the 1995 ballad. The aromatic, herbal combination of vermouths and bitters here make for a drink that is very much like a rose just past its prime—both beautiful and something worthy of contemplation. Still, the full-on alcohol profile—no fruit juices need apply—makes for a compelling mix.

2 ounces dry gin

½ ounce dry vermouth

½ ounce sweet vermouth

Dash aromatic bitters

Dash orange bitters

1 Combine all of the ingredients in a mixing glass, fill the glass three-quarters full with ice cubes, and stir rapidly until thoroughly chilled, 30 seconds.

2 Strain into a martini glass.

DEVIL'S OWN

GLASS: MARTINI | ICE: CUBED | MAKES: 1 DRINK

This fiendishly named drink hails from the 1937 *Café Royal Cocktail Book* and is credited to a fellow named Colin Simmons. With an ounce of orange liqueur, it is very orange-forward, but despite that fact, the proportions work to produce a well-balanced drink.

The viscous quality, a product of being liqueur-centric, and the soft salmon color make this a great choice for autumn—especially a cold, spooky October fright night (the name doesn't hurt either).

1 ounce dry gin

1 ounce dry vermouth

1 ounce orange liqueur

Dash aromatic bitters

1 Combine all of the ingredients in a mixing glass, fill the glass three-quarters full with ice cubes, cover with a Boston shaker tin, and shake vigorously until thoroughly chilled, 15 seconds.

2 Strain into a martini glass.

"Always do sober what you said you'd do drunk. That will teach you to keep your mouth shut."

—ERNEST HEMINGWAY

CHAPTER 7

Genever

CHAPTER 7

Genever

Every home bar should have a major surprise in it. Ours is genever ("geh-*nee*-ver" is the Americanized pronunciation but in Dutch it's more like "yeh-nay-fer"). When any one of our friends insists that they don't like gin, we pull out a bottle of this heady stuff. Technically, genever isn't gin at all. Having started its life as a medicinal, juniper-flavored spirit, it's more like gin's great-great-grandpa. Or, better yet, it's the spirit that spurred gin into existence.

So are genever and gin related? Well, yes and no. On the one hand, both spirits use juniper. In fact, the word *genever* (*jenever* in Dutch) means "juniper," which is gin's main botanical flavoring component as well. When the English discovered genever (courtesy of their Dutch cousins), they anglicized it to *geneva*, and then shortened the word to *gin*.

On the other hand, classic, old-style genever—the type we recommend for your bar—differs markedly from gin in its base of "malt wine" (rich with the combined flavors of malted rye, wheat, and corn) rather than grain-neutral (unflavored) spirit. The malted grains produce a spirit, bold and warm in flavor, that is redistilled with botanicals. Where London Dry is crisp and clean, genever is potent and whiskeylike.

Even in its earliest and crudest form, English gin didn't get its start until the early 1700s. Witness the deadly, turpentine-laced "gin" of the Gin Craze (see page 92). However, juniper-based tonics had existed in Holland and Belgium since the thirteenth century. You'll recall that juniper had a long history as a medicinal aide for everything from digestion to kidney troubles; the people of the Low Countries capitalized on this belief with various local tinctures. (Today, Holland and Belgium have their own unique versions of genever, which diverged as the two countries became more autonomous.)

However, since few Belgian genevers are available in the States, it's Dutch genever that gets our focus. In the 1600s, trade blockades with wine-producing countries such as Spain and Italy forced the Dutch to get inventive if they wanted to get lubricated. With their surplus of grains, which grow much better than grapes in colder climates, the Dutch started distilling grain-based spirits, or early genever. In 1664, genever production went commercial thanks to a fellow named Lucas Bols. If the name sounds familiar, it should be; Bols is well known in the United States for making liqueurs such as triple sec and Advocaat. With the exotic spices that Bols received from the Dutch East India Company's forays across the globe, the grain-and-spices recipe for genever was secured.

Genever
IN A NUTSHELL

DEFINING FEATURE: "Malt wine," a grain mash that combines malted rye, wheat, and corn

FLAVOR PROFILE: Warm, smooth, whiskeylike, heavy in the mouth, lightly botanical

WHY WE CHOSE IT: Every home bar should have an ace up its sleeve, and this one has pedigree. With a little tweaking, it can substitute in gin, whiskey, and tequila drinks alike.

EMBLEMATIC DRINKS: Kopstootje (page 161), John Collins (page 155), Death in the Gulf Stream (page 150)

Today, per the European Community rules, genever has its own protected status, a legal designation completely separate from gin's that is equivalent to the French Appellation d'Origine Contrôlée used for wine.

"Old genever and young women, but never the other way around." We first heard this saying in a dark, old Amsterdam bar from an anonymous patron, who was more than willing to talk genever. His comment is a bit rough around the edges, but it reveals the most basic rule of good genever. Avoid the "young" stuff like the plague. It's as different from classic genever as ping-pong is from tennis. So what is this old/young dichotomy? Genever is divided into two somewhat confusing categories, created to distinguish between the stronger, old-school style

The House of Bols:
A COCKTAIL AND GENEVER EXPERIENCE

IF YOU EVER find yourself in Amsterdam and are looking for a little bibulous education, check out the House of Bols in the Museum Quarter (it's right next door to the Van Gogh Museum and Rijksmuseum, natch). The glitzy, modern space is a celebration of all things Bols, which means you are afforded a glimpse into Bols's genever production in addition to learning how all thirty-plus of the company's liqueurs are made.

The spot is part history lesson and part amusement park (they offer guests the ability to experience Tom Cruise–style "flair bartending" in the Flair Booth, complete with Bols "flair" bottles, brightly colored and shaped like bowling pins to help with your juggling skills). Your tour ends in the Mirror Bar, where you can order the genever-based cocktail of your choice. Our suggestion? Go with a classic like the Holland House (bold with genever and perfumed with maraschino liqueur), the original Collins, or the Gold-Fashioned, a genever-based riff on the classic.

If you miss the Amsterdam experience in the city proper, not to worry. Bols has installed a more compact version at Amsterdam's Schipol airport, complete with cocktail bar. We're guessing no one minds if they have a layover there.

(*oude*) and the more modern, lighter version (*jonge*). While *oude* and *jonge* literally translate to "old" and "young," these designations aren't entirely accurate; when applied to genever, *oude* and *jonge* are all about maltwine content. Or, in simpler terms, *oude* genever is more like whiskey, relying on the complexities of the combined malted grains to produce deep, rich flavors; *jonge* genever lacks maltwine and is a "cleaner," colorless spirit like vodka, which evolved to cater to the younger Dutch generation more interested in getting a buzz than experiencing flavor.

In fact, if you want to start a fight, walk into an old Amsterdam bar and try to order a *jonge* genever. You will likely be fixed with a deadly stare from the bartender—and the patrons, none of whom is likely to be younger than fifty. To these die-hard *oude*-style genever

THE ORIGINAL "GIN"

WHILE GENEVER IS indeed a bit obscure to the average drinker, it is an essential addition to any classic bar. Now, don't get us wrong, genever and gin are not the same thing, but without the former, the latter might never have existed.

By 1732, Holland "gin," or Hollands, as it was often known, was available in every tavern of the thirteen American colonies. In the 1800s, at the height of the golden age of cocktails, five times as much genever was imported as English gin and featured strongly in the cocktails of the day.

In fact, a well-known gin drink, the Tom Collins, was originally a John Collins made with, that's right, genever. The original "Gin Cocktail," featured in *How to Mix Drinks, or the Bon Vivant's Companion,* Jerry Thomas's ground-breaking recipe book from 1862, contained genever, not gin.

sippers, there is no other genever, and those who ask for anything else are boorish folk who just don't know or care about their liquor. So now you've been warned.

THE BOTTLES TO BUY

Unfortunately, unlike gin, there are no "bargain" or even midrange brands when it comes to genever—at least none that you will truly want to use in your drinks. Given that fact, genever is the one required splurge in our arsenal, partly because it makes such remarkable cocktails, and also, as noted, because there is no solid cheap brand. (That said, you can snag two of the bottles below—the Anchor and standard Bols—for about thirty bucks each.)

To make your choice more challenging, genever offers markedly limited options for export, compared to the hundreds of gins we have available. In fact, the only true genever bottlings readily available in the States come from the Dutch company Bols, which makes two versions (for the American and British markets), based on classic, historical recipes.

Another worthwhile choice is Genevieve, from the San Francisco–based Anchor Distilling, the only American company that produces a "genever-style" gin. To us, it's neither truly gin nor genever, but a sort of sweet love child of the two.

Artisan/ Premium

($30–$50/750 ml)

ANCHOR DISTILLING GENEVIEVE

BOLS GENEVER

BOLS BARREL-AGED GENEVER

ANCHOR DISTILLING GENEVIEVE Anchor distills this re-creation of genever in an old-school copper pot still, using a grain mash of wheat, barley, and rye. As to botanicals, they are the same as those in Anchor's dry gin, "Junipero," which contains juniper as well as other proprietary elements.

BOLS GENEVER The "malt wine" of this genever (over 60 percent) is separately blended with a juniper distillate and an herbal (including anise, coriander, licorice, and angelica) distillate creating layers of complex flavors. There is also a "secret ingredient" that, until Bols included it in their recipes, hadn't been used for centuries in general distillation. Master Distiller Piet van Leijenhorst claims it is this mystery element that "leaves a twinkle on the tongue." The Bols smells yeasty and fruity simultaneously, with a smooth, malty taste. Unlike whiskey, however, which can come across as heavy, there is something fresh and zingy here, again that "secret ingredient."

BOLS BARREL-AGED GENEVER A grain mash of rye, wheat, and corn is triple-distilled in copper pot stills. Botanicals include subtle juniper, as well as the spice of cloves, anise, and licorice. The spirit is then aged for eighteen months in both old and new French oak barrels, further intensifying the flavor. Truly akin to but also different from a fine whiskey, it can be sipped neat or, despite what connoisseurs might say, used in cocktails that are really meant to impress. (We are all for using the good stuff.)

DUTCH COURAGE

HOW COULD YOU not love a spirit whose nickname is "Dutch Courage"? During the Thirty Years' War (1618–1648), which pitted the Protestant Dutch against the Catholic Spaniards, the English fought beside their Dutch cousins. Historically, desertion was common among soldiers, especially when faced with the horrors of the battlefield. However, during the Thirty Years' War, the English stayed the course thanks to their allotments of genever. Before a battle—or perhaps in the midst of one—they would slug back a dram of genever and sally forth, courage intact. For this reason, genever earned the apt nickname "Dutch Courage," a term the soldiers brought back to England along with their taste for the fortifying spirit.

Unfortunately for the English, they didn't have the same sophisticated distilling techniques as the Dutch, and their eager attempts at replicating Dutch Courage ended quite badly. While genever was imported and drunk by the rich, the masses consumed rotgut gin, flavored with turpentine and other masking agents to capture the essence of a juniper spirit. Eventually, the English figured out how to do it right, and produced the elegant but vastly different style of drink known as London Dry gin.

THE DRINKS

Sweet & Fruity

PINEAPPLE JULEP

GLASS: ROCKS | ICE: CRUSHED | MAKES: 1 DRINK

There's nothing about the Pineapple Julep that makes it truly a julep (herbs macerated in sugar and water), but it comes from Jerry Thomas, the Babe Ruth of bartenders, and most importantly, it's downright delicious. Our variation—replacing the original maraschino liqueur with the more readily available orange liqueur—covers all the bases: fruity, of course; sweet, and sparkling due to the Moscato; heady and complex (think whiskeylike) thanks to the genever.

OLD SCHIEDAM SINGLE-MALT GENEVER

WHILE WE MAY never know exactly what nineteenth century genever tasted like, we can taste its closest modern counterpart—a 100 percent malt-wine genever—at the Genever Museum in Schiedam, Holland.

Using malted barley and rye, the genever is triple-distilled, flavored lightly only with juniper, then matured for at least three years in oak barrels. It's most likely the purest evocation of the spirit available today, made exactly the same way it was made in the 1800s.

½ ounce genever

½ ounce orange liqueur

½ ounce strained, freshly squeezed orange juice

½ ounce Raspberry Syrup (page 372) or Grenadine, homemade (page 376) or store-bought

1 teaspoon strained pineapple juice

Sweet sparkling wine, such as Moscato d'Asti

Pineapple spear, for garnish

Raspberry, for garnish

Fresh mint sprig, for garnish

- -

1 Combine the genever, liqueur, orange juice, Raspberry Syrup, and pineapple juice in a mixing glass and stir to combine.

2 Fill a rocks glass with crushed ice and pour the drink into the glass.

3 Top with the sparkling wine and garnish with the fruit and mint.

- -

DUTCH CREAM

GLASS: COLLINS | MAKES: 1 DRINK

We can point to two drinks that were fundamental to the success of 12bottlebar.com: Buttered Beere (page 332), which became our most popular drink at the height of the Harry Potter craze, and this Dutch Cream, which caught the attention of regional food writer Daniel Berman of FUSSYlittleBLOG.com, and subsequently produced our first boom in readership. The conceit here is simple to a fault. To a traditional New York egg cream, add a shot of genever. Not only does the malt of the liquor perfectly complement the pairing of chocolate and soda, but the combination also makes historical sense: The Dutch once claimed the greater New York area as the colony of New Amsterdam.

- -

Fox's U-Bet chocolate syrup

Chilled whole milk

1½ ounces genever

Chilled club soda

FOX'S U-BET CHOCOLATE SYRUP

CREATED IN THE early 1900s, Fox's Chocolate Syrup is the *only* chocolate syrup used in a real egg cream.

The egg cream itself is a New York standard, the subject of many a debate—is it from Brooklyn or another borough? While it contains no egg and no cream, it is a likely descendant of the soda fountain milkshake, which originally contained both. As legend tells it, candy shop owner Louis Aster can lay claim to creating the egg cream, using his own chocolate syrup, in the 1890s. Aster took the recipe to his grave and others simply appropriated the most popular syrup of the day. That's right: Fox's.

1 Pour the chocolate syrup into a collins glass to a depth of ½ inch.

2 Add milk, filling the glass to the halfway mark. Do NOT stir. Add the genever.

3 Insert a bar spoon into the glass and chop the spoon up and down as you top the drink with club soda, to create a thick head. Continue until the glass is overflowing and you have a proper chocolate drink with a white foamy head.

AMSTERDAM HOT CHOCOLATE

GLASS: HEATPROOF GLASS MUG | MAKES: 1 DRINK

Our friend, bartender, writer, and general bon vivant Jacob Grier knows a thing or two about genever and cold weather—he's the former brand ambassador for Lucas Bols. Here, he summons one to combat the other, proving the potent marriage of malty genever and chocolate. This tastes best when the hot chocolate is made with an unsweetened dark chocolate (see Tip, page 146), and the orange liqueur is used to fill in the sweet notes. The *Amsterdam* in the name comes from genever's association with Holland.

¾ cup whole milk

1 tablespoon good-quality unsweetened cocoa, such as Valrhona or Ghirardelli, or to taste

3 to 4 tablespoons granulated sugar

¾ ounce genever

½ ounce orange liqueur

Whipped cream (optional)

1 Combine the milk, cocoa, and sugar in a small saucepan over low heat and cook, stirring, just until the sugar dissolves and the mixture comes to a simmer (do not let it boil).

2 Pour the hot chocolate into a heatproof glass mug, stir in the genever and orange liqueur to combine, and top with whipped cream if you like (and why wouldn't you?).

Tip: CHOOSING YOUR CHOCOLATE

IN A PINCH, you could make an Amsterdam Hot Chocolate with a store-bought cocoa packet, but your drink would be the worse for it. Do you really want corn syrup and partially hydrogenated coconut oil in your cocktail? We thought not.

A fine-quality cocoa makes an enormous difference in taste by allowing you to control the sweetness and chocolate levels, and it takes roughly the same amount of time to make homemade hot cocoa to taste as it does from a store-bought packet. Our suggestions for superb flavor follow.

VALRHONA UNSWEETENED COCOA POWDER. With 100 percent cacao, this is one of the richest, most chocolaty cocoa powders you will find. Costly, yes, but you're worth it.

GHIRARDELLI UNSWEETENED BAKING COCOA. A can of all-American goodness. This vastly cheaper—by more than half—alternative to the Valrhona has distinct chocolate flavor and none of the bitterness often found in cocoa.

Tangy & Citrusy

AMANDA PALMER

GLASS: MARTINI | ICE: CUBED | MAKES: 1 DRINK

Aside from the opportunity to go off-roading in the carts—often forfeiting our deposits—we're not ones for golf. We're even less into the modern American beverage stalwart that is the Arnold Palmer. There's something about throwing lemonade and iced tea together that's about as clever as mixing ketchup and mayo and calling it Special Sauce.

As part of our ongoing life goal to deconstruct every banal American sacred cow, we couldn't help strapping down the Arnold Palmer, injecting it with a healthy pour of genever, and tarting it up as a funky punky drink that's so old school it's all brand-new again.

The tannic sweetness of the tea syrup provides a multilayered base against which the herbal maltiness of genever and the tartness of the lemon take center stage. From whence comes the name? Amanda Palmer, who first rocked the music world as the lead singer of the Dresden Dolls. We hope she would approve.

2 ounces genever

1½ ounces Tea Syrup (page 378)

1 ounce strained, freshly squeezed lemon juice

1 Combine all of the ingredients in a mixing glass, fill the glass three-quarters full with ice cubes, cover with a Boston shaker tin, and shake vigorously until thoroughly chilled, 15 seconds.

2 Strain into a martini glass.

3 Turn on "Delilah" by the Dresden Dolls.

AMSTERDAM COCKTAIL

GLASS: MARTINI | ICE: CUBED | MAKES: 1 DRINK

f there's one mixed-drink ingredient that sounds great at first glance, but so easily disappoints in practice, it's orange juice. When it's perfectly ripe and ready for drinking, it can be too sweet and unstructured for a cocktail. Typically it's just bitter, bringing down even the best drink. Applied properly, as in the Amsterdam, which balances bitter and sweet elements, it can sing as part of a greater whole. The Amsterdam succeeds not only because it tempers the orange juice with orange liqueur and orange bitters, but because of its diminutive size, which makes it an ideal morning-after pick-me-up.

1 ounce genever

½ ounce orange liqueur

½ ounce strained, freshly squeezed orange juice

4 dashes orange bitters

1 Combine all of the ingredients in a mixing glass, fill the glass three-quarters full with ice cubes, cover with a Boston shaker tin, and shake vigorously until thoroughly chilled, 15 seconds.

2 Strain into a martini glass.

"Drinking Holland gin is like the fanciful cliché about eating olives—when you like one you always like them. For many years we had hated the stuff with a passion, holding its taste to be like fermented radishes mixed with spirits of turpentine."

—CHARLES H. BAKER,
"THE GENTLEMEN'S COMPANION" SERIES

BOLD, BRIGHT, AND FEARLESS COCKTAIL

GLASS: MARTINI | ICE: CUBED | MAKES: 1 DRINK

This is an adaptation of a recipe created by gaz regan, one of the cocktail world's most knowledgeable and generous author/bartender/educators, to toast the 144th anniversary of the *San Francisco Chronicle* in 2009. While any of our suggested genevers will work, regan recommends the local San Francisco bottling, Anchor Distilling Genevieve, to deliver the kick that makes the drink truly live up to its name—bold due to the genever, bright because of the citrus, and fearless because, well, it's a lovely thought, isn't it?

• •

1½ ounces genever

1½ ounces orange liqueur

1½ ounces pineapple juice

1½ ounces strained, freshly squeezed lemon juice

Dash aromatic bitters

Lemon twist, for garnish

• •

1 Combine all of the liquid ingredients in a mixing glass, fill the glass three-quarters full with ice cubes, cover with a Boston shaker tin, and shake vigorously until thoroughly chilled, 15 seconds.

2 Strain into a cocktail glass and place the lemon twist on top of the drink.

DEATH IN THE GULF STREAM

GLASS: COLLINS | ICE: CRUSHED | MAKES: 1 DRINK

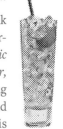

At some point in the mid 1930s, celebrated food and drink writer Charles H. Baker Jr., best known for our purposes for *The Gentleman's Companion, Being an Exotic Drinking Book, or Around the World with Jigger, Beaker, and Flask* (1939), found himself a bit worse for wear, having spent two long days fishing the Gulf Stream with his friend Ernest Hemingway. Hemingway mixed up a potion of his own devising and passed it to his friend, who would later recall: "It is reviving and refreshing; cools the blood and inspires renewed interest in food, companions and life." Baker likened the drink to a bitter English ale ("Its tartness and bitterness are its chief charm," he said), and advised against the sugar. This is one of the few points on which we disagree with him, as the small dose of sugar smoothes out the strength of the genever and sourness of the lime.

1 lime

4 to 5 dashes aromatic bitters

2 ounces genever

1 teaspoon superfine sugar (optional)

1 Remove the peel from the lime, taking as little of the white pith as possible. Juice the lime.

2 Combine the lime juice and peel in a collins class and muddle them.

3 Fill the glass with crushed ice and dash the bitters into it.

4 Add the genever and stir to combine. If the drink is too tart for your taste, add the sugar and stir to combine.

DUTCH COSMO

GLASS: MARTINI | ICE: CUBED | MAKES: 1 DRINK

In creating this drink we were inspired by the Double Dutch Cosmopolitan (which takes its name from the lemon, genever, Dutch curaçao, and Dutch cranberry juice it uses) from Amsterdam's first modern speakeasy, Door

PAPA DOESN'T ALWAYS KNOW BEST

PAPA HEMINGWAY LIKED his drinks strong. It wasn't uncommon for him to drink his martinis with a 7:1 ratio of gin to vermouth. Death in the Gulf Stream, above, was a Hemingway favorite, and he liked his tart and dry. No sugar, no garnish.

Of course, Hemingway was a diabetic, so heed his advice with a grain of . . . let's say sugar. Just because the man won a Pulitzer and a Nobel doesn't mean you should follow his recipes as written. As Papa himself once said, "No, that is the great fallacy: the wisdom of old men. They do not grow wise. They grow careful."

74, a bar that ranks on many "World's Best" lists. Our version here is a straight-ahead Cosmo, with the Door 74 substitution of genever for the more traditional vodka. While the drink is still shockingly pink, one sip of this heady and tart concoction and you'll know that you're a long way from Carrie Bradshaw and the Fifth Avenue boutiques. However, should a man find a lovely fashionista who prefers this strong and sour variation, we recommend he marry her on the spot.

2 ounces genever

1 ounce orange liqueur

¾ ounce strained, freshly squeezed lime juice

2 teaspoons unsweetened cranberry juice

½ to 1 teaspoon Simple Syrup (page 369), to taste *—does not need except for guests*

Lime wedge, for garnish

1 Combine all of the ingredients in a mixing glass, fill the glass three-quarters full with ice cubes, cover with a Boston shaker tin, and shake vigorously until thoroughly chilled, 15 seconds.

2 Strain into a martini glass and garnish with a lime wedge.

GAMBLER'S FIX

GLASS: MARTINI | ICE: CRUSHED | MAKES: 1 DRINK

This drink comes to us from our friend Justin Darnes, formerly of the Savoy London. If you're already a genever convert, then no matter how you look at it, this drink sounds delightful. Rich, deep pineapple caramel and a hint of cloves. The bite of lemon and spice of bitters. All this gambler is missing for a good time is a riverboat and pocket aces.

½ lemon, cut into wedges

2 ounces genever

2 dashes aromatic bitters

¾ ounce Caramelized
    Pineapple Syrup
    (page 373)

Lemon twist, for garnish

Tincture of Clove, for misting
    (page 380)

1 Muddle the lemon in a mixing glass to release the juice and oils.

2 Add the genever, bitters, and syrup, fill the glass three-quarters full with crushed ice, and stir rapidly until thoroughly chilled, 30 seconds.

3 Strain the drink into a martini glass and garnish with the lemon twist.

4 Mist the surface of the drink with tincture of clove.

GENEVER MAI TAI

GLASS: ROCKS | ICE: CUBED, CRUSHED | MAKES: 1 DRINK

John Clay, the Global Brand Ambassador to Bols, often cautions people not to link genever and gin too closely, lest one simply start substituting genever in gin drinks. While the transition works from the John Collins (genever) to the Tom Collins (gin), genever's dominant, malted personality is better served if you treat it almost like rum, not in terms of the flavors but in terms of how it mixes: It offers bold character and a full mouthfeel. This thought process led Clay to create the Genever Mai Tai, which aptly proves his point about genever's bold but not overly botanical style.

While the traditional Mai Tai is a rum drink, the substitution of genever spins this cocktail in an entirely new direction. While still embracing its tiki nature, this version also has that malty depth so central to quality-crafted genever, instead of the usual rumlike sweetness. Clay's version uses dry orange curaçao, but any of our orange liqueurs will capture the spirit of the drink just fine, with the bitters replacing the oft-applied amber rum float and countering any additional sweetness the orange liqueur might add.

2 ounces genever

1 ounce orange liqueur

1 ounce strained, freshly squeezed lime juice

½ ounce Orgeat Syrup, preferably homemade (page 379)

Dash aromatic bitters

Fresh mint leaves, for garnish

Orange slice, for garnish

1 Combine the genever, liqueur, lime juice, and syrup in a mixing glass, fill the glass three-quarters full with ice cubes, cover with a Boston shaker tin, and shake vigorously until thoroughly chilled, 15 seconds.

2 Fill a rocks glass two-thirds full with crushed ice and strain the drink into the glass.

3 Dash the bitters on top and garnish with the mint leaves and orange slice.

TRANSATLANTIC MAI TAI

GLASS: ROCKS OR COLLINS | ICE: CUBED OR CRUSHED | MAKES: 1 DRINK

The Mai Tai may be a tropical drink, but that doesn't stop it from taking a trip around the world in this inventive all-grain spin, courtesy of Portland, Oregon, bartender and drinks writer Jacob Grier. Fiery rye, most definitely the star player here, and malty genever are perfectly balanced by sweet orgeat syrup and orange liqueur.

Orgeat, a rather creamy, almond-flavored syrup, is always better when homemade, but as it is quite time-consuming to make, the bottled variety—B.G. Reynolds, for example—will suffice, although it won't be as complex.

• •

1 ounce genever

1 ounce rye whiskey

1 ounce strained, freshly squeezed lime juice

½ ounce orange liqueur

¾ ounce Orgeat Syrup, preferably homemade (page 379)

Brandied Cherry (page 367) or high-quality maraschino cherry (we like Luxardo brand), for garnish

• •

1 Combine all of the liquid ingredients in a mixing glass, fill the glass three-quarters full with ice cubes, cover with a Boston shaker tin, and shake vigorously until thoroughly chilled, 15 seconds.

2 Fill a rocks or collins glass with cubed or crushed ice. Strain the drink into the glass and garnish with the cherry.

• •

HOLLAND RAZOR BLADE

GLASS: MARTINI | ICE: CUBED | MAKES: 1 DRINK

As part of the inevitable backlash against the unearthing and fetishizing of any old cocktail, the Holland Razor Blade has been placed on some "better left forgotten" lists. We kindly disagree, especially when we follow the lead of bartender Eric Alperin and add a bit more sugar

to Charles H. Baker's original. Baker was introduced to the Holland Razor Blade by an intrepid Dutch fellow he met in Bali; during a hot, wet season, this margarita cousin provides something equally hot and wet, and infinitely bracing—the cayenne pepper is the requisite ingredient for producing a cooling sweat in the heat of the day.

2 ounces genever

¾ ounce Simple Syrup (page 369)

¾ ounce strained, freshly squeezed lime juice

Pinch cayenne pepper

1 Combine all of the liquid ingredients in a mixing glass, fill the glass three-quarters full with ice cubes, cover with a Boston shaker tin, and shake vigorously until thoroughly chilled, 15 seconds.

2 Strain into a martini glass and sprinkle the cayenne over the top.

JOHN COLLINS

GLASS: COLLINS | ICE: CUBED | MAKES: 1 DRINK

If you've heard of the Tom Collins but not his cousin John, then one of cocktaildom's greatest feats of appropriation has been successful. Two hundred years ago, many popular "gin" drinks were, in fact, made with genever. One such popular libation was the genever punch ladled out to the late nineteenth-century sporting set by John Collins, head waiter at Limmer's Hotel in London. It is said that it was the

THE LIMERICK OF JOHN COLLINS

This little ditty was published in 1892 in *Drinks of the World*, and it is from these verses that the John Collins takes its name.

My name is John Collins, headwaiter at Limmer's,
Corner of Conduit Street, Hanover Square,
My chief occupation is filling brimmers
For all the young gentlemen frequenters there.

combination of Collins's generous nature, his powerful punch, and a rainy day that led the Brothers Sheridan to compose the verse (see page 155) that immortalized the link between John and "gin" (meaning genever) punch forever—or at least until the rise of Old Tom gin, which muscled out not only the genever but the original name of "John" in the famous Collins.

Unlike the Tom Collins, in both its early, sweeter incarnation (due to the use of Old Tom gin) and its later, refreshing version (with the more modern London Dry), the John Collins is headier stuff thanks to the malty intensity of the genever.

2 ounces genever

1 ounce strained, freshly squeezed lemon juice

1 teaspoon confectioners' sugar

Club soda

Lemon slice, for garnish

1 Combine the genever, lemon juice, and sugar in a collins glass and stir until sugar is dissolved.

2 Add 2 or 3 ice cubes and top with club soda. Garnish with the lemon slice.

VARIATION

TOM COLLINS Substitute dry gin for genever.

AFTON CLUB PUNCH

GLASS: PUNCH OR MARTINI | ICE: BLOCK | MAKES: 10 TO 12 DRINKS

These days, no one is more of an expert on punch—and all things cocktailian—than cocktail historian David Wondrich, the man who brought Jerry Thomas to the attention of the modern public and the bartending populace at large. Along with Jerry Thomas's *Bar-Tender's Guide* (see page 365), you should most certainly have Wondrich's *Imbibe!* and *Punch* in your library.

Given Dave's turn of a phrase, we will let him explain the genesis of the Afton Club:

Whenever I'm overworked, bored, Power-Pointed, slight-delayed, chicken shat, I like to take my mind to the Afton Club. There, amidst the carved mahogany, the deep leather club chairs, the shelves groaning with first editions, foreign curios, and heavy regimental silver, jovial, pleasant men and witty women make clever, inconsequential chit-chat while portly, dignified waiters circulate among them with trays of hot anchovy toasts, bacon-wrapped whatnots, and cool bumpers of the Club's characteristic punch. It is the abode of amusement, the kingdom of comfort, the realm of relaxation. It is also, alas, entirely imaginary, a club of the mind. Afton Club Punch, however, is real. I came up with the recipe a couple of years ago on a warm February afternoon in Los Angeles. I've made it many times since. It's light, pleasant, a little intriguing, and drinking it reminds me that at least amusement, comfort and relaxation exist in this world if you know how to find them.

- -

4 lemons, plus extra lemon wheels, for garnish

¾ cup granulated sugar

2 cups genever

2 cups off-dry German riesling

2 cups sparkling water

- -

1 Peel 3 of the lemons with a vegetable peeler, removing as little of the white pith as possible. Combine the peels and sugar in a 1-pint jar with a lid. Muddle briefly, cover the jar, and let it sit until the sugar is aromatic with the scent of the peels, 3 to 4 hours.

2 Juice the peeled lemons and remaining unpeeled lemon and strain through a fine-mesh sieve, discarding any solids. Add 6 ounces of the lemon juice to the jar, reseal it, and shake it until the sugar has dissolved, 3 to 4 minutes.

3 Pour the contents of the jar into a 3-quart punch bowl or other large bowl and top with the genever and the Riesling, stirring gently to combine.

4 Float a large block of ice in the bowl and top the mixture with the sparkling water. Garnish with the lemon wheels.

MARGRIET

GLASS: MARTINI | ICE: CUBED | MAKES: 1 DRINK

A s we mentioned at the front of the book, people often ask us, "Where's the tequila?" Usually, this question precedes a follow-up inquiry about Margaritas. While we adore a good mingling of reposado and lime, we put forth that the Margriet is basically a traditional Margarita recipe that substitutes genever for tequila. Should you choose a bottle of Bols here, you'll have a glass of placid smoothness. Opt for Anchor Distilling's Genevieve and mezcal-like boldness will abound.

Margarita salt or kosher salt

Lime wedge

2 ounces genever

1 ounce strained, freshly squeezed lime juice

1 ounce Simple Syrup (page 369) made with raw sugar, such as Demerara

1 Cover a small plate with salt to a depth of ¼ inch. Halve the lime wedge widthwise and run a cut edge around the outer rim of a martini glass to dampen it. Roll the glass in the salt to coat the outer rim.

2 Combine the remaining ingredients in a mixing glass,

fill the glass three-quarters full with ice cubes, cover with a Boston shaker tin, and shake vigorously until thoroughly chilled, 15 seconds.

3 Strain into the prepared martini glass.

Strong 4.2r

THE BURGESS (VARIATION)

GLASS: MARTINI, CHILLED | ICE: CUBED | MAKES: 1 DRINK

C ocktail historian Ted Haigh created The Burgess for us back when Peychaud's bitters was still one of the bottles included on our site. The name memorializes Patrick Henry and his patriotic pro-independence speech to the Virginia House of Burgesses in 1775; the use of rum and genever aptly celebrates early American drinking habits. As the anise flavor that Peychaud's brings to the drink is a key component, we've reimagined it here, to meet the rules of the 12 Bottle Bar, by infusing the genever with star anise.

The Burgess contains a plethora of ingredients, but the effect on the palate is more akin to a symphony than to death metal. There may be a lot going on here, but Haigh's mastery of the craft keeps it all in balance.

- -

1 ounce genever

1 star anise pod

½ ounce amber rum

½ ounce rye whiskey

½ ounce orange liqueur

½ ounce dry vermouth

½ ounce sweet vermouth

2 dashes aromatic bitters

Lemon twist, for serving

Orange twist, for serving

- -

1 Combine the genever and star anise pod in a mixing glass and let them infuse until an anise scent is noticeably present in the genever, about 6 hours. Remove and discard the star anise.

2 Combine all of the liquid ingredients in a mixing glass, fill the glass three-quarters full with ice cubes, and stir rapidly until thoroughly chilled, 30 seconds.

3 Strain into a chilled martini glass and squeeze both twists over the surface of the drink to express the oils. Drop the twists into the glass.

4 Scream "Give me liberty or give me death!" and consume.

VARIATION

THE BURGESS (ORIGINAL) For the original, omit the star anise (but keep the 1 ounce of genever) and add 1 dash Peychaud's bitters in its place.

• •

CHERRY BLOSSOM GIRL

GLASS: MARTINI | ICE: CUBED | MAKES: 1 DRINK

S ometimes we can't help but update an old cocktail and put our own spin on it. We found the original Cherry Blossom in a 1945 recipe book from the Chicago Bartenders and Beverage Dispensers' Union, played with the proportions, and added Champagne to liven things up a bit. It tastes like a fizzy, juicy cherry with a nice alcoholic kick.

• •

2 ounces genever

1 ounce unsweetened cherry
   juice (see Note)

¼ ounce Simple Syrup
   (page 369)

2 dashes aromatic bitters

Champagne, chilled

Brandied Cherry (page 367)
   or high-quality maraschino
   cherry (we like Luxardo
   brand), for garnish

• •

1 Combine the genever, cherry juice, Simple Syrup, and bitters in a mixing glass, fill the glass three-quarters full with ice cubes, and stir rapidly until thoroughly chilled, 30 seconds.

2 Strain into a martini glass, top with a splash of Champagne, and garnish with the cherry.

NOTE: Unsweetened cherry juice can be purchased in generous bottles at natural foods supermarkets such as Trader Joe's and Whole Foods, as well as online. If you have any left over, it's also deliciously refreshing as a virgin drink, simply topped with club soda.

KOPSTOOTJE

GLASSES: CORDIAL AND COLLINS | MAKES: 1 DRINK

Meaning "head butt" in Dutch, the Kopstootje ("kop-stow-che") is perhaps the most traditional way to drink genever. While there's no denying that this is little more than a shot with a beer back, it's from the spaces of that "little more" that the differences emerge. First, the traditional way to enjoy the drink is to sip the genever first, hands-free, from a stemmed, tulip-shaped cordial glass, then proceed with the beer (permission granted to use your hands). After the first sip of genever, you're free to drink as you please. The choice of beer is equally important. A saison style (also known as Belgian Farmhouse Ale, such as Boulevard Brewing's Tank 7 Farmhouse Ale) is the prime choice, but should you be in a pinch, a nice pale ale or richer lager should suit just fine. After one head butt, you'll hardly know the difference anyway.

· ·

1 shot genever	1 glass saison-style ale

· ·

Serve the genever in a stemmed cordial glass with the beer on the side.

Great Bars
THEN & NOW

CAFÉ OOSTERLING | UTRECHTSESTRAAT 140,
1017 VT AMSTERDAM | 31-20-623-4140

WHILE AMSTERDAM MAY be more famous for other kinds of "imbibing," when we're in town we head straight to Café Oosterling. This historic locals' "brown" café (meaning a pub) is a great escape from noisy tourists and a cozy hideaway in which to enjoy a Kopstootje. In fact, it was here that we learned the Dutch genever-and-beer tradition from a rather inebriated fellow.

Simple to a fault, this is an unspoiled neighborhood gem, rarely seeing the likes of tourists but still welcoming when you stumble inside. Rumor has it that the same family has run the bar for well over a hundred years.

TURF COCKTAIL

GLASS: MARTINI, CHILLED | ICE: CUBED | MAKES: 1 DRINK

When you run across a drink called "Turf," you know that you've stumbled into the realm of the sporting set, where the men drank hard while betting fortunes—large and small alike—on the ponies. Of course, drinking hard doesn't mean drinking in discomfort, and so it was in establishments like New York's famed Waldorf-Astoria Hotel that those with the means bent their elbows while reveling in or seeking solace from the day's turn of luck. This powerfully herbal drink, really a variation on a Manhattan, possesses a certain rugged sophistication that simultaneously provides a loving caress and a bold slap in the face.

• •

2 ounces genever

1 ounce sweet vermouth

Dash aromatic bitters

Lemon twist, for garnish

• •

1 Combine all of the liquid ingredients in a chilled mixing glass, fill the glass three-quarters full with ice cubes, and stir rapidly until thoroughly chilled, 30 seconds.

2 Strain into a chilled martini glass and garnish with the lemon twist.

CHAPTER 8

Amber Rum

CHAPTER 8

Amber
Rum

f you are like us, there are two things that immediately come to mind when you think of rum—pirates and fruity drinks. And, while both are valid associations, rum is far more complex than a simple "Yo ho ho" and a Piña Colada.

n the scheme of booze, rum has the singular distinction of being made from—sorry to say but it's true—garbage. Let's clarify: When sugarcane is harvested and squeezed for its juice, which is then dried to produce sugar crystals, the by-product is molasses. If you have ever stuck your nose in a jar of the stuff, it's pretty nasty smelling and not exactly something you would want to eat by the spoonful. So, farmers on sugarcane plantations in the seventeenth century were stuck with this sticky gunk and had no idea what to do with it. That is, until they noticed that some enterprising slaves were fermenting the molasses into alcohol.

The plantation slaves weren't the first to figure this out. The Malay people in the East Indies have been drinking "brum," made from indigenous sugarcane, for thousands of years. There are fermented drinks made from cane juice that date back to ancient India and China, and, in the fourteenth century, Marco Polo commented on some "very good wine with sugar" that was served to him in Persia. Lucky guy. The bottom line is, like the evolution of pretty much every other spirit, if something can be distilled into the fuel for a Saturday night bender, mankind will figure out how to do it.

Amber Rum
IN A NUTSHELL

DEFINING FEATURE: Deep sugar-based character and rich flavors, generally longer aging than white rum

FLAVOR PROFILE: Spice, toffee, dried fruits, orange

WHY WE CHOSE IT: The world needs more tiki drinks and punches.

EMBLEMATIC DRINKS: Hurricane (page 186), Planter's Punch (page 195), Hot Buttered Rum (page 181)

"All roads lead to rum."

—W. C. FIELDS

Of course, rum's history, much like gin's, is pretty sordid. It involves everything from slavery and pirates to politicians using rum to buy votes (shame on you, George Washington). In the early fifteenth century, the Spanish and Portuguese cultivated sugarcane in the Canary Islands and Madeira; when Spanish and Portuguese explorers crossed the Atlantic searching for gold, they brought sugarcane with them, transplanting it in Brazil and the Caribbean. Columbus himself planted cane in Cuba. And, while the search for gold went bust, the cultivation of sugarcane flourished.

In 1655, the British Royal Navy captured Jamaica and its islanders' sugarcane plantations. Soon after, rum replaced French brandy aboard British ships, first served neat and later cut with water by the enterprising Admiral Edward Vernon, who had unwittingly created grog. In the American colonies, rum production flourished as part of one variation on the infamous Triangle Trade (see right). By 1667, Boston—with its local talents for cooperage and its abundant lumber, both needed to build the barrels used for aging—was the center of rum production, which was a good deal more like whiskey than our modern rums. Nearby, Rhode Island rum was produced to such high standards that it was briefly treated almost like gold in Europe.

Rum of yore is also irrevocably linked to the politics of the era. Beyond George Washington's aforementioned transgression, politicians were known to

PROOF POSITIVE

The concept of "proof" evolved in the British naval yards in Jamaica in the 1700s. British sailors were often paid partially in rum rations. Ever eager to ensure their fair share, the sailors demanded a way of knowing that their rum wasn't watered down. The answer was ingenious: The purser would mix gunpowder with the booze and ignite it. If the rum was watered down, it wouldn't burn, as alcohol catches fire at 57% alcohol by volume. Gunpowder that ignited when lit ensured that the rum was "100 degrees proof."

influence voters with rum; a candidate who "drank with the people" was considered an upright fellow. And, when enterprising Americans tried to obtain sugar outside the British supply lines, the Crown levied the Molasses Act of 1733 and its sequel, the Sugar Act of 1764, which were so vilified that they are considered additional causes of the American Revolutionary War. Perhaps quite fittingly, when Paul Revere embarked on his historic ride, repeating "The British are coming," he apparently stopped by the house of a Medford rum distiller (and captain of the local militia) for a drink.

In the early nineteenth century, rum's fortunes faltered due to restrictions on molasses from the British Caribbean islands, as well as the burgeoning development of American whiskey, which pushed the colonial mainstay aside. Whiskey remained America's tipple of choice until the 1950s, when the tiki craze swept across America. Accompanied by pupu platters, wild fruity rum drinks became all the rage. However rum was mostly relegated to these potent concoctions and the Rum and Cokes favored by college students until the early part of this century, when a new crop of distillers decided it was time to reintroduce the spirit. Returning to classic techniques, such as using pot stills to capture a more old-world flavor, this cadre of renaissance distillers has restored rum's subtle beauty.

Molasses TO RUM TO SLAVES

THE INFAMOUS TRIANGLE Trade of the sixteenth to nineteenth centuries evolved for very practical, albeit reprehensible, reasons. On some level, it began with the demand for sugar in England, which was in the throes of a full-on sugar addiction due to the newly emerging popularity of coffee and tea. So, England sent various goods to Africa to purchase slaves, who were needed to work the sugar plantations in the Caribbean and eventually in the American colonies, where rum was also made. Then it was back to England with rum and sugar, as well as other desirable goods like cotton, and on and on, into infamy. Over the centuries of trading, millions upon millions of slaves were shipped to the islands and America.

> "Rum's huge diversity and flexibility means that you can control
> how it appears in a drink by selection of style, quantity, or blend of
> rums. If you want something light and lively, where the rum will be
> neutral and fall away, that's possible. If you want it to be assertive,
> that's possible as well. Rum gives you a lot of choices."
>
> **—MARTIN CATE, OWNER, SMUGGLER'S COVE, SAN FRANCISCO, CA**

A RUM BY ANY OTHER NAME

I n choosing a way to classify our amber (that is, non-white) rum, we
ran into a serious conundrum. Rum is made in more than a hundred
countries, and styles—including how the rums are distilled, aged,
and blended—vary markedly. The Caribbean Community's economic-
political organization CARICOM offers international legal definitions
of what rum "is," but it never really speaks to the variety of styles out
there. Thus, for our purposes, one of the best ways to appreciate that
variety is to focus on where the rum is made.

English-style rum—meaning rum from islands once or still under
British control, like Barbados, Jamaica, Guyana—is one of the oldest rum styles and is specifically known for a very aromatic structure
and flavor. Often distilled in old-fashioned pot stills, it is generally
medium-bodied; the age in years on the bottle (5-year, 10-year) refers
to the age of the youngest rum used in the blend. Jamaica enforces
its own classification system to control quality.

As you will see from our bottle choices (page 170), we happen to
be big fans of the profile found in Barbadian rums, appreciating how
the smooth, often fruity/spicy character works so well with cocktails.
Both the Plantation and Cockspur rums we favor are from Barbados.
Smith & Cross, our premium amber rum choice, is from Jamaica and
is a naval-strength, or overproof, rum.

Spanish-style rums vary between those from areas like Cuba
and Puerto Rico to those from Central and South America. The former style is "cleaner" and lighter-bodied because it is distilled in the
more modern stainless steel column stills. The latter's profile is often
almost brandylike, as the Spanish settlers brought their brandy making skills with them when they immigrated to the New World. One of
our white rum choices, Flor de Caña, is from Nicaragua.

French-style rums made from sugarcane juice rather than molasses are called *rhum agricole*, and are produced in only a few places, including Martinique and Guadeloupe. This style has its own vegetal, earthy/funky flavor. Those from Martinique come with their own AOC (Appellation d'Origine Controllée), a French geographic/production certification.

So, that's a start. But it hardly scratches the surface. Another consideration, since it tends to be the visually defining feature of rum, is color. We really struggled to choose an appropriate name for our "darker" rums, vacillating between gold, amber, aged, and many combinations thereof.

If we simply called for an "aged" rum as our darker choice, we were saddled with an overly broad term, particularly since many white rums are aged to some degree. So "aged," given its breadth, was out. The United States recognizes the classification "dark rum," but this describes any rum aged to any degree, including those whose hue is derived from added caramel color. Martin Cate, rum expert and owner of Smuggler's Cove in San Francisco, likes the term "black rum" to classify rums that are "lightly aged and darkly colored," as he describes them. These rums can still vary from light to full-bodied styles. For this book, we've chosen the term "amber," which for us denotes a rum of medium to full body with a far richer flavor profile than its cleaner, white rum brother.

THE BOTTLES TO BUY

A s with any spirit, learning about rum can be a lifelong journey. There are gin and whiskey devotees, and so too there are rum lovers who will fight to the death (well, almost) about their favorite expression of fermented molasses.

Admittedly, we are not rum aficionados. We don't much like "funky," to which most longtime rum lovers pledge their undying love. We like pineapple, vanilla, butterscotch, and a bit of oak, but not the overly woody, tobacco-like, or musty character that some amber rums have. We lean toward English-style rums that display a fruity, light sweetness and smooth drinkability. Above all, we like rum that reminds us that it is a sugar spirit. That said, we also like to be hit in the face with over-proof goodness, hence one of our choices.

Midrange
($20–$30/750 ml)

COCKSPUR FINE RUM This is Cockspur's entry-level rum and, at this price, everyone should buy it. It tastes far more expensive than it is, with a faint sweetness probably due to aging in whiskey and bourbon barrels. The typical vanilla and stone fruits come out, too, making this rum from Barbados a dynamite mixer.

PLANTATION 5 YEAR OLD GRAND RESERVE BARBADOS RUM This is a very smooth, accessible rum whose slightly lower price point makes it a real value, especially considering how good it is. Similar in body and age to the Cockspur, it has its own identity. The first thing we taste in this rum can only be described as "banana custard." It is classic English-style rum, tropically fruity with notes of vanilla.

Artisan/ Premium
($30—$50/750 ml)

SMITH & CROSS TRADITIONAL JAMAICA RUM Ever had a Werther's Original butterscotch? Smell the Smith & Cross—it's buttery candy in a bottle. The flavor is spicy and jungle fruity. Complex is the byword here, since Smith & Cross is a 100 percent pot still product. It's also navy strength, which means 57% ABV (see page 196 if you plan to use this potent brew for mixing). You've been warned—pour accordingly.

THE DRINKS

Sweet & Fruity

STONE FENCE

GLASS: COLLINS, CHILLED | ICE: CUBED | MAKES: 1 DRINK

Apples are not indigenous to America, but rather were introduced by European settlers; by the colonial era, apple orchards had spread across the land. (Fact: Johnny "Appleseed," also known as John Chapman, was a real dude who planted apple seeds with abandon.) Now, here's an interesting botanical note: Eating apples are generally grafted from apple tree root stocks. Apples planted from seed, however, are quite bitter, but they happen to make excellent cider, both hard and nonalcoholic, as well as applejack, a distillate of cider.

As is often the case, when there is a proliferation of something, the locals invent a drink to showcase it. Here, it's the Stone Fence, as American a beverage as ever there was. The Stone Fence can literally, like a buck, be made with any spirit, but back in the colonial days, it would have been made with rum. Ethan Allen and his Green Mountain Boys would have drunk it with the sugarcane spirit, lots of it, as they plotted their revolutionary campaigns. (By the 1800s, during Jerry Thomas's era, rye had replaced the less-accessible rum as the spirit of choice.) As to the choice of cider, we have our favorites (see page 328), but encourage you to find your own house quaff as well.

• •

2 ounces amber rum   Hard apple cider

• •

Place a few cubes of ice in a chilled collins glass, add the rum, and top with the cider.

CHICKEN FOOT

GLASS: ROCKS | ICE: CUBED | MAKES: 1 DRINK

O ur friend Lars, a contributor to the 12 Bottle Bar site, is our go-to guy for all things New Orleans, as his family is born-and-bred New Iberian. On one of his many trips back to the family's NOLA digs, he returned with a gift that not only embodied his dry sense of humor, but also turned out to be the perfect accent to Lars's 12 Bottle Bar post for the Voodoo Cocktail.

The original Voodoo Cocktail's provenance is unclear; we originally found it online at absolutdrinks.com and from there we ran with it, making it our own. The Spiced Sweet Vermouth, which we also use in the Bloodbath (page 105), makes this a particularly autumnal drink, especially at home on Halloween, which is when we first featured it.

• •

4 ounces apple juice

2 ounces amber rum

1 ounce strained, freshly squeezed lime juice

1 ounce Simple Syrup (page 369)

1 ounce Spiced Sweet Vermouth (page 388)

Lime wedge, for garnish (optional)

• •

1 Combine all of the ingredients in a mixing glass, fill the glass three-quarters full with ice cubes, cover with a Boston shaker tin, and shake vigorously until thoroughly chilled, 15 seconds.

2 Place a large ice cube in a rocks glass and strain the drink into the glass.

3 Pre-Zombiepocalypse, garnish with a lime wedge or voodoo charm. Post-Zombiepocalypse, you shouldn't be worried about garnishes.

NOTE: This is an easily scalable drink, making it the perfect choice for a seasonal punch. Just finish with a fresh grating of nutmeg and a sprinkle of cinnamon.

RUM AND VOODOO

HISTORICALLY, RUM AND voodoo are forever linked, both products of the slave culture in the Caribbean islands. Rum is a standard offering for Ogoun, a Haitian warrior spirit. When he possesses people and gives them power, the newly possessed person often washes his or her hands in flaming rum, apparently with no painful effects. (Please do not try this at home.)

I DO

GLASS: MARTINI | ICE: CUBED | MAKES: 1 DRINK

Lesley here. One of the perks of having a husband who plays around with cocktails is that I am often lucky enough to have one created just for me. The "I Do," a drink recipe posted on the 12 Bottle Bar site that commemorated our twelfth wedding anniversary, is an example of David's romantic side. As I originally said when presented with this gift in drink form, that "I Do" was the best thing I ever did.

On a more serious note, this is one lovely drink. The rum and honey-melon combination really harmonizes, while the rum adds spice and the Angostura adds a touch of bitterness to counter what might become too cloying a profile.

1½ ounces amber rum

2 ounces Honey Melon Nectar (recipe follows)

Dash aromatic bitters

Rose petal (preferably organic or unsprayed), for garnish

1 Combine all of the liquid ingredients in a mixing glass, fill the glass three-quarters full with ice cubes, cover with a Boston shaker tin, and shake vigorously until thoroughly chilled, 15 seconds.

2 Strain into a martini glass and garnish beautifully with a rose petal.

Honey Melon Nectar

MAKES: ABOUT 4 OUNCES

∙∙

1 cup roughly chopped ripe
  Tuscan melon or other
  sweet, orange-fleshed
  melon, such as cantaloupe

1½ tablespoons honey

½ ounce strained, freshly
  squeezed lemon juice

∙∙

1 Place the melon in a mixing glass, add the honey and lemon juice, and muddle until the ingredients are as liquid as possible.

2 Strain the mixture into another glass, using the muddler to force all possible liquid from the pulp. Discard the solids. The nectar will keep, refrigerated, in an airtight container for about 2 days.

∙∙

TEA TIME

GLASS: COLLINS | ICE: CUBED | MAKES: 1 DRINK

There are few drink orders less appreciated by bartenders than the Long Island Iced Tea. Growing up, we often heard the myth, "If you combine all these liquors, it takes just like iced tea." Not our iced tea. The LIIT (which is what you'll become after consuming one) is a pain to make and goes out of its way to conceal the profiles of its composite ingredients.

What if there was an easy-to-assemble alternative that not only captured the spirit of iced tea—and sweet tea at that—but also knocked you on your tuckus? Riffing on the old-school-but-forgotten Tea Time from the *Old Waldorf-Astoria Bar Book*, we devised a stealth bomb in oolong clothing. A sweet tea that brings sweet dreams. Okay, enough with the hyperbole, just make the drink already.

∙∙

3 ounces amber rum

1 ounce Tea Syrup (page 378)

½ teaspoon strained, freshly
  squeezed lemon juice

Lemon twist, for garnish

Fresh mint sprig, for garnish

1 Combine all of the liquid ingredients in a mixing glass, fill the glass three-quarters full with ice cubes, cover with a Boston shaker tin, and shake vigorously until thoroughly chilled, 15 seconds.

2 Fill a collins glass with ice cubes and strain the drink into the glass. Garnish with the lemon twist and the mint.

HAWAIIAN PUNCH

GLASS: PUNCH | MAKES: 12 DRINKS

W e were on a roll one night, riffing on childhood memories. If you are a kid of the '70s, there's no getting away from the ubiquitous Hawaiian Punch. We decided to make a grown-up version, minus the shocking Red Dye #2 (or whatever number it was) and with a more authentic island flavor.

Historically, tea has been used in punch since the beginning of punch-making days; it's a great way to stretch out your ingredients and also add a surprising bit of bright, tannic flavor to the blend. We often serve this in coupes with a chunk of pineapple in the glass. Since we don't like to dilute this with ice, instead we chill the punch bowl in the fridge and then set it on a bed of ice to keep cold.

3 lemons

6 ounces light brown or raw sugar, such Demerara

About 2 cups hot brewed green tea (we use jasmine)

⅓ fresh pineapple, coarsely chopped into ¾-inch cubes

8 ounces amber rum

1 bottle (750 ml) Champagne or sparkling wine, chilled

Fresh whole nutmeg, for garnish (see Note, page 70)

1 Peel the lemons with a vegetable peeler, removing as little of the white pith as possible. Place the peels in a medium heatproof bowl, cover

them with the sugar, and set the mixture aside until the sugar has infused with the oil of the lemons, at least 1 hour.

2 Pour 6 ounces of the tea (refrigerate the rest) over the lemon mixture and stir to dissolve the sugar completely. Remove and discard the lemon peels and set the tea mixture aside to cool to room temperature.

3 Transfer the cooled tea mixture to a large bowl, add the pineapple, and stir to combine. Set aside to infuse at room temperature, covered with plastic wrap or a towel for at least 8 hours, or overnight.

4 To serve, place the pineapple mixture in a chilled punch bowl. Add the rum, then the Champagne.

5 Add the reserved chilled cold green tea to taste (we use 8 ounces total) and garnish with a fresh grating of nutmeg. Serve in the punch bowl, ladling into individual punch glasses.

MIDNIGHT PUNCH

GLASS: PUNCH | ICE: BLOCK | MAKES: ABOUT 12 DRINKS

A simple, rum-based punch that is as easy to make as it is crowd-pleasing. This one comes to us by way of the reliable *Boothby's World Drinks* (1934 reprint). We're always fans of a rum-and-ginger-beer combo, and the additions of grapefruit juice and grenadine contribute winning levels of both tartness and sweetness.

1 bottle (750 ml) amber rum

18 ounces ginger beer, such as Reed's Premium Ginger Brew

5 ounces strained, freshly squeezed grapefruit juice

5 ounces Grenadine, homemade (page 376) or store-bought

Grapefruit rings, for garnishing the punch bowl

1 Combine all of the liquid ingredients in a punch bowl and stir to combine.

2 Add a large block of ice and garnish with the grapefruit rings.

PUNCH À LA ROMAINE

GLASS: MARTINI | MAKES: 12 TO 14 DRINKS

Y ou just can't go wrong with the punch that was served on the *Titanic*. Granted, the ship sank, but your party will stay afloat long into the wee hours with this luscious, sweetly citrusy bowl of goodness. Making the lemon ice and the Italian meringue are time consuming, precise bits of work (and you'll need a candy thermometer for the meringue), but oh, the lovely product of that effort!

For a very serviceable quickie version, replace the lemon ice and meringue with 1 pint good-quality lemon sorbet, combine it with the rum and Champagne, then refreeze until semisolid.

1 recipe Lemon Ice
   (recipe follows),
   slightly thawed

1 recipe Italian Meringue
   (recipe follows)

8 ounces amber rum

8 ounces Champagne or
   sparkling wine, chilled

1 Combine the lemon ice and the Italian meringue in a chilled punch bowl and stir gently to combine.

2 Just before serving, slowly add the rum and Champagne, stirring constantly. The mixture should be thick and creamy but drinkable. Serve immediately (and we mean it) in martini glasses.

I VOTE FOR RUM PUNCH

IN 1755, George Washington ran for the Virginia House of Burgesses and lost. In 1758, he smartly offered voters a plentiful assortment of alcoholic beverages, including (according to Marvin Kitman's book *The Making of the President 1789*): "28 gallons of rum, 50 gallons of rum punch, 34 gallons of wine, 46 gallons of beer, and two gallons of cider royal."

He won the election.

Lemon Ice

MAKES: ABOUT 1 QUART

4 lemons

1½ cups superfine sugar

1 Peel the lemons, removing as little of the white pith as possible. Place the peels in a medium bowl, cover completely with the sugar, and let sit for 1 hour.

2 Juice the peeled lemons, for 1 cup of juice. Add the juice to the peel mixture in the bowl and stir to dissolve the sugar.

3 Strain the mixture through a fine-mesh sieve into a 1-quart casserole dish, discarding the solids.

4 Add enough water to the lemon syrup to make 1 quart of liquid. Cover and freeze until the edges are frozen, about 1½ hours. With a fork, break up the ice until slushy, then return to the freezer. Repeat this process 2 more times.

5 Freeze the ice one last time—the mixture should be set and scoopable, but not frozen solid, about 1 hour.

Italian Meringue

MAKES: ABOUT 1 CUP

Whites from 2 large eggs
¾ cup granulated sugar

3 ounces water

1 In a large, very clean, heatproof bowl, beat the egg whites to stiff peaks. Set aside.

2 Combine the sugar and water in a small saucepan and bring to a boil over medium-high heat, stirring occasionally to dissolve the sugar.

3 Set a candy thermometer into the sugar mixture and continue to cook until the mixture reaches the "soft ball" stage, 236–238°F.

4 Remove the syrup from the heat and, using a heatproof rubber spatula, carefully fold the syrup, in a very slow stream, into the beaten egg whites. Stir until all the syrup is added and the mixture is smooth. Use immediately.

COQUITO

GLASS: ROCKS OR MUG | MAKES: 9 DRINKS

This is a traditional Puerto Rican drink that is essentially eggnog made with coconut milk. The result is subtle and refreshing—not necessarily what one thinks of in a Christmas punch, but rewarding nonetheless. If you live in a cold-weather clime, the punch brings a bit of sunshine on a snowy day; if you live in California, as we do, the flavors are right at home, especially in the middle of December. While you might be tempted to add more rum, proceed with caution, as the proportions here are perfectly balanced.

8 ounces amber rum

4 cups (32 ounces) coconut milk (not coconut water)

1 can (14 ounces) sweetened condensed milk

½ cup water

Pinch of salt

1 teaspoon ground cinnamon

Fresh whole nutmeg, for garnish (see Note, page 70)

Cinnamon sticks, for garnish (optional)

1 Combine the rum, coconut milk, condensed milk, water, salt, and cinnamon in a blender and blend until smooth. Cover and refrigerate for 8 hours, or overnight.

2 To serve, stir the mixture gently, then pour a measured serving into a glass or mug and garnish with a grating of nutmeg. For a bit of flair, add a cinnamon stick.

ARAB STRAP

GLASS: HEATPROOF MUG | MAKES: 1 DRINK

T he Arab Strap evolved as many drinks do at 12 Bottle Bar—with the spark of an idea. We were toying with Valentine's Day sippers and wanted something to finish off an amorous evening, perhaps prolonging it with its "invigorating" qualities. As we are huge fans of Turkish coffee, we riffed on those spicy aromatics, using orange and cardamom. The molasses added a savory sweetness to the coffee element and the rum completed the recipe for the Arab Strap.

As to the name, well, that's a bit of a story; when we name a drink, it's always roundabout. The term "Arab strap" seems to have its genesis as a sexual device to prolong a man's erection. That titillating fact caught the attention of a Scottish indie band, who dubbed themselves Arab Strap. Neither of these facts would ever have hit our radar except that Belle and Sebastian, one of our favorite bands, put out an album called *The Boy with the Arab Strap,* referencing both the device and the band, and making the term something of a household word. As "strap" can also refer to blackstrap molasses (we've taken some liberty there), the spices we used were vaguely Arabic, and we wanted a bit of a "seductive" name . . . presto! A drink name was born.

· ·

2 cardamom pods

6 ounces strong, freshly brewed black coffee

2 cubes light brown or raw sugar, such as Demerara

Orange twist

1 ounce amber rum

1 tablespoon blackstrap molasses

· ·

1 Pinch the cardamom pods to break the outer hull slightly. Place them in a small saucepan with the coffee and sugar. Squeeze the orange twist over the pan to express the oils, then add the twist.

2 Bring to a boil over medium-high heat, then remove the pan from the heat and set it aside for a few minutes to steep.

3 Stir together the rum and molasses in a heatproof mug.

4 Return the saucepan to the heat and bring to a boil. Add the hot spiced coffee to the mug and stir to combine.

BLACK STRIPE

GLASS: HEATPROOF MUG | MAKES: 1 DRINK

Nothing goes together like rum and molasses—after all, one wouldn't exist without the other. Given that the two products were rife in the colonial era, it's a no-brainer that eighteenth-century imbibers put them together in a drink. Later, in Jerry Thomas's first edition of *Bar-Tender's Guide*, the maestro included the drink, suggesting its popularity hadn't waned.

If you don't want to buy a bottle of blackstrap molasses (which comes from the third boiling of sugar syrup), you can certainly opt for the standard style, but the flavor will be less intense—and less "healthful." Blackstrap actually possesses salubrious qualities, offering potassium, carbohydrates, and protein. Maybe the early American penchant for using cocktails as "medicine" wasn't so far off.

1 tablespoon molasses (preferably blackstrap)

2 ounces boiling water

2 ounces amber rum

Fresh whole nutmeg, for garnish (see Note, page 70)

1 Combine the molasses and water in a heatproof mug and stir to combine.

2 Add the rum and stir again. Garnish with a grating of nutmeg.

HOT BUTTERED RUM

GLASS: HEATPROOF MUG, WARMED | MAKES: 1 DRINK

This is as classic and old-school as punch can be. When the cinnamon, nutmeg, and cloves warm in the brew, the sweet-spicy aroma is positively magical. And, if you are into historic recreation, prepare it the old-fashioned way: Combine all the ingredients, cold, in a heatproof mug, then plunge a red-hot poker fresh from the fire into the glass to warm the drink. Note: Remove the poker before consuming.

The Spiced Butter called for in the recipe makes enough to butter ten to twelve cups of punch, making this easy to scale up.

2 tablespoons Spiced Butter
(recipe follows)

2 ounces amber rum

4 ounces boiling water

1 pat unsalted butter,
for serving

1 Heat the mug by running it under very hot water; dry it thoroughly.

2 Place the Spiced Butter in the bottom of the mug. Add the rum, then the boiling water, and stir to dissolve the sugar that's in the butter. Float the pat of unsalted butter on the surface of the drink.

Spiced Butter

MAKES: 1½ CUPS BUTTER; ENOUGH FOR 10 TO 12 DRINKS

½ cup (1 stick) unsalted
butter, at room temperature

2 cups light brown or raw
sugar, such as Demerara

1 teaspoon ground cinnamon

½ teaspoon freshly
grated nutmeg
(see Note, page 70)

Pinch ground cloves

Pinch salt

Combine all of the ingredients in a small bowl and cream together with a wooden spoon. Cover and refrigerate until firm, 8 hours or overnight.

The butter will keep, stored in an airtight container and refrigerated, for up to 1 week, or frozen for up to 1 month.

Tangy & Citrusy

BUMBO

GLASS: COLLINS | ICE: CUBED | MAKES: 1 DRINK

Y ou will immediately see the similarities between Bumbo and Grog (page 184). They contain the exact same ingredients, except the Bumbo uses different proportions and has the addition of spices. These small adjustments make for a drink that stands on its own and can also stand up to a bit more decorative "junk"—the garnish on top.

Bumbo has a bit more pizzazz than Grog, with those spices adding a bit of a sensory flourish, which is why we affectionately call it "pirate grog." After all, you'd never say Jack Sparrow didn't enjoy a little flourish. Notice that there is less water here than in Grog, necessitating a good shake to blend the spices. One sip and you might start singing "The pirate's life for me."

2 ounces amber rum

2 ounces water

½ ounce strained, freshly squeezed lime juice

2 teaspoons light brown or raw sugar, such as Demerara

2 pinches ground cinnamon

Pinch freshly ground nutmeg (see Note, page 70)

Lemon or orange slice, for garnish

Strawberries or blackberries, for garnish

1 Combine the rum, water, lime juice, sugar, and spices in a mixing glass, fill the glass three-quarters full with ice cubes, cover with a Boston shaker tin, and shake vigorously until thoroughly chilled, 15 seconds.

2 Place a cube or two of ice in a collins glass and strain the drink into the glass. Garnish with the citrus slice and the berries.

GROG

GLASS: COLLINS OR ROCKS | ICE: CUBED | MAKES: 1 DRINK

Old-timey sailors were a surly lot, but their daily rum ration placated them to some degree. Still, straight rum didn't seem such a great idea to the powers (namely one Admiral Edward Vernon), who ordered that his men's rations be cut with water and lime. Add a little brown sugar and, with that combination of strong, weak, sour, and sweet, you have a nascent punch, sailor-style. The drink gained a quick following among the men, who dubbed it "grog" after Vernon, whose nickname was "Old Grogram."

True to its purpose as a pick-me-up for the sailors, Grog is bracing, tart, and thirst-quenching, a perfect drink for a hot summer afternoon hoisting the mainsail, or just being a landlubber and hanging in a hammock.

COLONIAL COCKTAILS

THE EVER-ENTERPRISING BARTENDERS of the colonial era created their own riffs on Grog—four parts water to one part rum—ad infinitum. Here is just a partial list of the inspired "cocktails" they devised.

SLING (PAGE 33): water, rum

MIMBO: sugar, rum, water

BOMBO: molasses, rum, water (not to be confused with the Bumbo, page 183)

CHERRY BOUNCE: cherry juice, rum

BILBERRY DRAM: bilberries, rum

SYLLABUB: warm milk, rum, spices

SHRUB (PAGE 200): sweetened vinegar, rum

SAMPSON: hot cider, rum

BLACK STRIPE (PAGE 181): molasses, rum

FLIP: beer, rum, molasses, heated until foaming

½ ounce strained, freshly squeezed lime juice

2 teaspoons light brown or raw sugar, such as Demerara

4 ounces water

2 ounces rum (we like amber, but the pirate in you need not be picky)

Lime wheel, for garnish

1 Combine the lime juice and sugar in a collins or rocks glass. Add the water and stir to dissolve the sugar.

2 Add the rum and a few large cubes of ice and stir to chill. Garnish with the lime wheel.

BLACK TOT DAY

FOR MORE THAN three hundred years, the sailors of the British Royal Navy received rations of alcohol. Beer came first—roughly a gallon per man per day—but took up a good deal of room and was prone to spoilage during the warm months. Wine was occasionally issued in place of beer, but the ration that stuck in the history books was rum.

After capturing Jamaica from Spain, the Royal Navy switched the ration to half a pint of neat navy-strength (57% ABV) rum twice a day. This daily ration—or "tot"—was ultimately deemed excessive by Admiral Edward Vernon, who ordered that the rum be diluted with water. The mixture was called "grog" after Vernon's own nickname, "Old Grogram," taken from the silk and wool grogram fabric cloaks he was fond of wearing.

On July 31, 1970—a day known as Black Tot Day—the last rations of rum were doled out by the Royal Navy. The Queen was toasted as black armbands were worn and mock funerals were held for a tradition that was almost as old as the Royal Navy itself.

HURRICANE

GLASS: COLLINS OR ROCKS | ICE: CUBED | MAKES: 1 DRINK

I f you ever find yourself in New Orleans, you may end up at Pat O'Brien's, sipping one of the restaurant's legendary Hurricanes, a mind- and body-numbing alcoholic sweet-tart bomb. That recipe calls for 4 ounces of rum and 4 ounces of a mysterious red powder known as "O'Brien's Hurricane Mix." Our version tames the rum a bit and eliminates the ersatz red powder, harkening back to the simplicity and sweet-tart profile of the original.

3 ounces amber rum

2 ounces passion fruit juice or nectar (see Note)

1 ounce strained, freshly squeezed lime juice

½ ounce Grenadine, homemade (page 376) or store-bought

Orange slice, for garnish

Brandied Cherry (page 367) or high-quality maraschino cherry (we like Luxardo brand), for garnish

1 Combine all of the liquid ingredients in a mixing glass, fill the glass three-quarters full with ice cubes, and shake vigorously until thoroughly chilled, 15 seconds.

2 Pour the drink without straining it into a collins or rocks glass. Garnish with the orange slice and the cherry.

NOTE: We like Ceres brand passion fruit juice, which is available at most supermarkets.

Tiki:
PAGEANT AND POTENCY

"Tiki may continue to influence contemporary bars in the areas of experience and presentation—that there should be some drama to the drink and some atmosphere that makes it worth going out . . . historically quite a few of these drinks are powerful concoctions. I really think that to do it right, they should be at original strength, but it's a really good idea to caution guests about their potency."

—MARTIN CATE, OWNER, SMUFFLER'S COVE, SAN FRANCISCO, CA

INDEPENDENCE SWIZZLE

GLASS: COLLINS | ICE: CRUSHED | MAKES: 1 DRINK

Swizzles are their own class of drink, like a sour or a fizz, employing a healthy dose of spirit, plus lemon or lime juice, a sweetener, and usually bitters. The "swizzle" part of the name originates from the "swizzle stick," originally a small, three-pronged branch of wood that was used to blend rum-based drinks on West Indian sugar plantations. Swizzles have a sort of mysterious aura about them, perhaps because of the swizzle stick itself and the fire-starting vigor with which the drink is assembled, combining to produce a voodoo-quality frost on the glass.

The Independence Swizzle is a slight variation of the Trader Vic staple Barbados Red Rum Swizzle (simply rum, bitters, sugar, and lime), employing honey in addition to the sugar. It's a key addition. Even if you don't have a swizzle stick, this is one heck of a drink—one that particularly highlights the magic of the aromatic bitters employed. Angostura bitters are traditional here, and they work exceptionally well.

½ ounce strained, freshly squeezed lime juice

1½ teaspoons honey

1 teaspoon granulated sugar

2 ounces amber rum

3 dashes aromatic bitters

Mixed berries, for garnish

1 Combine the lime juice, honey, and sugar in a collins glass and stir to dissolve the sugar.

2 Fill the glass with crushed ice and add the rum and bitters. Swizzle with a swizzle stick or stir vigorously until a froth appears, at least 30 seconds. Garnish with any and all berries available.

THE SWIZZLE STICK

IF YOU WERE a child of the 1960s, then you grew up in what we can now reverentially refer to as the "Era of the Swizzle Stick." Back when mad men were king, swizzle sticks could be found everywhere—restaurants, bars, even airlines offered them with almost every drink. People took them as souvenirs as a matter of course; they were one of the best advertising gimmicks of their day. But, while the heyday of the swizzle stick may have been the Don Draper days, the swizzle stick has been around since sugar plantations rose up in the West Indies, producing rum which was then used in the drink called Switchel, or Swizzle.

The original swizzle stick was a branch of wood with three small prongs at one end; the more flamboyant plastic version we know today was created in 1934 by Jay Sindler. Sindler was an enterprising young fellow with a real problem—he couldn't get the olive out of his martini without dipping his fingers into the glass. His idea was simple and practical: a long stick of wood with a paddle on one end with which to retrieve said olive. The visionary part of the design was the advertising—each swizzle stick could be imprinted with the name of the bar or restaurant from which it came.

In post–World War II America, the swizzle stick assumed its plastic form and, as the 1960s arrived, the sticks took on whimsical shapes—those from Trader Vic's featured Menehune (mythological Hawaiian little people), the now-defunct TWA airlines showed a native American in full headdress, and many offered pinupstyle ladies to mix with aplomb. These days, the old-school ones are collector's items (Etsy and Ebay offer tons of them) meant for gently stirring one's drink in contemplative reverie. Should you want to officially "swizzle" your rum swizzle, you can find more practical and durable threepronged styles from cocktail suppliers (see Resources, page 393). Consider a swizzle stick a small investment in the magic that is drink preparation.

"The rum ration must be regarded as a food. The quantity which is served out per man be entirely assimilated by the body, and under the present regulations it is impossible for any man to have more than his share.

"In men exposed to cold, wet, shells, and all the other discomforts of trench life, it produces a sense of comparative wellbeing, makes life just bearable, and is often just the incentive necessary for hanging on to a newly captured position until relieved."

—GEOFFREY SPARROW AND JAMES NESS MACBEAN ROSS,
ON FOUR FRONTS WITH THE ROYAL NAVAL DIVISION (1918)

JAMAICA HONEY BEE

GLASS: MARTINI | ICE: CUBED | MAKES: 1 DRINK

This rum variation on the Bee's Knees (page 106) is a perfect three-season tipple (we'll opt for a Daiquiri in the peak of summer). The key here is the right honey. While some will wax about this rum or that rum, we're equally choosy about our honey. A savory varietal honey such as wildflower is required here to steer the drink away from Cloyingtown. And, certainly, if you have a nice Jamaican rum handy, like Smith & Cross, reach for that.

2 ounces amber rum

½ ounce strained, freshly squeezed lemon juice

½ ounce Honey Syrup (page 371)

1 Combine all of the ingredients in a mixing glass, fill the mixing glass three-quarters full with ice cubes, cover with a Boston shaker tin, and shake vigorously until thoroughly chilled, 15 seconds.

2 Strain into a martini glass.

DON AND VIC

ALONG WITH THE Xerox machine and color TV, 1950s America was blessed with a widespread fascination with tiki culture. In actuality, the first Polynesian-style restaurant had been opened back in 1934, in Hollywood, by a fellow named Ernest Raymond Beaumont-Gantt. Enamored of the South Pacific after sailing there, Ernie legally changed his name to Donn Beach and opened Don the Beachcomber. He is often credited with creating the first fruity rum drinks, including the Zombie, a recipe so varied that rum and citrus are often the only two constant components.

Three years after Don the Beachcomber opened, the hot spot got some healthy competition from Trader Vic's, founded by Victor Bergeron. In the ensuing decades, there were dozens of copycats as tiki culture grabbed the country's collective imagination, inspiring design trends, musical styles, and summer party themes. Like so many gimmicks, no matter how clever, the tiki trend faded for many years, although a few of the drinks continued to show up here and there. In the 1990s, along with swing culture, tiki had a resurgence and the potent drinks (see Martin Cate's advice, page 187) still appear on bar menus today.

MAI TAI

GLASS: ROCKS | ICE: CRUSHED | MAKES: 1 DRINK

This is the king of tropical/tiki drinks, and for good reason. It's powerful, it's fruity, and it's made with rum. Created by tiki maestro Victor Bergeron at the legendary Trader Vic's, the Mai Tai conjures up the epitome of island escapism. The orgeat, an almond syrup that is key to the recipe, is best when homemade, but as it is quite time-consuming to prepare, you can substitute high-quality store-bought syrup. The exact proportions of the sweet components vary slightly depending on the recipe you consult; you be the judge as to your own preferences. Ours errs on the side of not too sweet, not too alcoholic.

Trader Vic's original Mai Tai called for J. Wray & Nephew 17-year-old Jamaican rum. When that went the way of the dodo, Vic revised the recipe to include two rums—a Martinique rum, also known as rhum agricole (see page 169), and a dark Jamaican rum. As agricole may be too funky for many palates (and we don't call for it at 12BB), we use a traditional amber rum here. Sincere apologies to all purists, but better that 12 Bottle Bar contains a Mai Tai than not.

• •

2 ounces amber rum

½ ounce orange liqueur

¼ ounce Orgeat Syrup, preferably homemade (page 379)

¼ ounce Rich Simple Syrup (page 369)

½ ounce strained, freshly squeezed lime juice

Fresh mint sprig, orange slice, and/or Brandied Cherry (page 367) or high-quality maraschino cherry (we like Luxardo), for garnish

• •

1 Combine the rum, liqueur, syrups, and lime juice in a mixing glass. Fill the mixing glass three-quarters full with crushed ice and shake the drink vigorously until thoroughly chilled, 15 seconds.

2 Strain into a rocks glass and garnish with the mint, orange, or cherry.

KNICKERBOCKER

GLASS: ROCKS | ICE: CUBED | MAKES: 1 DRINK

The Knickerbocker is a flashback in a glass to the days just after the Civil War. It appears in *Jerry Thomas' Bar-Tender's Guide*, the first cocktail book, and is just as tasty now as it was a century and a half ago. As with the Knickerbocker Club (page 79), it takes its name from Washington Irving's tongue-in-cheek sobriquet for New York's blue bloods.

Why go to the trouble of making your own syrups? If the Knickerbocker and the raspberry syrup contained therein don't convince you of the benefits, nothing will. Here is a perfect example of a flavor as sublime and delicate as raspberry rising to the forefront against intimidating competition—and soaring.

½ lime

2½ ounces amber rum

¼ ounce Fresh Raspberry Syrup (page 372)

½ teaspoon orange liqueur

1 Squeeze the juice of the lime through a sieve into a mixing glass and drop the juiced shell into the glass. Add the remaining ingredients, fill the glass three-quarters full with ice cubes, cover with a Boston shaker tin, and shake vigorously until thoroughly chilled, 15 seconds.

2 Pour the drink, lime and all, into a rocks glass.

MIDDLETON

GLASS: MARTINI | ICE: CUBED | MAKES: 1 DRINK

One sip of the Middleton and you might as well be sitting at a bar in a painting by Henri de Toulouse-Lautrec. There is a grand Belle Epoque quality at work here, conjuring the rich decadence—thanks to the heady combination of genever and rum and the velvety texture of the grenadine and egg white—of can-can petticoats and late nights in Montmarte. The egg white and grenadine add a confectionary quality while the genever counters with its inherent funk. The drink is simultaneously dry, indulgent, and ephemeral.

2 ounces amber rum

½ ounce genever

¾ ounce Grenadine, homemade (page 376) or store-bought

1½ ounces strained, freshly squeezed lemon juice

White from 1 large egg

••

1 Combine all of the ingredients in a mixing glass, cover with a Boston shaker tin, and shake vigorously to combine the ingredients and froth the egg white, 15 seconds.

2 Fill the mixing glass three-quarters full with ice cubes, cover again, and shake vigorously until thoroughly chilled, 15 seconds.

3 Strain into a martini glass.

••

PKNY

GLASS: ROCKS | ICE: CRUSHED | MAKES: 1 DRINK

The drinks business is very much about economics, and economics often means branding. Enter Pusser's Rum vs. PKNY (formerly called Painkiller) Bar. Theirs is a story of how good business sense can be, in point of fact, very bad for business.

The story goes like this. Back in the 1970s, the Soggy Dollar bar in the British Virgin Islands came up with a drink called a Painkiller—a combination of rum, pineapple juice, cream of coconut, and orange juice—that caught the attention of Pusser's Rum. Pusser's bought the rights and trademarked the drink as "Pusser's Painkiller." The bartenders at PKNY, a bar originally and ironically called Painkiller, liked the drink, too—but not made with Pusser's. Pusser's insisted that the bartenders use Pusser's rum, and that the bar change its name; the owners kindly demurred and Pusser's took them to court—and won . . . sort of. Painkiller bar had to change its name, which it did, to PKNY, and it removed the Painkiller drink from its menu. But, as news spread of the debacle, the cocktail community rose up in what can only be called a Unitarian stance and protested Pusser's actions. Worse, they boycotted the brand and even started putting non-Pusser's Painkillers, often called PKNYs, on their menus.

Unfortunately, PKNY the bar is no longer with us. In its memory, we choose to make the drink with any rum we find tasty—and we hope you will as well—and have applied the PKNY moniker, lest the lawyers come knocking.

3 ounces amber rum

4 ounces pineapple juice

1 ounce Coconut Milk Syrup (page 381)

1 ounce strained, freshly squeezed orange juice

Fresh whole nutmeg, for garnish (see Note, page 70)

Seasonal fresh fruit, for garnish

1 Combine all of the liquid ingredients in a mixing glass, fill the glass three-quarters full with ice cubes, cover with a Boston shaker tin, and shake vigorously until thoroughly chilled, 15 seconds.

2 Fill a rocks glass with crushed ice and strain the drink into the glass. Grate fresh nutmeg generously over the top, garnish with the fresh fruit, and ignore the legal ramifications.

Great Bars
THEN & NOW

TIKI TI | 4427 SUNSET BOULEVARD
LOS ANGELES, CA 90027 | 323-669-9381 | TIKI-TI.COM

BACK IN 1961, a bartender named Ray Buhen, who had worked at Don the Beachcomber (see page 190) in the early years, opened Tiki Ti on Sunset Boulevard in the now-hipster Silverlake area. Still going strong in the same location, the spot—with only twelve seats and a no-reservations policy—is now run by Buhen's son and grandson, who serve more than ninety tiki-style drinks. Be forewarned—the drinks are potent, the hours are quirky, and, because there are no employees, this is one of the few bars in Los Angeles where people can still smoke.

PLANTER'S PUNCH

GLASS: COLLINS OR ROCKS | ICE: CUBED, CRUSHED |
MAKES: 1 DRINK

W hile the name has led people to believe that Planter's Punch originated at the Planter's Hotel in Charleston, South Carolina, history says differently. As with most rummy concoctions, Planter's Punch was born in Jamaica, but the variety of recipes for the cocktail has led many drink historians to classify it as a "collection" of drinks, rather than one recipe. Rather than split hairs, we will simply turn to Trader Vic's owner and man-about-town Victor Bergeron, purveyor of all things tropical, and cite his recipe for posterity. Experiment as you will, of course, and make Planter's Punch your own. Vic topped his with seltzer; we prefer it without.

3 ounces amber rum

1 ounce strained, freshly squeezed lime juice

½ ounce strained, freshly squeezed lemon juice

½ ounce Grenadine, homemade (page 376) or store-bought

¼ teaspoon granulated sugar

Seltzer (optional)

1 Combine all of the ingredients in a mixing glass, fill the glass three-quarters full with ice cubes, and stir rapidly until thoroughly chilled, 30 seconds.

2 Fill a collins or rocks glass with crushed ice and strain the drink into the glass. Serve with a straw. An umbrella is an optional but nice touch.

QUEEN ELIZABETH

GLASS: MARTINI | ICE: CUBED | MAKES: 1 DRINK

C ocktail names are—like drinks themselves—fluid, changing with the era and the bartender's fancy. In the case of the Queen Elizabeth, there is a far better-known drink of the same name with vastly different ingredients, the most common version of which is dry vermouth, Benedictine, and lime juice. That, of course, ain't a

12 Bottle Bar drink by a long shot, so here's a little beauty—basically a daiquiri with a bit of flash—that we stumbled on in the *Old Waldorf-Astoria Bar Book*.

The drink originally called for Jamaican rum specifically, as it has a very rich profile. Any of the amber rums we suggest will work here, but Smith & Cross is Jamaican; beware, though, as it is overproof, thus more alcoholic, and you will probably want to adjust your rum measure down a bit.

· ·

2 ounces amber rum

½ ounce strained, freshly
 squeezed lime juice

½ ounce Grenadine,
 homemade (page 376)
 or store-bought

· ·

1 Combine all of the ingredients in a mixing glass, fill the glass three-quarters full with ice cubes, and shake vigorously until thoroughly chilled, 15 seconds.

2 Strain into a martini glass.

· ·

SIR WALTER

GLASS: MARTINI | ICE: CUBED | MAKES: 1 DRINK

H ey, it's yet another variation on the sour—who would have thought? If you've gotten this far, you've obviously assumed our penchant for citrus-based cocktails. The Sir Walter (S'walter to its friends) applies the typical sour ingredients—and a lot of them—but twists them in an interestingly booze-heavy fashion. At first sip, you'll be inclined to think that this one's headed into stiff drink territory, but then the sweet-sour notes kick in, producing something simultaneously bracing, light, and very balanced.

· ·

1½ ounces amber rum

1½ ounces Cognac-style
 brandy

1 teaspoon orange liqueur

1 teaspoon Grenadine,
 homemade (page 376)
 or store-bought

1 teaspoon strained, freshly
 squeezed lemon juice

Traditional Royal Navy
TOASTS OF THE DAY

SUNDAY: To absent friends.

MONDAY: To our ships at sea.

TUESDAY: To our friends.

WEDNESDAY: To ourselves (as no one else is liable to concern themselves with our welfare).

THURSDAY: To a bloody war or a sickly season.*

FRIDAY: To a willing foe and sea-room.

SATURDAY: To sweethearts and wives (may they never meet).

* The likeliness of a promotion increased during times of war or sickness.

1 Combine all of the ingredients in a mixing glass, fill the glass three-quarters full with ice cubes, cover with a Boston shaker tin, and shake vigorously until thoroughly chilled, 15 seconds.

2 Strain into a martini glass.

TRAFALGAR   4. 5

GLASS: MARTINI | ICE: CUBED | MAKES: 1 DRINK

In 1805, in the midst of the Napoleonic Wars, Admiral Horatio Nelson was outnumbered by eight ships and outgunned by five hundred cannons, but he nevertheless led the British navy to one of its greatest maritime triumphs—the Battle of Trafalgar. Named in honor of that monumental victory, the cocktail combines a basic British grog with French brandy and orange liqueur, for the Spanish. The red wine float is in honor of the blood spilled by Nelson himself; he lost his life in the battle. The result is an inside-out sangria, tangy and refreshing.

1½ ounces amber rum

1½ ounces Cognac-style brandy

½ ounce orange liqueur

½ ounce Simple Syrup (page 369)

½ ounce strained, freshly squeezed lime juice

½ ounce red wine (we like Shiraz)

1 Combine the rum, brandy, liqueur, simple syrup, and lime juice in a mixing glass, fill the glass three-quarters full with ice cubes, cover with a Boston shaker tin, and shake vigorously until thoroughly chilled, 15 seconds.

2 Strain into a martini glass.

3 Hold a bar spoon against the inside wall of the glass, just below the rim and not touching the surface of the liquid. Slowly pour the red wine into the bowl of the spoon and down the inside of the glass so that it floats on the surface of the drink.

NELSON'S BLOOD

ENGLISH VICE ADMIRAL Horatio Lord Nelson, beloved by his fellow officers as well as the sailors who served under him, fought valiantly in the American and French revolutionary wars and the Napoleonic Wars. Tragically killed by a French sniper's bullet at the Battle of Trafalgar, he was mourned by king and country.

Unfortunately, after he died, Nelson's men weren't quite as respectful of their boss. In order to preserve Nelson's body on the trip back to England, it was placed in a cask of rum—although some claim it was brandy. Ever desperate to tap the last drop of liquor aboard ship, the resourceful sailors drilled a hole in the cask and drank the rum. Ever since, rum has sported the picturesque name of "Nelson's Blood" and the act of drinking rum is often known in naval circles as "tapping the Admiral."

WATERMELON RUM SHRUB

GLASS: ROCKS | ICE: CRUSHED | MAKES: 1 DRINK

I n a misguided attempt to impress a fellow writer early in our online career, we created a drink called the Watermelon Mojito. Only, it wasn't a mojito. It was a Watermelon Rum Shrub, so we're taking this opportunity to get the name correct.

Shrubs, with their vinegar base, are wonderful summer drinks—tart and thoroughly quenching. Here, we incorporated ingredients that marry well with watermelon, namely lemon, balsamic vinegar, and mint. If you have teetotaling friends joining you, they can partake of these minus the rum. Everyone wins.

1 cup cubed watermelon

Handful fresh mint leaves

2 ounces amber rum

½ ounce strained, freshly squeezed lemon juice

1½ ounces Watermelon Shrub Syrup (recipe follows)

½ ounce Simple Syrup (page 369)

1 to 2 ounces club soda

Fresh mint sprig or watermelon wedge, for garnish

1 Place the watermelon in a blender and blend until pureed. Strain the puree into a measuring cup through a fine-mesh sieve, pressing down to extract the juice; discard any solids.

2 Place the mint in a large rocks glass and muddle it, pressing it just enough to release the oils.

3 Add the rum, 3 ounces of the watermelon juice, the lemon juice, Shrub Syrup, and Simple Syrup and stir gently to combine.

4 Fill the glass three-quarters full with crushed ice, top with club soda, and stir gently again to combine. Garnish with the mint sprig or watermelon wedge, as desired.

What's a
SHRUB?

WHENEVER WE TALK "shrub" at 12BB, we are talking about the good old colonial days in America. Those early settlers got pretty thirsty tending the land and building the cities. What better way to relax and refresh than to sip a nice, cold glass of shrub? Made from fruit syrup, vinegar, and water—fizzy or otherwise—shrubs were madly popular back in the day.

Today, when everything old is new again, the shrub is a lovely, tangy twist on fruit juice. It's a perfect virgin drink if ever there was one, and a great base for cocktails, too. Rum has a natural affinity with shrubs because of the inherent sweet-tart flavor. You can make a modified Dark 'n' Stormy (rum and ginger beer), substituting ginger shrub. You can combine raspberry or blackberry shrub with dry vermouth for a modified Vermouth Cassis (see our Vermouth De Mure, page 298), cassis being a black currant liqueur very popular as a cocktail additive. You can even go the spritzer route, with dry vermouth or white wine, plus fruit shrub and club soda. Any way you serve it, shrub is a surprisingly versatile addition to the home bar.

HOW TO SHRUB There are two techniques to making shrub—hot and cold—both of them valid versions. We prefer the cold method because it results in brighter, less "cooked" flavors. It takes more time, but it's worth it. Below are some basic rules that apply to all cold-method "shrubbing."

Wash all fruits and vegetables. Soft berries like raspberries can be gently crushed with your hands. Stone fruits, such as peaches, should be pitted and chopped into medium-size pieces. Vegetables should be seeded and chopped. For the vinegar, you can use any of the following, individually or in combination: apple cider vinegar, balsamic vinegar, Champagne vinegar, rice vinegar, red wine vinegar, or white wine vinegar.

When mixing up a shrub drink, use the following basic proportions: For virgin shrubs, combine 1 ounce shrub syrup with 6 to 7 ounces club soda or ginger beer. For alcohol-based shrubs, use 1 to 2 ounces shrub syrup (you might want more if it's made from a delicate fruit, such as watermelon), 2 ounces spirit, 4 ounces club soda or ginger beer.

Watermelon Shrub Syrup

MAKES: ABOUT 1½ CUPS

1 cup finely diced watermelon

1 cup granulated sugar

½ cup apple cider vinegar

1 Place the watermelon and sugar in a nonreactive container, cover it, and chill in the refrigerator until the watermelon has partially disintegrated and combined with the sugar to make a thick syrup, 24 hours.

2 Pour the watermelon mixture into a large measuring cup through a fine-mesh sieve, pressing down on the solids to extract as much of the liquid as possible, and scraping out any thick sugar syrup in the bottom of the container.

3 Add the apple cider vinegar to the mixture and stir to combine.

4 Transfer to an airtight glass container and store in the refrigerator for up to 1 month. The mixture will separate; simply shake it to recombine.

BLACKBERRY RUM SHRUB

GLASS: COLLINS | ICE: CUBED | MAKES: 1 DRINK

Rum and shrub, both quintessentially American beverages: Combine them and you get some serious patriotic magic in a glass.

Here, blackberries and balsamic and red wine vinegars in the shrub bring a level of depth and complexity not found in your everyday mixer.

2 ounces amber rum

1 ounce Blackberry Shrub Syrup (recipe follows)

4 ounces club soda

Fill a collins glass with ice cubes, add the rum and Shrub Syrup, then top with the club soda.

Blackberry Shrub Syrup

MAKES: ABOUT 2½ CUPS

1½ cups blackberries, gently crushed

1½ cups granulated sugar

1 cup red wine vinegar

½ cup balsamic vinegar

1 Combine the blackberries and sugar in a large bowl and stir to combine. Cover and refrigerate until the fruit and sugar have formed a syrupy juice, at least 24 hours and up to 4 days.

2 Strain through a fine-mesh sieve into a clean bowl, pressing gently to extract every last bit of liquid from the fruit; discard the solids. If any sugar remains in the original bowl, scrape it into the new bowl.

3 Add the vinegars, whisking to combine and to dissolve any remaining sugar.

4 Transfer the shrub mixture to a clean, dry bottle with a secure closure. Seal the bottle, shake the contents well, then refrigerate it. The Shrub Syrup will keep for several weeks in the refrigerator.

VARIATIONS

BLACKBERRY-JALAPEÑO SHRUB SYRUP In step 1, add ½ of a medium jalapeño pepper, stemmed, seeded, and thinly sliced, to the blackberries and sugar. Replace the vinegars with an equal amount of apple cider vinegar.

RASPBERRY SHRUB SYRUP Replace the blackberries with raspberries, and the vinegars with 1 cup unseasoned rice vinegar.

Strong

PALMETTO

GLASS: MARTINI, CHILLED | ICE: CUBED | MAKES: 1 DRINK

Should you be a rum drinker on the prowl for your own cigar-and-poker tipple, we've got you covered. Essentially—make that literally—a rum Manhattan, the Palmetto gives you exactly what you'd expect: a powerhouse of a rum drink. More important, however, it offers a great sandbox in which you can try out different rum and vermouth combinations—one to go with a Montecristo #5 and another to go with a Cohiba Robusto.

2 ounces amber rum

1 ounce sweet vermouth

2 dashes orange bitters

1 Combine all of the ingredients in a mixing glass, fill the glass three-quarters full with ice cubes, and stir rapidly until thoroughly chilled, 30 seconds.

2 Strain into a chilled martini glass.

CHARLES DICKENS' OWN PUNCH

GLASS: HEATPROOF MUG | MAKES: ABOUT 12 DRINKS

Measurements were just different way back when. In *Convivial Dickens,* Charles Dickens' Own Punch, from 1847, calls for "two good handfuls" of sugar (meaning literally measured with one's hands) and "1 or 2 large wineglasses brandy." Converting these measures to create an accurate rendition of a recipe presents quite a challenge, so we have turned to David Wondrich's superb adaptation of this recipe in his book *Punch.* Wondrich recommends 6 ounces of rough sugar cubes (we use La Perruche Demerara, see Resources, page 393), but he doesn't specify whether those ounces are by weight or volume.

This produces a not too tart, not too sweet punch where the lemon, sugar, and alcohol offer a delicate dance of flavors. This is one of our all-time favorite holiday punches, not too boozy thanks to the addition of a goodly amount of water, but still offering that cozy feeling that only a warm punch can.

By the way, if you are game, lighting the ingredients on fire—a necessary step to temper the flavors—makes for showstopping party entertainment. It may take a bit of practice, but with or without an audience, it's loads of fun watching the spirits glow and knowing the flame is playing a major role in shaping the mellow profile of the drink. If your punch is too harsh or alcoholic, you most likely didn't let the flame burn long enough.

· ·

3 lemons

6 ounces raw sugar cubes (roughly 18 equally sized cubes)

2 cups amber rum, plus extra for flaming

10 ounces Cognac-style brandy

4 cups boiling water

· ·

1 Peel away the lemon zest with a vegetable peeler, leaving behind as much of the white pith as possible; juice the flesh into a small nonreactive bowl.

2 Combine the lemon peels, sugar, 2 cups of rum, and brandy in a fireproof bowl.

3 Warm a spoon under hot running water and dry it thoroughly. Pour rum into the spoon, hold it over the bowl, and carefully light it on fire with a match. Slowly, pour the flaming rum from the spoon into the bowl from just above the surface of the bowl, igniting the contents. Let the liquid in the bowl burn for 3 to 4 minutes, gently stirring it occasionally with a long-handled bar spoon, and being careful not to overstir and put out the flame.

4 Cover the bowl with a heatproof lid to extinguish the flame.

5 Add the reserved lemon juice and the boiling water to the mixture and stir to combine. Cover the bowl with a heatproof lid until flavors meld, 5 minutes, then stir it again.

6 Transfer the contents of the bowl to a medium saucepan and simmer, partly covered, over medium-low heat until the flavors combine and bloom, 15 minutes.

7 Serve the drink in heatproof mugs.

CHAPTER 9
White Rum

CHAPTER 9

*White
Rum*

Amber or white, rum can be a love-it-or-hate-it spirit. Like gin, its bold, often funky profile can scare people off, but if you take the time to really appreciate rum—especially the "tamer" white rums—you will soon find that it is indispensable in your mixing arsenal. In fact, because of their bright nature, white, or light/silver, rums are the go-to style for mixing in summer cocktails.

Still, we want our white rum to have some depth and complexity. To that end, we prefer a specific type, a style that is light-bodied, molasses based, and charcoal filtered (to remove any residual color from aging). Our chosen rums are all aged for several years, whereas in contrast Bacardi Superior uses a special "speedy" yeast for its light rum, which forces a very short fermentation period, so as not to allow too many strong flavor compounds to develop.

White rums are typically distilled in a column still, which removes much of the molasses intensity and produces a lighter, brighter spirit. As mentioned above, many white rums are typically aged for several years, either in metal tanks or wooden barrels. If aged in barrels, a white rum will be charcoal filtered to remove any color imparted by the wood. This way, the clear color remains, but so do the deeper flavors of the barrel.

While the best-known white rum is probably Bacardi Superior, which is originally from Cuba but now headquartered in Bermuda, the island of Puerto Rico is often called the "rum capital" of the world. In 1506, Juan Ponce de León brought Creole sugarcane to Puerto Rico from the Dominican Republic (where it grew courtesy of Christopher Columbus). In 1517, the country's first sugar mill was opened and, in the mid-1600s, rum production began in earnest.

Because of white rum's exceptionally clean and vivid flavors, it is our choice for bringing out the delicacy of the daiquiri, and for summer sippers. Its soft profile offers a light vanilla sugar without the robust, buttery qualities imparted by amber rum.

THE BOTTLES TO BUY

We find that the best way to test rums is to mix them with Coke in a 1:4 ratio, favoring the Coke. This offers a nice basis on which to judge the rum's mixability. Of course, you should try the rums on their own as well; the contrast in how the flavors express themselves is always interesting. We don't offer a premium option here simply because excellent examples of the spirit can be had without breaking the bank.

Budget
($20 or less/750 ml)

FLOR DE CAÑA 4-YEAR EXTRA DRY

EL DORADO CASK AGED 3 YEAR

FLOR DE CAÑA 4-YEAR EXTRA DRY Vanilla, butterscotch, and smooth, smooth, smooth. Add cheap to the mix and you have a low-priced winner. Made in Nicaragua.

EL DORADO CASK AGED 3 YEAR DEMERARA RUM Aged exclusively in American oak bourbon barrels (think: vanilla, vanilla, vanilla), El Dorado is the amber rum drinker's answer to white rum. Notes of butterscotch and banana, as well as other island fruits, come through, but the defining factor here is the oak aging, which adds a complexity that is especially shocking in such a reasonably priced rum. This is an incredibly versatile rum, eager to offer itself up as a foundation for a fruity, tropical drink but equally at home in cocktails where the spirit must anchor the cocktail. Made in Guyana.

Midrange
($20–$30/750 ml)

CAÑA BRAVA RUM

CAÑA BRAVA RUM When the independent upstart Eighty Six Company decided to make spirits, they wanted a rum that recalled the original Carta Blanca style that made Bacardi Superior famous. Don Pancho Fernandez, rum distiller extraordinaire, helped create the recipe, which evokes the brightness of white rums with the complexity of dark. Simply put, this is amazing in a daiquiri. Made in Panama.

White Rum
IN A NUTSHELL

DEFINING FEATURES: Brighter sweetness and clarity than amber rum

FLAVOR PROFILE: Vanilla, orange, and tropical fruits without the oaky character some darker rums have

WHY WE CHOSE IT: Hemingway (and his Daiquiri) can't be wrong.

EMBLEMATIC DRINKS: The aforementioned Daiquiri (page 216), Mojito (page 221), Cuba Libre (page 212)

WHY TWO RUMS?

Well, first of all, why not? We suspect rum enthusiasts will probably ask us why *only* two rums? Well, it is just a 12 Bottle Bar, gang, so that's our excuse.

Like gin, rum is available in a wide variety of permutations, from white to amber to dark, navy strength, rhum agricole, and cachaça from Brazil. Please feel free to experiment as always.

As to our choice of both white and amber rums, we made it for several reasons. While both styles can often be used interchangeably, certain drinks like the Daiquiri (page 216) or Palmetto (page 213) tend to shine more brightly with one style or the other.

Likewise, amber, medium-bodied rums are often an acquired taste for those who enjoy lighter spirits, and it would be a shame not to open wide the possibilities of the rum universe for those folks. Think of white rum, with its softer, less intense flavors, as your gateway rum. And for you confirmed rum lovers, you've also got the deeper, more intense caramel notes of amber.

THE DRINKS

Sweet & Fruity

CUBA LIBRE

GLASS: COLLINS OR ROCKS | ICE: CUBED | MAKES: 1 DRINK

S hould the name Cuba Libre be unfamiliar to you, you may know this drink as the college classic Rum and Coke. Truth be told, the Cuba Libre is a bit more than just a run-of-the-mill Rum and Coke—it's the lime that makes all the difference.

The origins of the drink date back to the aftermath of the Spanish-American War in 1898 and a cry of "Por Cuba Libre!" in celebration of the newly freed country. If you believe the Bacardi version of the story, that is. As with many a drink, the exact inception of the Cuba Libre may be lost to time. Fortunately the recipe isn't.

. . . .

1½ ounces rum (white or amber, take your pick)

6 ounces cola, preferably sugar-based (such as Boylan Cane Cola)

Lime wedge, for serving

. . . .

1 Fill a collins or rocks glass with ice cubes, add the rum, and top with the cola. Stir gently to combine (you don't want to de-fizz the soda).

2 Squeeze the lime wedge into the glass and drop it in.

3 Smile.

BACARDI AND THE BAT

THERE IS ONE name that overshadows all the rest when it comes to white rum, and that name is Bacardi. In 1829, Spanish wine merchant Don Facundo Bacardi moved to Cuba and was immediately intrigued by rum production. An insightful fellow, he noticed the growing trend toward a lighter rum style, far removed from the dark, aged varieties of the past. So, in 1862, when he bought a distillery, he turned his attention to devising a light rum.

Bacardi's success—and its fortunes—rose exponentially when it was rumored that the Spanish King Alfonso XIII was cured of influenza (the infamous 1918 Spanish Flu epidemic) by drinking copious amounts of rum. Then, during Prohibition, Cuba became a hotbed of frolicking socialites eager to get real booze any way they liked it, and Bacardi was happy to supply said booze.

But why the bat on the logo? The "official" story is that the distillery Don Facundo bought had fruit bats in the attic, and his wife suggested using the bat as a symbol, so that even illiterate islanders would be able to recognize the brand. The less "proper" version tells of how an early batch of Don Facundo's rum was left to age for a few days in his backyard. When Facundo went to check the spirit's progress, he discovered a bat flapping around in the vat. Upon being scooped out, the bat flopped around drunkenly and died, proving the potency of Bacardi's brew.

NOT-SO-BLUE HAWAII

GLASS: ROCKS | ICE: CRUSHED | MAKES: 1 DRINK

There is an abomination known as blue Curaçao—essentially the same stuff as orange Curaçao but with a sickly cerulean hue. Luckily, the flavor of the orange liqueur hidden beneath that Smurf-blue sea is unaffected by the food dye added to it. But why, we have always asked ourselves, would someone do that to a drink? If you take the "blue" out of the Blue Hawaii, you are left with a refreshing tropical drink with hints of pineapple and citrus, no gimmick needed. Thus, below is our "not-so-blue" version of bartender Harry Yee's Blue Hawaii, created in 1957 at the Hilton Hawaiian Village to showcase Bols's new blue kid on the block.

3 ounces pineapple juice

½ ounce strained, freshly squeezed lemon juice

½ ounce Simple Syrup (page 369)

½ ounce orange liqueur

¾ ounce white rum

¾ ounce vodka

Pineapple slice, for garnish

Brandied Cherry (page 367) or high-quality maraschino cherry (we like Luxardo brand), for garnish

1 Fill a rocks glass with crushed ice and add all of the liquid ingredients.

2 Stir gently to combine and garnish with the pineapple and cherry.

THE LAUGHING ZOMBIE

GLASS: MARTINI | ICE: CUBED | MAKES: 1 DRINK

When our good friend Thomas Roche published his noir horror/thriller *The Panama Laugh*, about crazed zombies who laugh until they die, we knew it was fodder for a Halloween drink. Similar to the original Zombie, with its traditional rum floatl our versiion separates out the pineapple component into a boozy foam. The key to enjoying this is to sip deeply enough to get some of both layers.

2 ounces white rum

½ ounce amber rum

1 ounce strained, freshly squeezed lime juice

½ ounce passion fruit juice (see Note, page 186)

1 ounce Grenadine, homemade (page 376) or store-bought

2 dashes aromatic bitters

1 recipe Pineapple Foam (page 380)

Fresh mint sprig, for garnish

1 Combine all of the liquid ingredients in a mixing glass, fill the glass three-quarters full with ice cubes, cover with a

Boston shaker tin, and shake until thoroughly combined, 15 seconds.

2 Strain into a martini glass, top with Pineapple Foam, and garnish with the mint.

PINEAPPLE FIZZ

GLASS: COLLINS | ICE: CUBED | MAKES: 1 DRINK

I f there's a drink that could best be called affable, it's the Pineapple Fizz. Rather than wax clever, let's call this one what it is—a pineapple soda that will get you drunk. There are certainly worse things in this world.

Whereas pineapple can often underperform in drinks, here it is bolstered to center stage by a support team that brings out only its best qualities. The sugar just takes off the edge, while the club soda brings a mild salinity reminiscent of Italian sodas. We don't mention the rum here because it goes down so easily that you'll hardly notice it. Again, there are worse things.

1½ ounces pineapple juice

1 teaspoon granulated sugar

1½ ounces white rum

Club soda

1 Combine the pineapple juice and sugar in a collins glass and stir to dissolve the sugar.

2 Fill the glass with ice cubes, add the rum, and top with the club soda. Stir gently to combine.

Tangy & Citrusy

DAIQUIRI

GLASS: MARTINI | ICE: CUBED | MAKES: 1 DRINK

I f pressed to use white rum for only one drink until the end of time, we'd pick the Daiquiri without a moment's hesitation. Not the "Big Ass Daiquiri" dispensed from a Bourbon Street vending machine or the chain restaurant "smoothie" that is often strawberry flavored and sickeningly sweet. No, we're talking about the hand-shaken kind from the heyday of the Buena Vista Social Club. The kind of Daiquiri that cuts through 100-degree heat and 100 percent humidity. The kind that quenches a thirst without peer. A decidedly elegant drink that is far simpler to make than anyone might imagine.

The key to a good Daiquiri is to do as little to it as possible. Take a lovely white rum and add only a bare minimum of sour and sweet—that'll hit the spot.

½ ounce strained, freshly squeezed lime juice

1 teaspoon granulated sugar

2 ounces white rum

1 Combine the lime juice and sugar in a mixing glass and stir to dissolve the sugar.

2 Add the rum, fill the glass three-quarters full with ice cubes, and shake vigorously until thoroughly chilled, 15 seconds.

3 Strain into a martini glass.

VARIATIONS

ORANGE DAIQUIRI Add 1 teaspoon strained, freshly squeezed orange or blood orange juice.

SANTIAGO Add ¼ teaspoon Grenadine, homemade (page 376) or store-bought.

A YEAR TO REMEMBER

IF YOU BELIEVE tall tales, two of the most famous white rum drinks—the Daiquiri and the Cuba Libre—were both created in 1898. That year, Teddy Roosevelt and the Rough Riders (the First United States Volunteer Cavalry) headed for Cuba at the outset of the Spanish-American War. In addition to aiding Cuba in her fight for independence, two enterprising fellows—an engineer and a soldier—also showed interest in the local beverage, rum.

While the engineer came up with the now classic Daiquiri, the soldier opted for the more prosaic but equally famous Cuba Libre, better known as the Rum and Coke.

Roughly thirty years later, when Prohibition went into effect, privileged Americans with a hankering for an open bar headed for Cuba, where they sipped both cocktails to their hearts' content.

EL PRESIDENTE

GLASS: MARTINI, CHILLED | ICE: CUBED | MAKES: 1 DRINK

This is truly a lost gem of a drink that is slowly making its way back into the repertoire. The El Presidente came to fruition in Prohibition-era Havana, and is named for one of Cuba's presidents—depending on whom you consult, either Mario García Menocal or Gerardo Machado. It's a drink from a time when those with the means drank on Caribbean shores; it's a bold and complex mix with just enough sweetness to take off the edge. As journalist Wayne Curtis noted in the May 2006 issue of *Lost* magazine, it is "one of cocktail history's missing links—part tropical treat, part sophisticated lounge drink, and wholly Cuban."

Like so many cocktails before and after it, the El Presidente is a drink that reflects the particular variations of its bartender, at home or otherwise. It is essentially a variation on the daiquiri (rum, sugar, lemon juice) that is altered by the substitution of another sweetening agent, classically grenadine and curaçao, but in some versions pineapple juice and other ingredients. Some recipes shake it; others stir it, as we do. Sloppy Joe's 1932–33 bar book calls for equal parts rum and vermouth; modern versions, like ours, often cut down the vermouth by half, and this proportion will vary depending on the vermouth you use (they are all slightly different in sweetness, even the dry ones). The *Bar La Florida Cocktails* book substitutes amber rum for a deeper flavor. You can even add lime juice and/or some bitters to counter too much sweetness. No matter how you mix it, if ever a drink called out for a real maraschino cherry (meaning homemade or high-quality bottled; anything but the Day-Glo ones used on sundaes), this is it.

• •

1½ ounces white rum

¾ ounce dry vermouth

1 teaspoon orange liqueur

¼ teaspoon Grenadine, homemade (page 376) or store-bought

Orange slice, for garnish

Brandied Cherry (page 367) or high-quality maraschino cherry (we like Luxardo brand), for garnish

• •

1 Combine the liquid ingredients in a mixing glass, fill the glass three-quarters full with ice cubes, and stir rapidly until thoroughly chilled, 30 seconds.

2 Fill a chilled martini glass with large ice cubes and strain the drink into the glass. Garnish with the orange slice and the cherry.

VARIATIONS

SUNSHINE (WALDORF-ASTORIA) Replace the first 4 ingredients with: 2 ounces white rum, ½ ounce dry vermouth, 1 ounce pineapple juice, dash grenadine.

AMERICAN PRESIDENT Replace the first 4 ingredients with 1½ ounces white rum, 1½ ounces dry vermouth, dash orange liqueur, dash grenadine.

PRESIDENTE COCKTAIL Replace the first 4 ingredients with 2 ounces amber rum, 1 ounce dry vermouth, dash orange liqueur, dash grenadine.

EL TAMARINDO

GLASS: COLLINS | ICE: CUBED | MAKES: 1 DRINK

When faced with a tequila-less bar, one is forced to improvise. So, when 12 Bottle Bar used to do its yearly Cinco de Mayo drink, we sought out equally Mexican ingredients and used them as the base for our drinks. Tamarind, sold in bulk buckets at Latin food markets, is just one of those ingredients.

Indigenous to Africa, this fruit is hard-shelled outside and gooey-pulped inside, and is used around the world in cuisines as varied as Latin, Arabic, and Asian. In America, we find it most commonly in Worcestershire sauce. What is particularly appealing to us is the fruit's sourness, which is especially refreshing in the traditional Agua de Tamarindo featured here.

1½ ounces white rum

1½ ounces Agua de Tamarindo (page 349)

3 to 4 ounces club soda

Lime wedge, for garnish

Fill a collins glass half full with ice cubes, and add the rum and Tamarindo base. Top with the club soda and stir gently to combine. Garnish with the lime wedge.

Bar Con: THE ALEXANDER HAMILTON

THE CON ARTIST sits at the bar, locating his mark. He pays cash for his drink, receiving $10 back. He turns the bill over and says to the mark, "We spend a lot of time looking at things, but how many of the specifics do we really see? For instance, I'll bet you the next round that you can't tell me the name of the president on the $10 bill. You can even ask other people in the bar." If the mark accepts the bet, he has already lost because it is not a president, but Secretary of the Treasury Alexander Hamilton. The drink's on the mark.

—TODD ROBBINS, AUTHOR, *THE MODERN CON MAN*

Tip:
CHOOSING AND USING LEMONGRASS

1. Choose stalks that are pale yellow on the bottom and green on top, with no brown or dry leaves.

2. Before using a stalk, cut off the lower bulb with a chef's knife

and remove the tough leaves on the outside.

3. Cut the stalk lengthwise into ¼- to ½-inch sections and then bend them in half a few times to help release the aromatics.

LEMONGRASS MOJITO

GLASS: COLLINS OR ROCKS | ICE: CUBED, CRUSHED | MAKES: 1 DRINK

Lemongrass is a tropical, lemon-scented plant much used in Thai and other Southeast Asian cooking. If you've never used it—the one-foot-tall stalks are sold in small bundles at most natural-foods supermarkets—don't be daunted. Once you get a whiff of this potent herb, you will be hooked for good. Here in the Lemongrass Mojito, Amy Stewart—author of *The Drunken Botanist*—recognized the ease with which you could substitute lemongrass for the usual lime in a classic mojito. The simple substitution gives the cocktail an entirely new and entirely captivating spicy lemon twist.

1½ ounces white rum

½ ounce Lemongrass Syrup (page 374)

3 to 4 sprigs fresh mint, plus a mint leaf for garnish

1 stalk lemongrass (see box, above)

¼ lime

Club soda

1 Combine the rum, lemongrass syrup, mint sprigs, and lemongrass in a cocktail shaker, then squeeze the juice from the lime into the shaker and drop the shell in. Muddle the ingredients gently to release the flavors.

2 Fill the shaker three-quarters full with ice cubes and shake vigorously until thoroughly chilled, 15 seconds.

3 Fill a collins glass with crushed ice and strain the drink into the glass. Top with the club soda and garnish with the mint leaf.

CACHAÇA

CAH-SHAH-SAH. The name alone conjures up a dreamy mindscape of swaying palms and sandy shores. As well it should, because it is Brazil's national spirit. Often called *pinga* by locals, cachaça was once a poor man's drink, but has gained respectability in recent years due to the popularity of the caipirinha, a mojito-like rum cocktail.

While often termed "Brazilian rum," cachaça is now recognized as its own distinct spirit, much as genever and gin are differentiated. However, as it is made with sugarcane juice, it has much in common with the French West Indies style of rum known as rhum agricole (for more on this, see page 169). While Americans tend to know the unaged white version, there is also an aged gold cachaça, which gets its color and flavor from time spent in wood barrels, and is often sipped on its own, neat or on the rocks.

MOJITO

GLASS: ROCKS | ICE: CRUSHED | MAKES: 1 DRINK

Well before the mojito made it into the repertoire of every chain restaurant bartender in America (not a bad thing, we say), we were smitten by the nonalcoholic Minty Lime Cooler (page 352) served up by our local faves, the Too Hot Tamales. That drink has a bit of everything—sour, fizz, and aromatic mint. Being young and uneducated in the ways of drink, we never thought it could get better—until someone dashed some white rum into the mix, that is.

The illegitimate love child of the Mint Julep and the Daiquiri, the Mojito captures the best of simple mixological flair—compounding a drink in the serving glass—with the perfect ratio of sultry summer-busting ingredients. It's impossible to make a proper mojito in front of someone without adopting a bit of Tony Montana swagger. Both in the making and the drinking, it's a potion that instills confidence.

1 lime, quartered

1 teaspoon granulated sugar

3 fresh mint leaves, plus extra
   for garnish

2 ounces white rum

Club soda

1 Combine the lime and sugar in a rocks glass and muddle them until the sugar dissolves.

2 Add the three mint leaves to the glass and gently muddle them against the inside of the glass.

3 Fill the glass with crushed ice, add the rum, and top with the club soda. Stir gently to combine the ingredients. Garnish with additional mint leaves.

RALEIGH

GLASS: MARTINI | ICE: CUBED | MAKES: 1 DRINK

There are a lot of Raleighs in this world—motorcycles, bicycles, Sir Walter, and North Carolina, to name a few—and we can safely say that this Raleigh is our second favorite (see the Introduction for our first). While this is a sour like so many other sours, the Raleigh stands out by offering an orange primary note. Orange juice has a tendency to go sideways in mixed drinks, becoming muddied or too sweet, but the Raleigh gives us a bracing hit of sour by combining orange and lime. If you're a fan of a tart Daiquiri, do yourself a favor and give this one a try.

> "There's nought, no doubt,
> so much the spirit calms as rum and true religion."
> —LORD BYRON

1½ ounces white rum

1 ounce strained, freshly squeezed orange juice

½ ounce strained, freshly squeezed lime juice

½ teaspoon Grenadine, homemade (page 376) or store-bought

1 Combine all of the ingredients in a mixing glass, fill the glass three-quarters full with ice cubes, cover with a Boston shaker tin, and shake vigorously until thoroughly chilled, 15 seconds.

2 Strain into a martini glass.

RUM RICKEY

GLASS: COLLINS | ICE: CUBED | MAKES: 1 DRINK

The original 12 Bottles featured on our site didn't include white rum. This did not go unnoticed by our friend Daniel Berman, proprietor of FUSSYlittleBLOG.com. Daniel lamented our lack of white rum and our omission of many classic summer cocktails. When it came time to put together this book, we not only had an opportunity to include white rum, but we had a fine reason to solicit Daniel for a drink contribution. He chose the Rum Rickey.

Daniel tells us, "It's hard to think of summertime cocktails without thinking of sours. The Margarita really rules the roost. While the classic rum daiquiri doesn't enjoy quite the same popularity, it's closely related. But neither of these cold, citrus-centric drinks is truly refreshing. The rickey fulfills the refreshing promise of the sour without any of the fuss. There is no shaking, as the seltzer does all the hard work of keeping the spirit mixed with the citrus. And there is no mucking around with multiple bottles. Is it bracing? Oh yeah."

2 ounces white rum

½ lime

Seltzer

1 Fill a collins glass with ice cubes and add the rum.

2 Squeeze the juice from the lime into the glass and drop in the shell.

3 Top with seltzer and stir gently to combine.

SMALL-DINGER

GLASS: MARTINI | ICE: CUBED | MAKES: 1 DRINK

There are several curious things about the Small-Dinger. It's found on the title page of the *Bar La Florida Cocktails* book, and not among the recipes. There's that hyphen in the middle of the name for reasons of which we're not sure. It combines gin and white rum, which, while odd as drinks go, works nicely. Fortunately, it tastes out of this world and has long been one of our summertime favorites. Light and perfectly balanced on the sweet-tart pendulum, the Small-Dinger is a real humdinger. (Come on, how many chances do we get to throw in a joke like that?)

1 ounce white rum

1 ounce dry gin

½ ounce strained, freshly squeezed lime juice

½ ounce Grenadine, homemade (page 376) or store-bought

1 Combine all of the ingredients in a mixing glass, fill the glass three-quarters full with ice cubes, cover with a Boston shaker tin, and shake vigorously until thoroughly chilled, 15 seconds.

2 Strain into a martini glass.

SLOPPY JOE'S #1

GLASS: MARTINI | ICE: CUBED | MAKES: 1 DRINK

Cocktail history can be a bit muddy. Not only are there two world-famous, Hemingway-blessed, Daiquiri-slinging bars called Sloppy Joe's (see sidebar), there are two Sloppy Joe's cocktails: #1 and #2. Number Two can be traced to the famed Cuban haunt sharing the Joe's moniker (it's the original Sloppy Joe's), but we haven't been able to track down the origin of #1.

Exact history aside, the drink is specifically tasty. Though the recipe may be a bit complicated—¼ ounces are no fun to measure (1½ teaspoons works best for the job)—follow it exactly and you will be well rewarded.

1 ounce strained, freshly squeezed lime juice

¾ ounce white rum

¾ ounce dry vermouth

¼ ounce Grenadine, homemade (page 376) or store-bought

¼ ounce orange liqueur

1 Combine all of the ingredients in a mixing glass, fill the glass three-quarters full with ice cubes, cover with a Boston shaker tin, and shake vigorously until thoroughly chilled, 15 seconds.

2 Strain into a martini glass.

Great Bars
THEN & NOW

SLOPPY JOE'S BAR | 201 DUVAL STREET
KEY WEST, FL 33040 | 305-294-5717 | SLOPPYJOES.COM

DESPITE ITS over-commercialization in recent decades, Sloppy Joe's Bar is forever linked to author Ernest Hemingway, making it an essential stop on our worldwide historical barhopping tour.

The day Prohibition was repealed (December 5, 1933), an enterprising illegal speakeasy operator named Joe Russell went legit and opened a tiny joint named the Blind Pig. The name changed to the Silver Slipper with the addition of a dance floor. Frequent patrons didn't much care for either choice and nudged Joe to change the name to Sloppy Joe's, cribbing the name from the popular Cuban joint of the time (see below).

In 1937, after refusing to pay a rent increase from three dollars to four, Joe moved the bar across the street to the corner of Duval and Greene, where it remains to this day.

Sure, the place has a touristy souvenir shop next door, and granted there is an annual "Papa" look-alike contest, but you can't argue the fact that while Ernest Hemingway called Key West home, Sloppy Joe's was where he held court.

SLOPPY JOE'S BAR | ZULUETA 252 ANÍMAS Y VIRTUDES,
HABANA VIEJA, HAVANA, CUBA | 537-866-7157

HEMINGWAY MAY BE forever tied to Sloppy Joe's, but the question is *which* Sloppy Joe's or, perhaps more correctly, why not both? Other than a name and a claim to Papa, the two Sloppy Joe's have nothing to do with each other. The Havana location was among the city's hottest spots, and during Prohibition the celebrities flowed as freely as the booze.

Fire up a copy of the Alec Guinness film *Our Man in Havana* to get a gander at how Joe's looked not long before it closed in 1965. A renovation of the site was completed in 2013 and, for the first time in more than fifty years, one of cocktailia's most sacred locales is back in business.

Just don't ask us which Sloppy Joe's invented the titular sandwich.

Strong

CLIPPER COCKTAIL

GLASS: MARTINI, CHILLED | ICE: CUBED | MAKES: 1 DRINK

W e're too young to remember the halcyon days of air travel—the days when you dressed up like ladies and gentlemen and were treated like ladies and gentlemen—but we do know that if there was a classy way to fly, it was aboard a Pan Am Clipper. The flight attendants were straight out of a fashion magazine, and the passengers were pampered with table dining and amenity kits containing cologne or perfume, compacts, sewing kits, and more. And of course, there were signature cocktails.

The Clipper Cocktail comes from Pan Am's North Pacific run, connecting North America to Asia, in the 1930s, and it's a delightful distraction during any voyage, whether by plane or boat, or merely contemplating life in your favorite armchair. If you find martinis too strong—and not pink enough—this may be your perfect drink. It's serious but not unkind.

1½ ounces white rum

1½ ounces dry vermouth

½ teaspoon Grenadine, homemade (page 376) or store-bought

Lemon twist, for garnish

1 Combine the rum, vermouth, and grenadine in a mixing glass, fill the glass three-quarters full with ice cubes, and stir rapidly until thoroughly chilled, 30 seconds.

2 Strain into a chilled martini glass and garnish with the lemon twist.

The Insanely Rageful
BARTENDER

ONE OF THE essential yet often overlooked ingredients to running a thriving bar—and one that should be secured even before other essentials, for example, a stuffed moose wearing a propeller beanie—is an insanely rageful bartender.

Let me explain.

Years ago I worked at a very popular bar and grill, a national chain, and though, yes, a great deal of its success can be attributed to the general manager, a small, pinched man with a fondness for short-sleeved cotton-blend business shirts in dull brown patterns, and a particular style of horn-rim glasses last popular around the time Hamilton Jordan was White House chief of staff, great credit must also go to its service bartender.

A largely affable and handsome young man, when under stress he would, what is the term, "go absolutely eye-clawingly insane with violent, screeching rage"? Yes, I believe that fits. Invective was hurled, along with anything nearby that could serve as a projectile—pieces of fruit, handfuls of ice, and, memorably, a bottle opener he managed to stick into the wall with the expertise of a circus knife-thrower.

But his quirkiest trait, and probably his raison d'être, was revealed about when presented with an even remotely unorthodox drink order. His eyes narrowing with menace, he would stalk around the bar, grab the terrified service person by the arm, and drag them to the dining area. "Who ordered that?" he'd demand.

"Wha—? What difference does it make?"

"*Who ordered that?*" he'd repeat.

"It's from table 47."

"Who? Which person? I want to look into their eyes."

"There. That lady."

Loosening his grip on the service person he'd then stand staring for half a minute, uttering curses not loud but deep, his heart filled with the blackest of malice, all directed at a data entry worker who had the nerve to order a Peach Fizz.

This astonishing bit of theatrics was acted out at least once per night, and I like to think it made our little TGI Something's more than just a bland, cookie-cutter suburban chain restaurant with an old canoe hanging from the ceiling.

Here's looking at you, Insanely Rageful Bartender. (Though not directly in the eyes, because I know you hate that and it might set you off.)

—**MICHAEL J. NELSON,**
AUTHOR, HOST OF *RIFFTRAX*

CUBAN OLD FASHIONED

GLASS: ROCKS | ICE: CUBED (OPTIONAL) | MAKES: 1 DRINK

There's no denying that this is a tried-and-true cocktail in the most literal sense. If you like a short, bracing drink, you'll certainly be pleased here. Moreover, take a gander at the ingredients—rum, sugar, bitters (Angostura is called for in the original), orange liqueur—and ask yourself how much more Caribbean one drink can get. Should you be enjoying this on a blistering tropical day, we won't begrudge you an ice cube.

1 cube sugar

2 dashes aromatic bitters

2 teaspoons water

1½ ounces white rum

Dash orange liqueur

Lime twist, for garnish

1 Place the sugar cube in a rocks glass and dash the bitters over it, to saturate it. Add the water and muddle to dissolve the sugar.

2 Add the rum and liqueur and stir to combine. Add an ice cube, if desired, and garnish with the lime twist.

CHAPTER 10

Rye Whiskey

CHAPTER 10

Rye
Whiskey

P rohibition can be blamed for many things, among them the demise in popularity of our beloved rye whiskey. In the mid-eighteenth century, the golden age of cocktails, rye was America's most popular spirit, utterly eclipsing bourbon, which came on the scene in the late 1700s as well. In fact, classic cocktails like the Manhattan and the Old Fashioned originally called for rye, and luckily, bartenders are quickly rediscovering the reason for that choice: Rye's inherent spicy-fruity balance adds serious zing to mixed drinks that had previously relied on bourbon and other whiskeys.

N ow, when we talk about rye, we mean U.S. rye, not Canadian rye whisky, which can contain 75 percent or more of corn in the mash, or sadly, even no rye at all. In fact, Canadian rye in many ways gave U.S. rye a bad rap, as people came to consider the spirits one and the same, particularly during Prohibition, when our northern cousins sneaked a goodly amount of booze across the border to cater to thirsty Yankee drinkers. By the end of Prohibition, the United States had lost its taste for the inferior rye—and rye in general.

But, you might ask, why do we at 12 Bottle Bar prefer rye to bourbon or any other whiskey? Granted, there are myriad choices out there and we'd be happy to get into a serious discussion about another favorite of ours: Irish Whiskey. But here's

Rye
"I'M YOUR HUCKLEBERRY"

Famous gunfighter and gambler Doc Holliday knew a good thing when he saw it. Whenever he strode into a saloon—which he did quite often—his drink of choice was rye, specifically Old Overholt.

Rye Whiskey
IN A NUTSHELL

DEFINING FEATURES:
Spice and fruit

FLAVOR PROFILE: Spicy,
fruity, dry, and less sweet
than bourbon. Some ryes veer
toward heavier spicing; others
are more subtle.

WHY WE CHOSE IT: George
Washington distilled rye (when
he wasn't getting voters drunk
on rum), and it adds greater
complexity to mixed drinks
than bourbon.

EMBLEMATIC DRINKS:
Manhattan (page 47), Whiskey
Sour (page 251), Mint Julep
(though Southerners will call
this treason; page 238)

the thing. Unlike Scotch or Irish whiskeys, American rye is undeniably American, being one of the country's earliest spirits after Applejack. It is also far more old-school than bourbon, no matter how much the bourbon folks will try to tell you otherwise.

And then, perhaps most important, there's the flavor. Made from at least 51 percent rye (a grass grown as a grain), rye whiskey is drier and less sweet than bourbon and has a knockout blend of fruit and spice components—often with dashes of vanilla and leather thrown in—that make any rye-based cocktail more complex. Plus, with its comeback a relatively recent occurrence, we can't help but root for the underdog.

So please, feel free to stock your shelves with Irish, Scotch, Tennessee, and Kentucky whiskeys. Far be it from us to dissuade you from expanding your selection. But if we can choose only one from the whiskey pantheon, rye it is and will ever be.

THE BOTTLES TO BUY

As with gin, a really decent bottle of rye can be had for less than $25. No need to spend a fortune when the selection below will make a mighty-fine cocktail.

Budget
($20 or less/750 ml)

Midrange
($20–$30/750 ml)

OLD OVERHOLT Sweeter and less complex than other ryes, but still offering that one-two punch of spice and fruit. It makes a great rye for bourbon devotees or for anyone wary of 90-plus proof spirits, which ryes generally are.

BULLEIT RYE Since Bulleit bourbon has such a high percentage (28 percent) of rye in it, it's only logical that the company would decide to bottle a rye as well. The spirit is 95 percent rye, with 5 percent malted barley. The very reasonable price is pretty amazing, especially since rye is a notoriously finicky and expensive spirit grain. Spicier than Rittenhouse, Bulleit has layer upon layer of fruit and spice flavor, including dark cherries and cinnamon and even a hint of tobacco character. It is equally at home in cocktail as when it's sipped solo in a glass.

RITTENHOUSE 100-PROOF BOTTLED IN BOND RYE We can't get enough of Rittenhouse rye, whose amazingly affordable price tag and bold flavor makes it our go-to bottle of rye for cocktails. It's sweet and spicy up front, with an assertive amount of heat (it is 100 proof after all). Vanilla and even orange comes through. There's so much going on in this stuff, it's no wonder bartenders love it. But beware, this is a cocktail rye—it's a bit too rough around the edges for solo sipping, but it makes a killer Manhattan.

*Artisan/
Premium*

($40–$60/750 ml)

**MICHTER'S
US *1 SINGLE
BARREL RYE**

**HIGH WEST
WHISKEY
RENDEZVOUS**

If you find yourself a confirmed rye lover and tend to sip your spirits neat as well as in cocktails, then Michter's US *1 Single Barrel Rye and High West Whiskey Rendezvous are both winners. But at their $40 to $60 price, using them in a cocktail simply isn't cost effective or respectful of the remarkable products they are.

MT. VERNON'S RYE

REMEMBER WE MENTIONED that, along with rum, George Washington had a hankering for rye? With rum, Washington had to import it, but rye he could make himself. On the advice of the plantation's overseer, James Anderson, he agreed to construct a distillery in 1797. Anderson created the recipe, first using wheat, which he then abandoned for a balance of 60 percent rye, 35 percent corn, and 5 percent malted barley.

In the first year of production, the distillery yielded only 80 gallons from two stills. The following year, the stills produced 11,000 gallons at a $7,500 profit, which was astronomical for the day. Even more amazing is that the majority of this profit came from Washington's friends and neighbors, who lived within a five-mile radius. Records from the old distillery suggest that the rye was often traded as well, for everything from wheat to herring.

Today, Washington's recipe has been painstakingly recreated from the meticulous records he kept. The modern Mt. Vernon distillery—reconstructed from excavations of the site, as well as construction records—opened in 2007 with five pot stills placed on the original still footprints. The distillers followed the old recipe, double distilled in copper pot stills. The first batch sold out within hours. Sadly, it is only available at the distillery, so hop on a plane, train, or in an automobile if you want a taste of history.

THE DRINKS

Sweet & Fruity

RYE ROGERS

GLASS: COLLINS | ICE: CRUSHED | MAKES: 1 DRINK

Remember those cloyingly sweet Roy Rogers and Shirley Temples from childhood—the ones that let you feel like a grown-up because they were made at the bar, using bar ingredients (grenadine!) and came with a garnish (ersatz maraschino cherries and, if you were lucky, a plastic monkey or sword)? What if you could relive those days, but in a more adult manner? Meet the Rye Rogers.

We've yet to meet the person who didn't smile when presented with a Rye Rogers—first mishearing the name, then intrigued by the thought of a kid's drink turned boozy. Homemade grenadine, a real-sugar cola, a splash of lime, and those clown-nose cherries make all the difference here. Images of childhood may be conjured, but this is a balanced adult affair that just screams to be paired with a big trough of barbecue.

2 ounces rye whiskey

1 ounce Grenadine, homemade (page 376) or store-bought

½ ounce strained, freshly squeezed lime juice

4 ounces cola, preferably sugar-based (such as Boylan Cane Cola)

2 imitation maraschino cherries (i.e., the Day-Glo kind)

1 Fill a collins glass halfway with crushed ice. Add the rye, grenadine, lime juice, and cola and stir.

2 Garnish with the cherries and sing a round of "Happy Trails."

MINT JULEP

GLASS: SILVER CUP OR, IN A PINCH, A CHILLED ROCKS GLASS |
ICE: CRUSHED | MAKES: 1 DRINK

There are as many ways to make a Mint Julep as there are to pick a winning horse. Some prefer brandy (which would still keep the drink in the 12 Bottle Bar family) or a dash of amber rum, while most call for bourbon. As the Mint Julep is the official swig of the Kentucky Derby, it makes it hard to argue against bourbon, but argue we will.

Among the many spirits that have been associated with the mint julep over the centuries, we choose rye on taste alone. The spiciness of the spirit brings a depth to the drink that easily handles and complements the sweetness of the sugar, the herbal brightness of the mint, and, of course, the excessive amount of ice. Despite all of the other layers, the character of the rye shines through.

Handful of fresh mint leaves, plus 1 sprig, for garnish

1 ounce Simple Syrup (page 369)

2 ounces rye whiskey

1 Place the handful of mint in a silver cup or a rocks glass and muddle it. Add the Simple Syrup.

2 Fill the cup or glass with crushed ice and add the rye. Stir gently but quickly to chill thoroughly and to frost the cup or glass, at least 30 seconds.

3 Add more ice, if needed, and garnish with the sprig of mint. Serve the cup or glass wrapped in a napkin to prevent the drinker's hand from heating the drink.

The Mint Julep:
A LITTLE HISTORY

NEW ORLEANS BARTENDER Chris McMillian, a twenty-plus-year veteran of the trade whose showmanship, wisdom, and hospitality are legendary, has succinctly stated, "What the martini was to the twentieth century, the Mint Julep was to the nineteenth century." It is an essential evocation of a civilized era when high society enjoyed lawn parties and languid afternoons sipping equally genteel drinks.

The word *julep* originated in ancient Persia from the word *gulab*, which means "rose water." Back then, people would sip on what they considered a therapeutic beverage made from water and rose petals. As the recipe traveled around the Mediterranean, the local cultures often replaced the rose petals with fresh mint. The modern julep is clearly a cousin of these beverages, marrying the herbaceous aromatic syrup so essential to the julep with another, more bracing liquid.

The first written reference to the drink is in 1803, from Londoner John Davis, in his book *Travels of Four Years and a Half in the United States*, who described it as " a dram of spirituous liquor that has mint steeped in it, taken by Virginians of a morning."

This early morning wake-up call is pretty standard for an era when mixed drinks were conveniently considered medicinal tinctures of sorts. The medicinal angle traces back to the Arabs in medieval times distilling wine into brandy and flavoring it with syrup essences thought to have health benefits. These tinctures evolved into more recreational creations using various spirits beyond the original brandy, like our friend the julep.

Footnote: In the 1920s, the acerbic critic and rye-loving northerner H. L. Mencken thought to use rye instead of bourbon in his julep, sparking this response from fellow writer and Kentucky native Irvin S. Cobb: "Any man who'd put rye in a mint julep . . . would put scorpions in a baby's bed." We beg to differ, sir.

Tip:
CHOOSING AND BRUISING YOUR MINT

WITH ITS TONGUE-TINGLING flavor, fresh mint adds a layer of complexity, particularly in conjunction with sugar and citrus. There is nothing like a sprig of the herb, either in a cocktail or simply as garnish, to give a drink a unique profile. The scent alone is a proven pick-me-up.

When it comes to choosing mint for your cocktails, don't grab just any variety. According to our friend Amy Stewart, author of *The Drunken Botanist*, you are looking for spearmint specifically because of its bright, sweet mint character.

And when it comes to muddling your mint, don't crush it. Take a line from Joshua Soule Smith, who wrote of the herb in his "Ode to the Mint Julep": *"Like a woman's heart it gives its sweetest aroma when bruised."* He's not kidding.

Whereas other ingredients, such as a sugar cube, might require a bit of force to muddle, delicate fresh herbs like mint require the gentlest touch. Using the muddler, simply rub the mint leaves around the inside of the glass. Now smell. You'll be amazed at how much oil the mint will give up when softly bruised.

WHISKEY HOT TODDY

GLASS: HEATPROOF MUG | MAKES: 1 DRINK

Toddies are drinks of the old school, dating back to colonial days. There's not much mystery to them, but if done right, you'll be surprised how well a toddy can slide down and warm the bones, much like Grog (page 184). Two ounces of booze, no matter how much or little it's diluted in a drink, is still two ounces of booze, and while this one may seem thin up front, you'll most likely feel the onset of effects soon enough.

Of course, if you're feeling a bit nostalgic about home remedies, the hot whiskey toddy was traditionally believed to cure just about whatever ailed you. As always, feel free to adjust any of the ingredients to suit your particular tastes.

2 ounces rye whiskey

1 cube sugar, preferably
   raw sugar, such as Demerara

Lemon twist

4 ounces boiling water

Fresh whole nutmeg,
   for garnish (see Note,
   page 70)

1 Combine the rye and sugar in a heatproof mug.

2 Squeeze the lemon twist over the surface of the drink to express the oils, and drop it in. Top with the boiling water and stir. Garnish with a grating of nutmeg.

WHISKEY BUCK

GLASS: COLLINS | ICE: CRUSHED | MAKES: 1 DRINK

If there's a go-to three-season drink at our house, it's the buck, which also goes by the appellation Mamie Taylor or mule. What's particularly great about the buck is how flexible it is—it can be made with rum, brandy, gin, or vodka, as well as with lime or lemon. While everyone has their spirit of choice, ours is rye when it comes to the buck, because rye's spicy character meshes so well with the other two ingredients.

The key to a great buck is the ginger beer. You'll want something with some body and some bite. We suggest Reed's, Bundaberg, or Blenheim (technically labeled an ale).

1½ to 2 ounces rye whiskey,
   to taste

½ lemon

4 to 6 ounces ginger beer

1 Fill a collins glass halfway with crushed ice and add the rye.

2 Squeeze in the juice from the lemon through a sieve to catch the solids, then drop in the shell.

3 Top with the ginger beer and stir gently to combine.

ROBERT BENCHLEY ON DRINKING

"Drinking makes such fools of people, and people are such fools to begin with that it's compounding a felony."

. . . .

"A real hangover is nothing to try out family remedies on. The only cure for a real hangover is death."

. . . .

"I know I'm drinking myself to a slow death, but then I'm in no hurry."

Tangy & Citrusy

THE BENCHLEY

GLASS: MARTINI | ICE: CUBED | MAKES: 1 DRINK

Oftentimes, a cocktail that seemed like a good idea at the time it was created comes off as insipid in hindsight. The Algonquin—simply rye, dry vermouth, and pineapple juice—comes immediately to mind. There's just "something" missing. We decided that *something* was Thai hot sauce.

Named for Vicious Circle founding member Robert Benchley, this drink is both dry and biting—much like Benchley's humor. The Sriracha brings in depth as well as heat, which is kept in check by the sweet pineapple. This is a great drink to pair with sweet, fatty meat dishes.

1½ ounces rye whiskey

¾ ounce dry vermouth

¾ ounce Pineapple Sriracha Syrup (recipe follows)

1 Combine all of the ingredients in a mixing glass, fill the glass three-quarters full with ice cubes, cover with a Boston shaker tin, and shake vigorously until thoroughly chilled, 15 seconds.

2 Strain into a martini glass.

Pineapple Sriracha Syrup

MAKES: 6 OUNCES

½ cup pineapple juice

½ cup granulated sugar

¼ teaspoon Sriracha hot sauce, or to taste

1 Combine the pineapple juice and sugar in a small saucepan over low heat and stir to dissolve the sugar. Stir in the Sriracha. Remove from the heat.

2 Allow the syrup to cool to room temperature, transfer it to an airtight container, and refrigerate. It will keep, refrigerated, for up to 1 month.

Great Bars
THEN & NOW

THE PALACE BAR | 120 SOUTH MONTEZUMA STREET
PRESCOTT, AZ 86303 | 928-541-1996

IF YOU WANT to whet your whistle where Doc Holliday and the Earp brothers enjoyed their last draughts, the Palace Bar is your spot. Virgil Earp lived in town, and siblings Wyatt and Morgan collected him there before heading to Tombstone. Doc joined the Earps eight months later, having enjoyed a $10,000 winning streak in a poker game that may have been played at the Palace.

The original Palace Saloon opened in 1877 as part of the local "whiskey row," only to be destroyed by a fire in 1900. The Brunswick Bar's back bar architecture was saved and carried across the street, then reinstalled in the rebuilt bar. It remains today. With many of its original trappings, the Palace is a living monument to the saloon's essential role in the Old West.

BLINKER

GLASS: MARTINI | ICE: CUBED | MAKES: 1 DRINK

What do you get when you mix bold, spicy rye with tart grapefruit and a bit of sweet grenadine? A tasty variation on the classic whiskey sour. By most accounts, the Blinker is a Prohibition-era drink, and its combination of spirit, fruit juice, and sweetener certainly fit the bill.

Cocktail historian Ted Haigh resurrected the Blinker from the dusty cocktail vaults, substituting thick raspberry syrup for the original grenadine. Our version harkens back to the 1930s original, but we tweaked the mix to more modern proportions.

1½ ounces rye whiskey

1 ounce strained, freshly squeezed ruby grapefruit juice

½ ounce Grenadine, homemade (page 376) or store-bought

1 Combine all of the ingredients in a mixing glass, fill the glass three-quarters full with ice cubes, cover with a Boston shaker tin, and shake vigorously until thoroughly chilled, 15 seconds.

2 Strain into a martini glass.

GO-TO GRAPEFRUITS

THERE ARE THREE types of grapefruit available:

WHITE: The least sweet type, although it does have a perceived sweetness.

RED, OR RUBY: Your go-to cocktail choice, being the sweetest and least bitter. The skin on this variety is yellowish-orange, while the fruit is a deep pink-red.

PINK: A hybrid of the other two, and more tart. These are the ones people usually sprinkle with sugar.

WARNING: Regrettably, some of us must avoid grapefruit-based cocktails, as they may interfere with certain medications. Be sure to ask your guests if they have any restrictions.

THE LANNY-YAP

"WE PICKED UP one excellent word—a word worth travelling to New Orleans to get; a nice limber, expressive, handy word—'lagniappe.' They pronounce it lanny-yap.... It has a restricted meaning, but I think the people spread it out a little when they choose. It is the equivalent of the thirteenth roll in a 'baker's dozen.' It is something thrown in, gratis, for good measure. The custom originated in the Spanish quarter of the city. When a child or a servant buys something in a shop—or even the mayor or the governor, for aught I know—he finishes the operation by saying—'Give me something for lagniappe.' The shopman always responds; gives the child a bit of licorice-root, gives the servant a cheap cigar or a spool of thread, gives the governor—I don't know what he gives the governor; support, likely. When you are invited to drink, and this does occur now and then in New Orleans—and you say, 'What, again?—no, I've had enough,' the other party says, 'But just this one time more—this is for lagniappe.'"

—MARK TWAIN,
IN *LIFE ON THE MISSISSIPPI*

LAGNIAPPE

GLASS: MARTINI | ICE: CUBED | MAKES: 1 DRINK

Among Cajuns, the term *lagniappe* means "that little bit extra." We created this drink, which takes its inspiration from Cajun and New Orleans cooking—the Tabasco, blackberries, rye—with exactly that sentiment in mind.

Our Cajun friends like the drink on the hotter side, but we prefer a careful balance of never-too-hot and never-too-sweet. Be sure to include the andouille sausage garnish "for lagniappe."

1½ ounces rye whiskey

¾ ounce strained, freshly squeezed lemon juice

2 dashes Tabasco Sauce

¾ ounce Blackberry Syrup (page 373)

Andouille sausage wheel, for garnish

1 Combine the rye, lemon juice, Tabasco, and raspberry syrup in a mixing glass, fill the glass three-quarters full with ice cubes, cover with a Boston shaker tin, and shake vigorously until thoroughly chilled, 15 seconds.

2 Strain into a martini glass and garnish with the andouille sausage.

BROWN DERBY

GLASS: MARTINI | ICE: CUBED | MAKES: 1 DRINK

One of the greatest books we've ever inherited from a relative is an original copy of the Prohibition-era *Hollywood Cocktails,* a thin pamphlet that records the drinks of the golden age of Tinseltown for, as the book proclaims, "whenever it becomes legal to serve."

The Brown Derby cocktail, so named for one of Hollywood's most memorable celebrity and tourist haunts, is a whiskey sour in different clothing. Imagining the spicy fruitiness of rye, silken sweet honey, and a jolt of tangy citrus (we've replaced the traditional grapefruit with pomelo and lime), we think people may have made the move out West for the drinks, not the chance at stardom.

1½ ounces rye whiskey

¾ ounce strained, freshly squeezed pomelo juice

¼ ounce strained, freshly squeezed lime juice

½ ounce Honey Syrup (page 371)

1 Combine all of the ingredients in a mixing glass, fill the glass three-quarters full with ice cubes, cover with a Boston shaker tin, and shake vigorously until thoroughly chilled, 15 seconds.

2 Strain into a martini glass.

SCOFF-LAW

GLASS: MARTINI | ICE: CUBED | MAKES: 1 DRINK

After four years of Prohibition, there were anywhere between 30,000 and 100,000 speakeasies in New York City. What was any civic-minded member of the Anti-Saloon League to do? If you were multimillionaire Delcevare King, you'd throw a contest for the best term describing "the idea of lawless drinker, menace, scoffer, bad citizen, or whatnot, with the biting power of 'scab' or 'slacker.'" Which is exactly what King did. The winning entry: *scofflaw*.

And of course, in true scofflaw fashion, it wasn't two weeks later that the Scoff-law (the original spelling) cocktail popped up on the menu at Harry's Bar in Paris. With the cocktail renaissance, the Scoff-law has seen a great resurgence as of late, and there's a fine reason for that: The balance of sweet, citrus, herbal, and spice is worth the trip to the City of Lights. Fortunately, nowadays, we can make one at home.

1½ ounces rye whiskey

1 ounce dry vermouth

¾ ounce strained, freshly squeezed lemon juice

¾ ounce Grenadine, homemade (page 376) or store-bought

Dash orange bitters

1 Combine all of the ingredients in a mixing glass, fill the glass three-quarters full with ice cubes, cover with a Boston shaker tin, and shake vigorously until thoroughly chilled, 15 seconds.

2 Strain into a martini glass.

NEWTON AND THE HIVE

GLASS: MARTINI | ICE: CUBED | MAKES: 1 DRINK

T his drink was originally called the Honey Fig Redemption when we threw it together with our friend, chef Tim Kilcoyne, and his staff. The "Redemption" part came from Redemption Rye. Since that's not on our 12 Bottle Bar list, the drink begged for a new name. Given the honey element, an image of Sir Isaac Newton sitting not beneath a precarious apple tree but a beehive came to mind. We'll let you fill in the rest.

Our core inspiration came from the Black Mission figs Chef Tim was featuring on his menu the night we came in. The bartender asked if we had any thoughts about what drink to make with the figs, and a few tries later, what you see on the page was born. Every element of the drink is balanced to complement the natural goodness of figs. If figs are your thing, you'll be very happy cozying up to this drink.

Note that the recipe calls for a puree and a syrup; each one is easily made, can be assembled in advance, and yields enough to be used for multiple drinks—in other words, this quaff is dinner party gold.

1½ ounces rye whiskey

¾ ounce Honey Mint Syrup (page 371)

2 teaspoons Fig Puree (recipe follows)

½ ounce strained, freshly squeezed lemon juice

½ ounce red wine (preferably Shiraz)

1 Combine the rye, syrup, fig puree, and lemon juice in a mixing glass, fill the glass three-quarters full with ice cubes, cover with a Boston shaker tin, and shake vigorously until thoroughly chilled, 15 seconds.

2 Strain the drink through a fine-mesh sieve into a martini glass.

3 Hold a bar spoon against the inside wall of the glass, just below the rim and not touching the surface of the liquid. Slowly pour the red wine into the bowl of the spoon and down the inside of the glass so that the wine floats over the surface of the drink, without mixing in.

Fig Puree

MAKES: ¼ CUP

3 Black Mission figs, stemmed and halved lengthwise

1½ teaspoons granulated sugar

½ teaspoon strained, freshly squeezed lemon juice

2 teaspoons water

Combine all of the ingredients in a blender and puree until smooth. Strain through a fine-mesh sieve (see Tools of the Trade, page 16) into an airtight container. The puree will keep, covered, in the refrigerator, for up to 1 week.

WARD EIGHT

GLASS: MARTINI | ICE: CUBED | MAKES: 1 DRINK

What were they drinking in Boston at the end of the nineteenth century? Funny you should ask, because the Ward Eight is exactly the tipple you are looking for. Its ancestry is more than a bit cloudy, with most records claiming it was created to commemorate the 1898 Boston political victory of one Martin Lomasney, whose winning votes came from the Eighth Ward. More than anything else, the Ward Eight (ours is from the *Savoy Cocktail Book*; there are multitudes of variations) offers a nice change-up on the venerable whiskey sour, thanks to the substitution of orange juice and grenadine for the usual sugar. The key here is to use just enough sweetness to dull the alcoholic edge while still maintaining a high degree of tartness.

1½ ounces rye whiskey

¾ ounce strained, freshly squeezed lemon juice

¾ ounce strained, freshly squeezed orange juice

1 teaspoon Grenadine, homemade (page 376) or store-bought

1 Combine all of the ingredients in a mixing glass, fill the glass three-quarters full with ice cubes, cover with a Boston shaker tin, and shake vigorously until thoroughly chilled, 15 seconds.

2 Strain into a martini glass.

THE CLARET SNAP

A NINETEENTH-CENTURY invention—"men who drink . . . sours expect a claret at every bar"—that ultimately found a home in New York, the "Claret Snap," a float of red wine on top of a sour, is one of those wow-factor flourishes on a drink that always leaves people speechless. And the best part of it is, it's simple to do once you've mastered the basic process.

While the standard wine choice is a Bordeaux style, we prefer a nice jammy red wine like a Shiraz. You will also need a moderately steady hand. First, measure your wine into a jigger or equally small vessel—precision and patience are key here. Then, working with a freshly mixed whiskey sour, place a bar spoon in the glass so that the bowl of the spoon rests against the inside edge of the glass right atop, but not touching, the liquid. The handle should rise at a slight angle. Slowly pour the red wine into the bowl of the spoon, letting it trickle down the side of the glass and spread out over the surface of the drink.

Make sure your guests sip through the snap when drinking, not just from the top. Otherwise, all they'll get is wine.

WHISKEY SOUR

GLASS: MARTINI | ICE: CUBED | MAKES: 1 DRINK

O f all classes of mixed drinks, we love sours the best. The basic formula is simple: 2 parts spirit, 1 part tart, 1 part sweet. Follow that ratio and you'll seldom go wrong. Since the drink is called a "sour," however, we recommend scaling back the sweetness a bit and allowing the tartness to come through.

Of all the sours—daiquiris, margaritas, pisco sours—whiskey sours are our favorite. Here is a drink so flexible that it's almost impossible to do it harm. To that end, the basic recipe below is followed by some tasty variations.

. . . .

1½ ounces rye whiskey

¾ ounce strained, freshly squeezed lemon juice

½ to ¾ ounce Simple Syrup (page 369), to taste

. . . .

1 Combine all of the ingredients in a mixing glass, fill the glass three-quarters full with ice cubes, cover with a Boston shaker tin, and shake vigorously until thoroughly chilled, 15 seconds.

2 Strain into a martini glass.

VARIATIONS

FANCY SOUR Reduce the Simple Syrup to ½ ounce and add 1 teaspoon orange liqueur.

EGG SOUR Add the white of 1 large egg, and first shake all the ingredients without ice to emulsify the egg, 15 seconds. Shake again with ice and strain. You want a nice foamy head to the drink.

HERBAL SOUR Use rosemary, thyme, or other herb-infused syrup in place of the Simple Syrup (see page 369).

HONEY SOUR Replace the Simple Syrup with Honey Syrup (page 369).

NEW YORK SOUR Float ½ ounce of red wine atop the glass (for instructions, see box, page 251). Our favorite version!

Strong

MANHATTAN

GLASS: MARTINI, CHILLED | ICE: CUBED | MAKES: 1 DRINK

R eaching the Manhattan in a cocktail book is akin to finally turning the page to the "Riddles in the Dark" chapter of *The Hobbit*. This is the big moment everyone talks about. In the realm of cocktails, there are few drinks more important than the Manhattan. It is believed to predate the Martini and, as the apocryphal origin story goes, was invented at a party hosted in 1874 by Jenine Jerome (Winston Churchill's mother) for New York Governor Samuel Tilden.

If you haven't tried the Manhattan, add it to your bucket list. It's certainly a cold weather drink, mahogany deep and rich like belting leather. It's also a perfect canvas for experimentation. We highly recommend using Carpano Antica vermouth (see page 296). And you'll find another variation of this drink—one incorporating orange liqueur—on page 53.

2 ounces rye whiskey

1 ounce sweet vermouth

Dash aromatic bitters

Orange twist, for garnish

1 Combine the rye, vermouth, and bitters in a mixing glass and place it in the freezer to chill, 10 minutes.

2 Fill the mixing glass three-quarters full with ice cubes and stir rapidly to chill further, 30 seconds.

3 Strain into a chilled martini glass and garnish with the orange twist.

MONTICELLO COCKTAIL

GLASS: ROCKS | ICE: POMEGRANATE ICE CUBES
(SEE HEADNOTE) | MAKES: 1 DRINK

A few years back, we competed in and won a national dinner party competition hosted by a large pomegranate grower and producer of pomegranate-based drinks. Our focus was on the pomegranate through the ages, and the Monticello commemorates both the 1771 planting of the first pomegranates at Thomas Jefferson's famous plantation as well as the distillation of rye spirit at Monticello.

At its core, the Monticello is a classic "fancy" cocktail—a drink with liqueur added to the base recipe—gussied up in some fruity trappings. The astringency of the unsweetened pomegranate, frozen into juicy ice cubes, ensures that this doesn't run into candyland. Should the drink prove to be too strong at first, let the ice melt a bit.

• •

8 ounces unsweetened pomegranate juice (such as POM)

1½ ounces rye whiskey

1 teaspoon Grenadine, homemade (page 376) or store-bought

¼ teaspoon orange liqueur

Dash orange bitters

1 Fill about 4 sections of a standard ice cube mold with the unsweetened pomegranate juice and freeze.

2 When the ice is ready, combine the remaining ingredients in a rocks glass and stir to combine. Add one or more pomegranate ice cubes as desired.

AMERICA'S FIRST WHISKEY

MICHTER'S DISTILLERY traces its origins back to 1753, when a Pennsylvania Swiss farmer named John Shenk found that he had too much rye and could think of nothing better to do with it than distill it (good man). The story goes that George Washington was a fan of Shenk's whiskey (we have yet to find a spirit George didn't like) and the general provided it to his men to help stave off the harsh Valley Forge winter chill. True or not, we'll happily crack a bottle whenever the temperature drops.

CHAPTER 11

Vodka

"**V**odka martini. Shaken not stirred." With those immortal words, James Bond did more for the future of vodka than any ad campaign ever could. Bond actually drank an assortment of other drinks—everything from Campari and Soda to beer—but it was with vodka, ironically from the Slavic word *voda*, meaning water, that he made his bibulous mark.

When we first started the 12 Bottle Bar site, we made a very conscious and vocal choice not to include vodka. First, it was not one of the classic spirits used during the golden age of cocktails, which is what our site celebrates. More important, though, vodka isn't really a spirit for people who enjoy the taste of alcohol, which is the real point of a well-made cocktail. Bottom line: If you came to a party at our house, you damn well didn't ask for a Vodka Tonic. All that told us was that you wanted to get a flavorless buzz on.

Granted, Eastern Europeans might argue the point that vodka is an alcohol delivery system and nothing more. But then, Eastern Europe's early forays into vodka making weren't exactly stellar, failing to produce the clean, pure product known today. As a result, vodka was often rank with impurities that had to be disguised with herbs and other flavorings, or filtered out by aging, freezing (impurities rise to the surface),

Vodka
IN A NUTSHELL

DEFINING FEATURE: Its ability to "blend in" with other drink ingredients

FLAVOR PROFILE: Its lack of flavor is its profile.

WHY WE CHOSE IT: Being essentially flavorless, it is the ultimate alcohol delivery system, great for making liqueurs and pleasing those who don't like the flavor of alcohol.

EMBLEMATIC DRINKS: Moscow Mule (page 276), Cosmopolitan (page 271)

or adding coagulants like milk, egg white, or isinglass (derived from the air bladder of the sturgeon fish) to the murky vodka (the impurities would literally adhere to the sticky additives).

Nowadays, with distilling techniques at their apex, purity isn't an issue. Indeed, since vodka is essentially just ethyl alcohol and water, there is a lot of freedom in the distillation process. While there is an incredibly long history of using potatoes (Chopin) as the base for vodka, these days almost anything is fair game, including grains (rye: Belvedere; wheat: Absolut and Stolichnaya; barley: Finlandia), grapes (Cîroc), honey (Comb), and even milk (Black Cow Pure Milk Vodka).

Here in the States, vodka is classified as "without distinctive character, aroma, taste, or color." Still, it got us thinking, because an alcohol delivery system—or neutral spirit, to use the parlance of the industry—can be a very useful thing. For instance, vodka is a base for making liqueurs (if you learn to make your own liqueurs you vastly expand your 12 bottles without adding a new spirit) or for boozing up drinks in which you want to highlight the flavor of other ingredients. Suddenly, Plain Jane vodka possesses a super power that no other spirit can equal.

This blank canvas is what has made vodka the bestselling spirit in the States, a fact that, in and of itself, makes it an essential part of any modern bartending collection. Some people won't drink anything else. So here we are, with vodka a very important part of our 12 Bottle Bar collection, and we don't feel one bit guilty for it. And now, bottom line, if you come to a party at our house and ask for a Vodka Tonic, you still won't get one, but we will mix you up a vodka *something* that delivers a lot of flavor and personality.

IT LEAVES YOU BREATHLESS

WHAT'S THE CHIEF appeal of vodka? Smirnoff knew over half a century ago. "It Leaves You Breathless" ran their brilliant 1952 ad campaign. Not only were they marketing vodka to impress—Bond, James Bond, anyone?—but they knew there was a huge market for alcohol that couldn't be smelled on your breath. Ah, the halcyon days before Breathalyzer tests.

THE BOTTLES TO BUY

With vodka, everyone who drinks it has a favorite. How many times has someone sidled up to the bar next to you and asked for a Grey Goose, Ketel One, or Whatever and Tonic? So, if you already love vodka, choose your favorite tipple. The bottles we recommend below have been chosen for their strength (in one case), as well as their availability and mixability.

Budget
($20 or less—750 ml)

ABSOLUT Vodka can start turf wars and Absolut has not escaped the crosshairs—it has its supporters and detractors. Much of its fame has come from its inventive ad campaigns. We like it because of its neutral, mildly sweet character, which offers a foundation for drinks, but doesn't compete with them as some premium vodkas do. Remember, in our book (literally), there is no such thing as a vodka martini, so "flavor" is not the issue here.

Midrange
($20–$30/750 ml)

STOLICHNAYA 100 Stoli 100 is the bomb. It's basic, it's old school, it's high proof, and, while it's made in Latvia (once but no longer a Russian dominion), its recipe is Russian in origin. It offers a great conduit for flavor extraction in liqueur because of the higher proof, and is quite respectable as basic vodka goes. Disclaimer: Be aware of the higher proof if you use this in mixed drinks or it will knock you on your popka.

THE RISE OF SMIRNOFF

PYOTR SMIRNOV came into this world on the eve of the birth of Russian capitalism and, in 1864, employed that capitalist spirit to make what would eventually be the world's number one selling vodka brand, now known as Smirnoff. Pyotr was the first to use the charcoal filtering process that removes impurities from the grain-neutral spirit. He was also the first to "advertise."

While organized publicity was still a vague concept, Smirnov shrewdly gathered a group of beggars, offered them a warm meal and plenty to drink at his home, then paid them to pop into Moscow's major bars demanding Smirnoff. The man was a PR genius far ahead of his time. No wonder he became the official vodka supplier to the tsar in 1886.

THE DRINKS

Sweet & Fruity

CHI CHI

GLASS: COLLINS | ICE: CRUSHED | MAKES: 1 DRINK

n the 1970s, when slushy tropical drinks reigned supreme, everyone under the sun was drinking Piña Coladas and getting caught in the rain. For those folks who didn't like rum, the spirit in the Piña Colada, the Chi Chi was invented, although its official origins are a mystery. Many versions blend the drink with—the horror—vanilla ice cream, but we feel this destroys the fresh island flavors, not to mention adding about three hundred calories to the drink. There's something completely retro about this drink. It doesn't have the flash of a modern cocktail, yet the inherent affinity of the coconut and pineapple flavors make it something of a classic in its own right.

We have purposely avoided cream of coconut, which most recipes call for, because of all the additives it has, opting instead for a homemade syrup made from coconut milk that is lighter and fresher tasting. You can certainly blend the ingredients if you choose, as this drink was so familiarly made in bygone days. And yes, you can try it with the ice cream.

• •

2 ounces pineapple juice

2 ounces Coconut Milk Syrup (page 381)

1½ ounces vodka

Pineapple slice, for garnish

• •

1 Combine the pineapple juice, syrup, and vodka in a mixing glass, fill the glass three-quarters full with crushed ice, cover with a Boston shaker tin, and shake

vigorously until thoroughly
chilled, 15 seconds.

2 Fill a collins glass with
crushed ice and strain the
drink into the glass. Garnish
with the pineapple.

MO CHI CHI

GLASS: ROCKS | ICE: CRUSHED | MAKES: 1 DRINK

More cocktails have been created—and improved upon—
by using classics as the jumping-off point. Here, Los
Angeles bartender Dan Long plays with the traditional
Chi Chi (page 263), itself originally a vodka version of a
Piña Colada. In a Mo Chi Chi, the nuttiness of amontillado sherry complements the coconut vodka, while the toasted coconut garnish offers a
crunchy, sweet treat on top. This same sherry is used in the Sherry Berry
Bramble (page 102), but it's also a useful addition to both your kitchen
and your after-dinner drink selection: Choose the style, dry or sweet,
based on your flavor preference. A drink like this could easily become
too rich and heavy, but Long's proportions—as well as his choice to
serve it tiki-style, over crushed ice—make this a light, refreshing sipper. We dare you to drink just one. (If you wish, the drink can also be
made without the sherry. Likewise, if you prefer a less tangy version,
cut down the lime and up the Simple Syrup to ½ ounce.)

1½ ounces "Coconutty" Vodka
  (page 384)

1 ounce pineapple juice

¾ ounce strained, freshly
  squeezed lime juice

¼ ounce amontillado sherry

¼ ounce Simple Syrup
  (page 369)

Toasted Coconut, for garnish
  (recipe follows)

1 Combine all of the liquid
ingredients in a mixing glass,
fill the glass three-quarters full
with crushed ice, cover with a
Boston shaker tin, and shake
vigorously until thoroughly
chilled, 15 seconds.

2 Pour the drink, without
straining, into a rocks glass and
top with crushed ice and the
coconut.

Toasted Coconut

MAKES: 2½ CUPS

2 ½ cups shredded, sweetened
  coconut (about half a
  14-ounce bag)

1 Preheat the oven to 300°F with a rack in the middle position.

2 Spread the coconut evenly in a thin layer on a rimmed baking sheet and bake, stirring every 5 minutes or so, until it browns lightly and evenly, 12 to 15 minutes.

3 Remove the coconut from the oven and allow it to cool to room temperature. Transfer it to an airtight container and store at room temperature for up to 1 week.

Bar Con:
THE BIRTHDAY BILL

AS SEEN IN the 1973 movie *Paper Moon*, this involves two con artists working together. The first one goes into a bar and orders a drink, paying with a $20 bill and getting change. Before going in, the con artist has written a note written on the twenty, saying "Happy Birthday Jim [or some name], Love Grandma" and the date. Meanwhile, the accomplice enters the bar, orders a drink, and pays with a $10 bill. When the bartender returns with the change, the second con artist insists he paid with a twenty, claiming the money was a gift from his grandma and she wrote a "Happy Birthday" note on it with his name and the date. The confused bartender goes to the till, finds the marked-up twenty, and returns with the "correct" change.

This con—an old-school trick—is, of course, predicated on a drink costing less than $10!!

—TODD ROBBINS, AUTHOR, *THE MODERN CON MAN*

LIMONCELLO DROP

GLASS: MARTINI | ICE: CUBED | MAKES: 1 DRINK

The Lemon Drop is one of those drinks that falls into the same "hang your head in shame" class of drinks as the Sex on the Beach. We have embraced the Lemon Drop, however (unlike the SOTB), because of its simplicity and sweet-to-tangy malleability. In other words, while it may be a "girlie" drink, the Lemon Drop has its place. After all, there's nothing wrong with what is essentially a boozy lemonade.

For our Limoncello Drop, we've replaced a portion of the vodka lemon juice with a healthy measure of homemade limoncello, a lemon liqueur common in southern Italy. Equal parts of simple syrup and lemon juice—tinker with the ratio depending on your sweet-tart preferences (ours run on the sweeter side)—round out what is a simple to remember, simple to make, and supremely simple-to-consume drink.

• •

Superfine sugar, for rimming the glass

Lemon wedge

1 ounce vodka

1 ounce Limoncello (page 386; see Note)

1 ounce Simple Syrup (page 369)

1 ounce strained, freshly squeezed lemon juice

Lemon peel, for garnish

• •

1 Cover a small plate with sugar to a depth of ¼ inch. Halve the lemon wedge widthwise and run a cut edge around the outer rim of a martini glass to dampen it. Roll the glass in the sugar to coat the outer rim.

2 Combine the liquid ingredients in a mixing glass, fill the glass three-quarters full with ice cubes, cover with a Boston shaker tin, and shake

vigorously until thoroughly chilled, 15 seconds.

3 Strain into the prepared martini glass and garnish with the lemon peel.

NOTE: If you don't wish to make your own limoncello, it's available at most liquor stores; we like the inexpensive Pallini and the more pricey Ventura County Limoncello.

CAPRESE-TINI

GLASS: MARTINI | ICE: CUBED | MAKES: 1 DRINK

Ventura, California, chef Tim Kilcoyne has always been a champion of working with farmers to procure the best produce for his restaurants and food truck. He was a locavore before there was even a word for it and he has always, always cooked seasonally. During summer, when tomatoes are at their peak, Tim uses them in every way he can, including in this clever take on a Caprese salad—in a glass. Because the tomato flavor is the star here, do take care in choosing the sweetest, freshest off-the-vine fruits you can find and have fun experimenting with heirloom varieties whose flavors can vary from tangy to almost rich and creamy. Note: The color of the tomato will determine the color of your drink. Miniature mozzarella balls can be found in the grocery store cheese section—choose fresh buffalo mozzarella if at all possible.

1 ripe medium tomato or 6 cherry tomatoes

1½ ounces vodka

½ ounce Basil Simple Syrup (recipe follows)

Cracked pepper, to taste

Sea salt, to taste

Mini mozzarella ball, for garnish

Cherry tomato, for garnish

Basil leaf, for garnish

1 Place the tomato in a mixing glass and muddle to extract the juice. Strain 1½ ounces of the tomato water to a separate mixing glass.

2 Add the vodka, syrup, pepper, and salt, fill the glass three-quarters full with ice cubes, cover with a Boston shaker tin, and shake vigorously until thoroughly chilled, 15 seconds.

3 Strain into a martini glass.

4 Skewer the mozzarella, cherry tomato, and basil leaf and place it atop the glass.

Basil Simple Syrup

MAKES: ABOUT 1½ CUPS

1 cup Simple Syrup
(page 369)

1 cup small to medium fresh
basil leaves, stems removed

1 Combine the simple syrup and the basil leaves in a blender and blend until pureed.

2 Strain the syrup through a fine-mesh sieve into an airtight container, pressing down on the solids to extract the syrup. Discard the solids.

3 The syrup will keep, covered, in the refrigerator for up to 1 week.

CELERY CUP NO. 2

GLASS: COLLINS | ICE: CUBED | MAKES: 1 DRINK

When barman and cocktail consultant H. Joseph Erhmann created his original Celery Cup No. 1, he so named it because he hoped other bartenders and cocktail enthusiasts would create their own versions. Thus, we introduce Celery Cup No. 2, a drinkable salad in the best possible way. Where Erhmann used agave syrup to sweeten the mix, we have used simple syrup. Our addition of celery salt on the glass rim adds a zippy component to the vegetal crispness of the drink.

Celery salt

Lemon wedge

2-inch piece of tender celery
(taken from close to the
heart), chopped, plus an
additional leafy stalk for
garnish

2-inch piece of English
cucumber, chopped

6 to 7 fresh cilantro leaves

1 ounce strained, freshly
squeezed lemon juice

1½ ounces Cucumber-Infused
Vodka (page 385), or vodka

¾ ounce Simple Syrup
(page 369)

½ ounce Cheater's Cup
(page 389)

1 Cover a small plate with celery salt to a depth of ¼ inch. Halve the lemon widthwise and run a cut edge around the outer rim of a collins glass to dampen it. Roll the glass in the salt to coat the outer rim.

2 Combine the chopped celery and cucumber, the cilantro, and lemon juice in a mixing glass and muddle them to a pulp.

3 Add the vodka, Simple Syrup, and Cheater's Cup, fill the glass three-quarters full with ice cubes, cover with a Boston shaker tin, and shake vigorously until thoroughly chilled, 15 seconds.

4 Carefully fill the prepared collins glass with ice cubes and strain the drink into the glass. Garnish with the remaining celery stalk.

Tangy & Citrusy

BUNNY MOTHER

GLASS: COLLINS | ICE: CUBED, CRUSHED | MAKES: 1 DRINK

The provenance of the Bunny Mother is unknown, at least to our inquiring minds, but it is clearly in the sour class of drinks, with citrus notes predominating. Numerous vodka-based sours have crossed our mixing table; few have survived, as most of them were relatively insipid, especially because the vodka contributed no major flavor to the drinks.

The Bunny Mother, however, is a super-tart cooler (you could almost say it's a vodka swizzle)—just the remedy for sweltering summer heat—and we were surprised by the kick of the citrus when we first made the drink. If the drink seems too lemony for your taste, you can cut the lemon juice by half. We also found that when we added ¼ ounce of grenadine to the existing recipe, the tang of the lemon mellowed quite a bit.

- -

1½ ounces vodka

1 ounce strained, freshly squeezed orange juice

1 ounce strained, freshly squeezed lemon juice

1 teaspoon granulated sugar

¼ ounce Grenadine, homemade (page 376) or store-bought

¼ ounce orange liqueur

Orange slice, for garnish

Brandied Cherry (page 367) or high-quality maraschino cherry (we like Luxardo brand), for garnish

- -

1 Combine all of the liquid ingredients in a mixing glass, fill the glass three-quarters full with ice cubes, cover with a Boston shaker tin, and shake vigorously until thoroughly chilled, 15 seconds.

2 Strain into a collins glass and add crushed ice to the glass. Garnish with the orange slice and cherry.

COSMOPOLITAN

GLASS: MARTINI | ICE: CUBED | MAKES: 1 DRINK

Yes we know, the Cosmo has been there and done that. But in the vodka arsenal, it is an essential. This recipe comes to us from preeminent bartender and author Dale DeGroff, who adds the showstopping touch of a flamed orange rind. Just as the Moscow Mule (page 276) was the PR baby of the Cock 'n Bull restaurant, the Cosmo finds its lineage in a 1960s cocktail marketing blitz from cranberry giant Ocean Spray. Their drink, the Harpoon, featured cranberry juice, lime juice, and vodka.

In the 1980s, Florida bartender Cheryl Cook added Absolut Citron and triple sec to the Harpoon, creating the cocktail that inaugurated *Sex and the City* into the cocktail zeitgeist, not to mention launching Manolo Blahnik's career. While citrus vodka is standard, we find the drink works just as well with plain vodka.

· ·

1½ ounces vodka

¾ ounce orange liqueur

1 ounce cranberry juice

¼ ounce strained, freshly squeezed lime juice

Orange peel, preferably flamed (see page 8), for garnish

· ·

1 Combine the vodka, liqueur, cranberry juice, and lime juice in a mixing glass, fill the glass three-quarters full with ice cubes, cover with a Boston shaker tin, and shake vigorously until thoroughly chilled, 15 seconds.

2 Strain into a martini glass and garnish with the flamed orange peel.

CUCUMBER GIMLET

GLASS: MARTINI | ICE: CRUSHED | MAKES: 1 DRINK

C ucumber, basil, and lime have a natural affinity for one another, so it's not surprising that they show up again and again in cocktails. Some people might choose to label this drink a "martini," but purists that we are, we opted for "gimlet" instead, because of the lime juice and simple syrup. However you slice the cucumber, this is as crisp and clean a gulp of summer as you will ever find. It's a perfect example of how vodka works as a blank canvas to deliver potency, but not compete with the drink's key flavors. Our version muddles cucumber with the basil, but you could also use Cucumber-Infused Vodka (page 385), for an even deeper cuke crunch.

8 to 10 fresh basil leaves, depending on size, plus 1 for garnish

2-inch piece of English cucumber, coarsely chopped

½ ounce strained, freshly squeezed lime juice

2 ounces vodka or Cucumber-Infused Vodka

½ to ¾ ounce Simple Syrup (page 369), depending on desired sweetness

1 Fill a mixing glass halfway with crushed ice, place the 8 to 10 basil leaves and the cucumber in the glass, and muddle until the ice starts taking on a greenish hue, about 15 seconds.

2 Add the vodka and Simple Syrup to the glass, fill the glass three-quarters full with crushed ice, cover with the Boston shaker tin, and shake vigorously until thoroughly chilled, 15 seconds.

3 Strain into a martini glass and garnish with the remaining basil leaf.

DE-CONSTRUCTED MARY

GLASS: MARTINI | ICE: CUBED | MAKES: 1 DRINK

Our friend Chef Tim Kilcoyne (see page 267) loves to play with familiar dishes and drinks by breaking them into their basic components. Here, he softened the flavor and mouthfeel of a basic Bloody Mary with tomato water, creating a more elegant, martini-style drink.

•••

Celery salt

1 lemon

1 ripe medium tomato or
   6 cherry tomatoes

1½ ounces vodka

Cracked black pepper,
   to taste

Sea salt, to taste

¼ to ½ teaspoon bottled
   horseradish, to taste

•••

1 Cover a small plate with celery salt to a depth of ¼ inch.

2 Cut a wheel from the lemon and reserve it for garnish. Cut a wedge from the remaining lemon, halve it widthwise, and run a cut edge around the outer rim of a martini glass to dampen it. Roll the glass in the celery salt to coat the outer rim.

3 Place the tomato in a Boston shaker tin and muddle to obtain at least 1½ ounces of strained tomato water.

4 Strain 1½ ounces of the tomato water into a mixing glass. Add the vodka, pepper, and salt, fill the glass three-quarters full with ice cubes, cover with a Boston shaker tin, and shake vigorously until thoroughly chilled, 15 seconds.

5 Strain into the prepared martini glass and float the lemon wheel on the top of the drink.

6 Gently dollop the horseradish on top of the lemon wheel.

KAMIKAZE

GLASS: MARTINI | ICE: CUBED | MAKES: 1 DRINK

The Kamikaze will raise the hairs on the back of your neck with its one-two punch of sour and bitter, thanks to the lime juice. Back in the '70s—notice how so many "bad drink" stories begin in the '70s—the drink was a shooter whose ability to lay you flat begat its tell-all name. The proportions vary depending on whose recipe you use, and some versions even include a bit of sugar or simple syrup (as we do) to soften the effects. Sugar or no, a few of these babies and you are going down for the count. Just make sure you know who has your car keys.

1½ ounces vodka

¾ ounce orange liqueur

½ to 1 teaspoon Simple Syrup (page 369) (optional)

¾ ounce strained, freshly squeezed lime juice

Lime wedge, for garnish

1 Combine the vodka, liqueur, Simple Syrup to taste, and lime juice in a mixing glass, fill the glass three-quarters full with ice cubes, cover with a Boston shaker tin, and shake vigorously until thoroughly chilled, 15 seconds.

2 Strain into a martini glass and garnish with the lime wedge.

VARIATION

BALALAIKA 1 ounce each of vodka, orange liqueur, and lemon juice. Garnish with a lemon wedge.

LEMONGRASS IS ALWAYS GREENER

GLASS: ROCKS | ICE: CUBED, CRUSHED (OPTIONAL) |
MAKES: 1 DRINK

William Grant & Sons brand ambassador and all-around charming lass Charlotte Voisey offered up this original vodka cocktail for the book and we thank her kindly. The name comes from Charlotte's observation of "the endless choices we seem to have at cocktail bars these days when ordering, and the subsequent quiet worry that we might have chosen the wrong drink."

In its flavor profile, this drink resembles a Limoncello Drop (page 266) to some degree—the vodka, lemon juice, and simple syrup components. However, using lemongrass adds a distinctly spicy, almost ginger-like quality to the mix. Accented by the fresh mint and served over ice, this is an unexpected and delightful variation on the sour. While making a flavored syrup might seem time-consuming, the lemongrass version required is simply lemongrass-infused simple syrup that requires a 12-hour resting period (no work involved) before use. It's worth it.

2 ounces vodka

¾ ounce Lemongrass Syrup (page 376)

¾ ounce strained, freshly squeezed lemon juice

10 fresh mint leaves, plus 1 sprig for garnish

Lemongrass straw (page 276), for garnish

1 Combine the vodka, syrup, lemon juice, and 10 mint leaves in a mixing glass, fill the glass three-quarters full with ice cubes, cover with a Boston shaker tin, and shake vigorously until thoroughly chilled, 15 seconds.

2 Fill a rocks glass with ice cubes or crushed ice and double strain the drink through a fine-mesh sieve into the rocks glass. Garnish with the mint sprig and lemongrass "straw."

HOW TO MAKE A LEMONGRASS STRAW

IT'S ACTUALLY QUITE easy to transform a stalk of lemongrass from woody herb to drinking implement. First, use a paring knife to cut away both ends of the stalk. Then slice lengthwise down the stalk to cut through the first few layers of the lemongrass; peel away and discard these tough outer layers to reveal the tender pale yellow layers beneath.

Finally use your fingertips to push out and remove the core from the stalk, creating a hollow straw. Now drink.

MOSCOW MULE

GLASS: COLLINS | ICE: CRUSHED | MAKES: 1 DRINK

The Moscow Mule is simply a vodka buck that has been given a fancy name and packaged by shrewd PR men (see opposite). It came about in the 1950s, at the height of the vodka boom, when people were looking for truly neutral spirits. The frosty copper mug it was traditionally served in (for obvious cost reasons, we use a basic collins glass) was pretty dandy, too, securing it a place in cocktail history.

1½ to 2 ounces vodka, to taste
½ lime

4 to 6 ounces ginger beer, such as Reed's Premium Ginger Brew

1 Fill a collins glass halfway with crushed ice and add the vodka.

2 Squeeze in the juice from the lime, then drop in the shell.

3 Top with the ginger beer and stir gently to combine.

MOSCOW MULE, OR SMIRNOFF DOES IT AGAIN

THE CREATION OF the Moscow Mule cocktail is the best example of how public relations dictated the fortunes of a spirit. Up until the 1930s, vodka was present in the United States, but was drunk only by a minuscule population, mostly Eastern European immigrants, of whom—proportionally speaking—there were not all that many.

After Heublein, one of the twentieth century's most powerful spirits producers and distributors, purchased Smirnoff, the company was hungry for an opportunity to raise vodka's profile. Enter "Jack" Morgan, who owned the Cock 'n Bull restaurant—a celebrity haven on L.A.'s Sunset Boulevard—and whose company made ginger beer. One fateful night, he and Heublein president John G. Martin, plus Heublein's vodka man, Smirnoff prez Rudolph Kunett, were drinking and knocking heads. *What if we combined vodka, lime juice, and Morgan's ginger beer,* they wondered, riffing on the Mamie Taylor cocktail, which combined Scotch, lime, and ginger ale or ginger beer.

Add a copper mug to the mix—the "classic'" way of serving a Moscow Mule—and a legend was born. Many argue that a Moscow Mule doesn't taste the same without that copper mug. Regardless, it's likely that vodka's fortunes would never have flourished had the Hollywood set not embraced the drink with such ferocity.

Strong

BLUSHING MARY

GLASS: COLLINS | ICE: CUBED | MAKES: 1 DRINK

When we came upon *The Drunken Botanist*, by Amy Stewart, we wondered how we had ever made cocktails without it. Amy has an utterly original approach to cocktails and the spirits from which they are made, writing about every plant under the sun that is used to distill a liquor. Reading her book will convince you that mankind's sole purpose on earth is to distill booze and get drunk on it.

Hidden toward the back of the book is this cocktail, which Amy told us is the best evocation of a seasonal, "cocktail garden" kind of drink. We wholly agree with her and would happily sip this lighter, more effervescent version of what is essentially a Bloody Mary. The original recipe called for celery bitters, but we use aromatic and find the drink just as lovely.

2 ounces vodka

5 cherry tomatoes, halved

½ medium red bell pepper, stemmed, seeded, and thinly sliced, 1 slice reserved for garnish

2 dashes Worcestershire sauce

2 fresh basil leaves

6 to 7 fresh cilantro leaves

4 ounces tonic water

Dash aromatic bitters

Cracked black pepper, to taste

Celery salt, to taste

1 In a mixing glass, combine the vodka, cherry tomatoes, bell pepper, Worcestershire, basil, and cilantro and muddle until the tomatoes have released their juices, 10 to 15 seconds.

2 Fill the mixing glass three-quarters full with ice cubes, cover with a Boston shaker tin, and shake vigorously until thoroughly chilled, 15 seconds.

3 Strain into a collins glass. Add the tonic water and stir to combine. Add the bitters, and top with a dusting of pepper and celery salt. Garnish with the reserved red pepper slice.

NO BLOODY MARY HERE

QUEEN MARY I may be known as the "Bloody Queen," but it's doubtful the Bloody Mary cocktail was named after her (it's more likely that the gal just took after her dad, Henry VIII). Serious history aside, the Bloody Mary's origins have been claimed by many a bartender over the decades, the most likely gent being Fernand "Pete" Petiot, of the Paris-based Le Harry's New York Bar.

Why is the Bloody Mary considered a brunch drink? Well, we may be dating ourselves, but we recall that with continental breakfasts you were often given the choice of orange, apple, grapefruit, or tomato juice. Somehow, tomato juice got a reputation as a sort of "hair of the dog" morning-after pick-me-up and the rest, as they say . . .

So, where's the recipe, you ask? Nope, we ain't giving you one. At least not the traditional tomato juice version. Everybody claims to have the best Bloody Mary, and we have no intention of jumping into that fray. It's one of the reasons we have purposely avoided the recipe and instead included two gin-based, non-tomato variations: the fruity/herbal Green Snapper (page 118) and the veggie-rich Montford Snapper (page 119). Both could easily take vodka instead of gin if you prefer the neutral spirit.

Still, we do understand the popularity of the Bloody Mary, so we have included two drinks that are clearly inspired by this boozy brunch bomb. Both the Blushing Mary (opposite page) and the De-constructed Mary (page 273) are lighter, more refreshing versions of the standard.

If you are still intent on holding to tradition, create your own Bloody You-Name-It. For all intents, a Bloody Mary is a glass of tomato juice, or a variation thereof (Clamato, V-8, and so on), some prototypical spices like celery salt and pepper, and a few aromatic components, which could include everything from Worcestershire sauce to horseradish (fresh or bottled), from olive brine to Old Bay seasoning. Almost every spirit out there, from tequila to aquavit, has spawned a Mary variation (see page 120). As for toppings, we've seen everything imaginable—the standard-issue celery stalk, a crab's claw, pickled green beans, even beef jerky. So give it a try. The whole point of this book is to give you the confidence to play with flavors and customize cocktails to your personal palate. The Bloody Mary, which has only two basic components—tomato juice and booze—is a great place to start.

VODKA MARTINI

There is no such thing. A Martini is gin and vermouth (see page 130). The reason we direct you to the Gin Martini isn't snobbery, it's practicality. By its very nature, a martini is a vermouth drink. Vermouth and gin marry famously, but when you replace the gin with vodka, the balance is gone. To compensate, the vermouth is cut back until it no longer exists in the drink.

If you order a Vodka Martini, "and just pass the vermouth cap over the top of the glass," all you are drinking is a "long" shot of vodka. And, sorry friends, that's no Martini.

LIGHTS, CAMERA, VODKA

EVER A FAN of the well-made drink, James Bond drank numerous cocktails throughout Ian Fleming's novels and the subsequent movies, everything from the Campari-based Americano, the first drink mentioned in the book version of *Casino Royale,* to the Stinger, a once popular combination of brandy and white crème de menthe. But the spirit that will forever be associated with Bond is vodka, and the main reason for that—aside from Fleming's inclusion of multiple Vodka Martinis in the Bond books—is a then-unknown company called Smirnoff.

Smirnoff vodka was first distilled in Russia, but the family was forced to flee during the Russian Revolution. Upon the death of Smirnoff's founder, Pyotr Smirnov, his son Vladimir took over and eventually sold the company to Russian emigrant Rudolph Kunett, who took Smirnoff to the U.S. Kunett, in turn, sold the company to G. F. Heublein & Bros. in 1934. At the time, vodka was little known—let alone consumed—outside Eastern European immigrant circles. Heublein helped to change that and, when James Bond appeared on screen in 1962's *Dr. No,* the series' first film, he drank a Vodka Martini—made with Smirnoff. The Martini would never be the same again.

CHAPTER 12

Orange Liqueur

By far, orange liqueur is the most essential liqueur when it comes to mixing cocktails. You are probably familiar with some of the usual suspects already—Triple Sec, Cointreau, Grand Marnier, and the more mysterious "Curaçao." While other liqueurs certainly define the drinks in which they are found (crème de cassis in a Kir Royale, crème de cacao in a Brandy Alexander), orange liqueur is the bottle that bartenders—and we—grab most frequently, thus it is the only liqueur that made the 12 Bottle Bar cut.

You will notice that there are only two orange liqueur–based recipes in this section. This is because, while orange liqueur is a defining element in many drinks, the main spirit in the drink is a stronger player. Conversely, the two recipes we have placed in this chapter each use a whopping two ounces of orange liqueur, making the liqueur the dominant flavor.

Unlike orange juice (or any other citrus for that matter), orange liqueur offers a trifold benefit—the power of alcohol, the concentrated flavor of orange, and the sweetness of sugar. Depending on type, orange liqueur can be syrupy and

Orange Liqueur
IN A NUTSHELL

DEFINING FEATURES: Orangey sweet, with a bitter note

FLAVOR PROFILE: From sweet to bitter, with tones of vanilla and caramel

WHY WE CHOSE IT: It's the #1 go-to liqueur for cocktails.

EMBLEMATIC DRINKS: Pegu Club (page 122), The Sidecar (page 52), Curaçao Punch (page 287)

light-textured, cloyingly sweet and slightly bitter. As one might expect, all of this has to do with what oranges and what base spirit (grain neutral or brandy) are used in your liqueur. Here's what's what:

ORANGE CURAÇAO We'll begin with this because it's a generic term for bitter orange liqueur, originally made by the Dutch who settled on the Caribbean island of Curaçao. The story goes that the Spanish planted Valencia orange trees there, but weren't prepared for the overly bitter fruit they produced. The Dutch, however, known for their talent for liqueurs, quickly snapped up the island oranges and used them to flavor a pot-distilled fruit brandy. As for blue curaçao, which also tastes like orange, the only thing that differentiates it is its almost neon-blue hue (you may break out the blue curaçao only in the event you're making a Papa Smurf, and certainly only after you've sold your copy of this book on eBay).

TRIPLE SEC *Triple Sec,* literally meaning "triple dry," is simply the French version of Curaçao, and essentially tastes the same. While *sec* truly does mean dry, the *triple* part is more amorphous, meaning triple distillation, or a liqueur that's three times more orangey, or in fact triple dry (that is, far less sweet), depending on whom you ask. Because it uses a grain-neutral base, triple sec is always clear, (Curaçao can be orange, blue, green, or clear, as it's often used to add color to drinks).

Today, most bottlings generically labeled as "triple sec" will have an unremarkable character. Some of the very cheap versions can be as low as $5. In contrast, liqueurs like Cointreau (see below) or the similar Combier, which posits itself as the original triple sec, weigh in at around $30. With orange liqueurs, you really do get what you pay for.

COINTREAU This is the "rich man's," as well as the bartender's, higher-end triple sec, made with bitter orange peels from the island of Curaçao as well as sweeter Spanish orange peels. It's

> **Tip:**
> # STAY IN THE CLEAR
>
> **IT WOULD BE A SHAME** if your carefully measured and sparkling clear gin cocktail suddenly turned a muddy shade of orangey-brown because you used Grand Marnier in it. For best results, reserve your brandy-based Curaçao for your brown drinks.

clear and made with a neutral grain base like generic triple sec, but smoother and perfect for mixing. There is a reason that every good bar has a bottle.

GRAND MARNIER With its Cognac base and rich, syrupy character, Grand Marnier is more akin to the style of the original Dutch brandy–based Curaçao. It further sets itself apart through an additional step in its production—barrel aging, which in effect mellows and rounds the flavors. The liqueur is ideal in some cocktails, but its deeper flavor can often overpower more delicate ones. However, if you are a devotee of crêpes Suzette—which relies on Grand Marnier for its velvety texture and deep orange flavor—you will need to add a bottle of this to your arsenal.

THE BOTTLES TO BUY

While the prices for quality orange liqueur might be high (the majority average $30-plus for a 750-milliliter bottle), in cocktails they are used in such small proportions that a little bit goes a very long way. We may not all be able to live in mansions or drive exotic cars, but when it comes to orange liqueur, best of breed is well within reach.

Artisan/ Premium
($30–$50/750 ml)

COINTREAU If our backs were up against a wall and you forced us to choose only one orange liqueur, it would be Cointreau. Not only is the balance of sweet to bitter ideal, but the clear color and clean orange flavor make it the most flexible of easy-to-get, quality triple secs.

GRAND MARNIER With its Cognac base and barrel aging, Grand Marnier, which is close in style to Dutch Curaçao, is slightly less pronounced in flavor, and certainly less clear than its triple sec cousins. That shouldn't deter you from picking up a bottle. Should you lean toward darker spirits in general, Grand Marnier will certainly please.

AN ORANGE BY ANY OTHER NAME

ORANGE LIQUEURS are a great way to experiment with the interplay of flavors and to see how a slightly different spirit (neutral in the "triple sec" style versus the brandy-based version) and a different orange character will affect a drink.

Along with the familiar names, there are many other orange-flavored liqueurs out there. Just for kicks—if you have money burning a hole in your pocket—line up a bunch of them and start mixing cocktails. When you think you have a handle on triple sec versus Curaçao, pick up a bottle of Clément Créole Shrubb, with its rhum agricole (see page 169) base. Here are a few lesser-known versions worth trying:

AURUM: An Italian brandy-based liqueur that uses an infusion of orange rind and whole oranges as well as saffron, which contributes to the vivid yellow color.

CLÉMENT CRÉOLE SHRUBB: You will see this popping up in a lot of drinks, as it is something of a bartender's darling. It gets its unique flavor profile—vanilla, pepper, chocolate, orange—from the rhum agricole, which is infused with bitter orange peels and creole spices, stored in oak casks, then sweetened with sugarcane syrup.

GRAN GALA: Hailing from Italy, Gran Gala is similar to Grand Marnier. It uses Mediterranean oranges and a brandy base, but it costs roughly half of its French cousin and is still relatively easy to come by at large chain liquor stores.

MANDARINE NAPOLEON: This Belgian liqueur uses tangerine skins, sourced exclusively from Sicilian tangerines, for a more intense tart sweetness.

VAN DER HUM: This is a South African equivalent of Curaçao, the name of which literally means "what's his name." It is made with a mandarin orange/tangerine variety known as a *naartjies* that's indigenous to South Africa and infused into Cape brandy; the flavor marries the tangerine citrus element with herbs and spices.

THE DRINKS

CURAÇAO PUNCH

GLASS: COLLINS | ICE: CRUSHED | MAKES: 1 DRINK

The first notation of this worthwhile but rarely made punch is in Harry Johnson's *New and Improved Bartender's Manual* from 1882. In the recipe notes, it suggests that you "ornament with grapes, pineapple, oranges, berries, and cherries (if in season)." One can't help but appreciate Harry's enthusiasm, as well as his admonishment that "the above drink, if mixed correctly, is very delicious." He is referring to the technique of "building" the drink in the glass, instead of mixing or shaking the components separately.

½ tablespoon granulated sugar

2 or 3 dashes strained, freshly squeezed lemon juice

1 ounce club soda

2 ounces orange liqueur

1 ounce Cognac-style brandy

½ ounce amber rum

Grapes, berries, a pineapple spear, orange slice, or cherries, for serving (but let's not get carried away)

1 Combine the sugar, lemon juice, and club soda in a collins glass and stir to combine.

2 Fill the glass with crushed ice, add the remaining ingredients, and stir well. Serve with a straw.

NAME CHANGE

COINTREAU WAS originally called "Triple Sec White Curaçao," but the distillery owners got a mite perturbed when other companies started selling their Curaçaos as "triple sec." The Cointreau boys decided that their own name was just fine, *merci beaucoup.*

11 Drinks Not to Order for
THE OPPOSITE SEX

SAM GREENSPAN, *proprietor of 11Points.com and author of the 11 Points Guide to Hooking Up, has a knack for holding up a fun-house mirror to the ordinary and revealing to us just how silly it looks. And so it was to Sam that we—happily conjugaled and long removed from the pickup scene—turned for some advice on how to appear slightly better than hapless when sidling up to an attractive stranger with the offer of a free round. Here's what he had to say:*

Unless you meet someone at an AA meeting, a Mormon church function, or during a kidney transplant, alcohol will probably show up at some point in your relationship. Perhaps every single time you get together for the first few months.

Here's some advice when you're buying someone a drink—whether it's to start a conversation at a bar, continue a conversation at a bar, or make the conversation more interesting on a date. Since the goal isn't to stifle your creativity on drink orders—you didn't buy this book so you could become a connoisseur of rum and Diet Coke—this isn't a list about what you should order. Instead, it's what you should NOT order.

1. THE CHEAPEST DRAFT BEER. There's a time and a place for Bud Light: college, sporting events, all-day beer pong tournaments, fishing, or when you're out to dinner with the Belgians who now own Anheuser-Busch. Instead, go ahead and order the second-cheapest draft beer, like Stella Artois or Bass. Yeah, they're *also* owned by those same Belgians, but at least they sound more exotic and cost one classy extra dollar.

2. BLENDED MARGARITA, especially strawberry or peach. Unless you're at a Mexican restaurant or bar, you probably shouldn't order margaritas. I'm not sure your average Irish pub has the credibility to make them (much like you wouldn't get fish and chips at a Chinese restaurant or a BLT at a Jewish deli). And when you are ordering margaritas at a Mexican restaurant, get the original gangsta version on the rocks, not the blended version that's more Slurpee than tequila.

3. SEX ON THE BEACH, LABORIOUS INTERCOURSE, SLIPPERY NIPPLE, SLOW COMFORTABLE SCREW, RED-HEADED SLUT, and so on. Full disclosure, I made one of those drinks up. All of them are too contrived to be sexually suggestive.

4. IRISH CAR BOMBS. No one looks attractive dropping a shot of Bailey's into a pint of Guinness and chugging it. You have to chug it quickly, lest the combination begin to repulsively congeal . . . and it's wildly unattractive to have motor oil–colored booze dripping from your chin as you gulp down a drink with an underratedly offensive name.

5. MOJITOS. I have many friends who are bartenders. Well . . . two. Two friends who are bartenders. But they're both quite loud and talkative, so I believe them to be a representative sample. And 100 percent of bartenders agree: Bartenders hate mojitos. They're the most labor-intensive drink (mashing the mint, mixing the variety of ingredients, shaking). So as the bartender makes you a mojito he's classifying you as a pariah, making it far more challenging to get his attention for future drinks.

6. SCREWDRIVER. This is an amateur drink. It's what a nineteen-year-old orders the first time he gets into a bar with a fake ID. If you must order a juice-plus-vodka drink, at least go with cranberry and vodka. You can always explain how it's delicious *and* fights bladder infections.

7. GRAIN ALCOHOL, 151-PROOF RUM, OR GENUINE ABSINTHE. Ostensibly you're trying to woo the other person, not kill them.

8. WELL TEQUILA. If you're going to go with tequila shots, at least have the courtesy to go with tequila shots that don't induce instant nausea. Nausea later in the night, sure. But not instant nausea.

9. SOMETHING THE BARTENDER HAS NEVER HEARD OF. There's the finest of lines between "hip" and "annoying." The cred you'd get from ordering a Furious Three will be completely shattered when the bartender says, "I don't know that one" and you're left scrambling to either shout out the ingredients or panic-order two vodka sodas.

10. RUSTY NAIL. I assume that if you're reading this book, you just gasped at the mere concept of mixing fine Scotch with another liquor and exclaimed, "Oh, my heavens" as your brandy violently swished around its snifter, nearly spilling onto your Egyptian cotton leisure robe. What if you order a Rusty Nail and get a similarly horrified reaction?

11. COSMOPOLITAN. If you're a woman, this sends a signal that you're still stuck in the *Sex and the City* tractor beam, probably as a Carrie but arguably as a Charlotte. Either way, pass. If you're a man, it sends the signal that your knowledge of women only extends to the most generic of all tropes, possibly ones you read in, coincidentally, *Cosmopolitan*.

WALDORF

GLASS: MARTINI | ICE: CRUSHED | MAKES: 1 DRINK

O ur version of the Waldorf comes not from the *Old Waldorf-Astoria Bar Book,* as you might expect, but from the *Chicago Bartenders and Beverage Dispenser's Union Local No. 278 Recipes* of 1945. It serves as a fine, and rare, example of an orange liqueur–centric cocktail. There's no denying the overt sweetness, but if you're inclined toward liquid confections, this one's for you.

2 ounces orange liqueur

1 ounce sweet vermouth

½ teaspoon Grenadine, homemade (page 376) or store-bought

Brandied Cherry (page 367) or high-quality maraschino cherry (we like Luxardo brand), for garnish

1 Combine the liqueur, vermouth, and Grenadine in a mixing glass, fill the glass three-quarters full with crushed ice, cover with a Boston shaker tin, and shake vigorously until thoroughly chilled, 15 seconds.

2 Strain into a martini glass and garnish with the cherry.

If You Don't Know the Bartender, WHAT DO YOU ORDER?

"When in doubt, I always order the simplest, most normal drink on the menu. If that comes out well, I'll try something more complex. If the place doesn't have a menu and isn't much on cocktails, I'll sometimes— if it's not too busy—ask for a slug of their best bourbon on the rocks with a couple of dashes of bitters and a splash of Grand Marnier."

—DAVID WONDRICH, COCKTAIL HISTORIAN AND AUTHOR

CHAPTER 13

Dry & Sweet Vermouth

CHAPTER 13

Dry & Sweet Vermouth

According to European law, all vermouths must contain three ingredients—wine, wormwood, and an additional spirit to fortify them. While the fortification raises the alcohol level above that normal to wine, in its heart of hearts, vermouth is more wine than spirit. It is made from grapes, then flavored with a variety of herbs, spices, flowers, and bitter roots or tree bark.

Originally a wormwood-based soporific, vermouth has been around for centuries. In his *Naturalis Historia* (circa A.D. 77), Pliny the Elder laid out a recipe for "wormwood wine," claiming it had many medical benefits. In 1660, Samuel Pepys's diary cited the popularity of—and his personal fondness for—wormwood wine, wormwood ale, and wormwood and sack (an old-fashioned term for what was essentially, but not exactly, sherry). About a century later, the Germans were chugging down wormwood wine made with the much-regaled Roman wormwood.

One of the first modern vermouths was created in 1786 by a young Italian fellow named Antonio Benedetto Carpano, who worked in a Turin wine shop where he created his own blend of aromatized wine. The wine got two thumbs-up from Duke

Dry & Sweet Vermouth IN A NUTSHELL

DEFINING FEATURES: Sweet or dry, with a clearly intentional bitterness at the center

FLAVOR PROFILE: Both white (dry) and red (sweet) are intensely herbal, sometimes floral, with a slight to strong sweet note.

WHY WE CHOSE IT: Vermouth is the salt to bitters' pepper—essential to balancing and marrying flavors in mixed drinks.

EMBLEMATIC DRINKS: Martini (dry vermouth, page 130), Manhattan (sweet vermouth, page 253)

WERMUT

THE WORD *VERMOUTH* derives from the German *wermut*, for wormwood, that notorious herbal component that caused absinthe to be banned in the States for almost a century. Wormwood, an aromatic shrub with a bitter flavor, was a major component in German fortified wines in the sixteenth century and was historically considered a medicinal aide. Contrary to popular belief (which has now been scientifically refuted), wormwood's main component, thujone, is not present in high enough doses in absinthe to cause hallucinations. Consequently, Americans once again can enjoy absinthe.

Vittorio Amedeo; presto, a simple nod from the nobility and the first commercial production of sweet vermouth began.

Not to be outdone, the French came along in 1800, eager to put their stamp on vermouth history. It was then that Joseph Noilly created the first dry vermouth, which is sometimes called French vermouth, for obvious reasons. Many others in both the red (sweet) and white (dry) categories—familiar names like Cinzano, Martini (formerly Martini & Rossi), and Dolin—followed.

No two vermouths are alike. While most cocktail folk, particularly Americans, think of vermouths as mixers, they were historically sipped on their own, which allowed for the full expression of their complexity. Particularly in Europe, Argentina, and Chile, vermouth, both dry and sweet, is still drunk as an aperitif (chiefly over ice) and, if it is a quality bottle, it can stand up to solo sipping beautifully.

Like bitters, vermouth is essential for making great mixed drinks. Granted, it is more of a "seasoning" than a main ingredient, but no bartender would do without it, just as no chef would cook in a kitchen without salt or pepper. In the drinks world, a bar without vermouth means a world without the Martini or Manhattan. And that would be a sad world indeed. If you're interested in making drinks beyond sours and highballs, you need vermouth. At approximately one-third to one-half the alcohol by volume of most spirits, vermouth can tame an otherwise unruly cocktail, giving the bigger booze a scratch behind the ears and making it purr like a kitten.

You may notice that, like the chapters on orange liqueur and bitters (our other secondary but crucial cocktail players), this chapter does not offer up a great deal in the way of recipes. We have tried to focus on drinks where the herbal or sweet notes of the vermouth are at the forefront of the drink—often because both sweet and dry varieties are used in concert, but also because the quantity of the vermouth (usually two or more ounces) is greater than any other spirit used. As to classifying the drinks by profile (sweet and fruity, tangy and citrusy, etc.), this is less essential than simply recognizing these as vermouth-based drinks.

THE BOTTLES TO BUY

There are many, many choices when it comes to vermouth. Luckily, the price difference between the swill ($5) and the good stuff ($15–$20) is not extreme. If you can afford the slightly higher price, don't skimp on vermouth; it would be akin to serving orange juice from concentrate versus freshly squeezed. The following price ranges include quality options for both dry and sweet.

Budget
($10 or less/750 ml)

NOILLY PRAT
EXTRA DRY
VERMOUTH

MARTINI SWEET
VERMOUTH

NOILLY PRAT EXTRA DRY VERMOUTH Back in 2009, Noilly Prat replaced their classic dry vermouth (sold only to the American market) with their international "aperitif-style" formula, which has a sweeter profile. The outcry was swift and, soon enough, the company brought back the pre-2009 bottling, now labeled "Extra Dry." There is still some sweetness here, but this is an infinitely serviceable vermouth at an easy price point.

MARTINI SWEET VERMOUTH Formerly Martini & Rossi, this has an almost Campari-esque bitter orange profile, which is tempered by an unmistakable sweetness. Among our choices, it's the most easygoing, offering workmanlike fortitude but lacking the complexity of the other brands. It's great in a Negroni, where that sharp character works so well.

PERFECT COCKTAILS

IF YOU'VE SPENT any time at a bar, at one point or another you've certainly heard someone ask for their drink "perfect." Are they demanding that the bartender not compromise when mixing? What does that say about the quality of *your* drink? Simmer down—a "perfect" cocktail calls for equal parts dry and sweet vermouth.

Midrange
($10–$20/750 ml)

DOLIN DRY VERMOUTH

PUNT E MES SWEET VERMOUTH

Artisan/ Premium
($20–$40/750 ml)

CARPANO ANTICA FORMULA

DOLIN DRY VERMOUTH Dolin's white wine character comes through beautifully in this bottle, but the seventeen botanicals in the blend express themselves, too. It's certainly dry, as it should be, but it is gentle, never harsh. Unlike the cheaper brands, it is enjoyable on its own over ice.

PUNT E MES SWEET VERMOUTH Punt e Mes wasn't available in the States until recently. We couldn't be happier, as it rounds out the flavors of cocktails and adds a level of complexity not found in many sweet vermouths. Rather than relying on the sweetness as its defining characteristic, it offers up intense chocolate and sour cherry notes. Originally made by the same family as Carpano Antica, it is a softer version of its big brother (see below).

CARPANO ANTICA FORMULA [SWEET] Carpano is the monster truck of sweet vermouths. It's not for everyone or every drink, but the tobacco, cinnamon, cloves, and bitter chocolate can be stellar in the right drink, like a Manhattan. What can we say? When you fall in love, you fall in love. Taste it and you too may be a convert, suddenly finding yourself rationalizing, "Well, $30 isn't really *that* much for a bottle of vermouth. . . ."

THE DRINKS

HAKAM-HICCUP

GLASS: MARTINI | ICE: CUBED | MAKES: 1 DRINK

Sweet, vermouth-heavy drinks like the Hakam-Hiccup offer much in the way of herbal, vegetal notes. Today, most imbibers aren't fans of drinks with a generous vermouth pour, but these quaffs do hold a place in the lower-alcohol corner of the mixological pantheon. We offer the H-H, courtesy of Harry McElhone's *Barflies and Cocktails,* as an example of how such a drink can succeed, especially if you employ a lighter vermouth and a higher-proof spirit.

2 ounces sweet vermouth

1 ounce dry gin

2 dashes orange liqueur

Dash orange bitters

Size Matters . . .
AND SO DOES TEMPERATURE

WE BET YOU didn't think that, when you cracked a cocktail book, you'd get not only a lecture on size, but also advice that smaller is vastly superior. At least when it comes to vermouth.

Although vermouth is fortified, it tends to oxidize and lose flavor. To counter this, always buy the smallest bottles you can find (375 ml). Though it may be costlier, it's better to buy two smaller bottles than one bigger one.

Because vermouth is essentially a wine, albeit an aromatized one, it should never be left on the countertop or bar like a bottle of spirits. Like wine, it will spoil and the flavor will change for the worse. Refrigerate always, usually for no more than a few months.

1 Combine all of the ingredients in a mixing glass, fill the glass three-quarters full with ice cubes, and stir rapidly until thoroughly chilled, 30 seconds.

2 Strain into a martini glass.

VERMOUTH DE MURE

GLASS: COLLINS | ICE: CUBED | MAKES: 1 DRINK

If you're looking for a light summer drink, dry vermouth mixed with a touch of liqueur can be a lovely solution. We've always been partial to the Vermouth Cassis, which consists solely of dry vermouth and crème de cassis, a black currant liqueur, with a lemon twist. Since we don't include the latter liqueur in our selection, we created this riff on the original drink using homemade blackberry liqueur, which has a similar flavor.

Like its inspiration, the Vermouth de Mure, whose name comes from the blackberry ("*mure*" in French) substitution, is a semisweet, vaguely herbal frolic. It is also a prime example of how to expand the repertoire of your bar while keeping within the 12-bottle framework.

3 ounces dry vermouth

½ ounce Blackberry Liqueur (page 373)

Club soda

Lemon twist, for garnish

1 Combine the vermouth and liqueur in a collins glass and add 2 or 3 ice cubes.

2 Top with club soda and stir gently to combine.

3 Garnish with the lemon twist.

"I drink to make other people more interesting."

—ERNEST HEMINGWAY

REVERSE COCKTAILS

JULIA CHILD, the doyenne of American cooking, was well known for her affection for the "Reverse Martini," five parts vermouth to one part gin. While most purists would consider these proportions an abomination, Child knew what she was doing—drinks with lower alcohol content tend to pair better with food (why we traditionally opt for wine over spirits when the entree arrives).

If you are so inclined, you can experiment with other combinations, like a Reverse Manhattan, or substitute vermouth for the spirit in drinks like the Gin and Tonic (page 115) or the Mojito (page 222). Will they taste like the original? Definitely not, but it's a fascinating exercise in flavor, not to mention a great solution for paring down the alcohol level in a drink.

THE VAMPIRE

GLASS: MARTINI, CHILLED | ICE: CUBED | MAKES: 1 DRINK

The Vampire's provenance is something of a mystery, the recipe having been scribbled on a hand-written page found tucked into a copy of a 1900 edition of *Cocktail Boothby's American Bar-Tender,* and later included in a modern reissue of the 1891 first edition of Boothby's book.

The drink is intriguing because it is the link between the old-style martini, which contained equal, minuscule parts of gin and vermouth with a dash of bitters, and the modern martini of dry gin and vermouth with no bitters. A standard garnish would be a lime twist. If the name has inspired you to serve it for Halloween, nothing but a speared garlic clove will suffice as garnish.

• •

1½ ounces dry gin

1½ ounces dry vermouth

5 drops strained, freshly squeezed lime juice

Lime twist (or garlic clove, to keep away the bloodsuckers), for garnish

1 Combine the gin, vermouth, and lime juice in a mixing glass, fill the glass three-quarters full with ice cubes, cover with a Boston shaker tin, and shake until thoroughly combined, 15 seconds.

2 Strain into a chilled martini glass and garnish with the lime or the garlic.

VICTORY

GLASS: MARTINI | ICE: CUBED | MAKES: 1 DRINK

O f the number of cocktails called Victory, we're laying odds that this is the least well known. As with the other vermouth drinks we've included, it's a light, herbal affair—although here, both vermouths are used and the herbs are tempered by citrus and sweetness. Should you have a guest who would like to participate in the evening's festivities but not the hard alcohol, the Victory offers a light, pleasing alternative.

¾ ounce dry vermouth

¾ ounce sweet vermouth

1 teaspoon strained, freshly squeezed lemon juice

1 teaspoon strained, freshly squeezed orange juice

1 teaspoon Grenadine, homemade (page 376) or store-bought

1 Combine all of the ingredients in a mixing glass, fill the glass three-quarters full with ice cubes, cover with a Boston shaker tin, and shake vigorously until thoroughly chilled, 15 seconds.

2 Strain into a martini glass.

VERMOUTH HOUR

IN ARGENTINA AND Chile, vermouth is such a favored son that the cocktail hour is called "La hora del vermut."

CHAPTER 14

Aromatic & Orange Bitters

I n the early days of America, there wasn't a pharmacy on every street corner. Medicine was simple and often archaic—laudanum, mustard plaster, gentian violet, and bitters. Back then, bitters were sold by snake oil salesmen who hawked their cure-all capability for everything from dropsy to indigestion. Prospectors and cowboys could have made their own from roots, seeds, bark, and flowers, whatever they found in the wild.

I n their most basic form, all bitters still conform to the old-style recipes, which require various flavorings (usually herbal, fruity, or floral) plus a bittering agent and alcohol. The resulting product is approximately 45% ABV. In this era of the cocktail renaissance, it seems that a new bitters company is popping up every day.

When it comes to bitters, it's all in the name. If you taste bitters directly from the bottle, you realize just how bitter these cocktail accents can be. Solo, they are by turns aggressive, harsh, and alcoholic, but in drinks—where they are used in relatively infinitesimal amounts—they make the spirits come alive, much like seasoning does in cooking.

In the modern era, bitters have become much more

Aromatic & Orange Bitters
IN A NUTSHELL

DEFINING FEATURES: Bitter with an alcoholic kick

FLAVOR PROFILE: By turns intensely herbal or fruity

WHY WE CHOSE IT: Bitters are like pepper for drinks.

EMBLEMATIC DRINKS: Since bitters are essentially cocktail seasoning, there are no drinks that truly feature them. However neither the original Cocktail (page 309) nor the Old Fashioned (page 229) would exist without them.

sophisticated: Examples include classics like orange, Angostura, and Peychaud's; modern re-creations of old formulas featuring dandelion and burdock root; and more esoteric variations like Bittermens' cacao- and spice-spiked Xocolatl Mole Bitters.

THE BITTER LIFE

We adore bitters. Using them is one of the easiest and most subtle ways to change a cocktail's profile. And since they're relatively inexpensive, they're a great way to beef up your arsenal of variations. Many a cocktail has been given a different name simply because the bitters were switched out. While we suggest only two styles (see page 5) in keeping with the 12 Bottle philosophy, you might become a bitters junkie yourself once you start to experiment.

Our two bitters choices are perhaps predictable, but they're central to making most classic cocktails. While there is no reason not to experiment with every bitters bottle you can get your hands on, we find that, if pushed against a wall with a cocktail glass shoved in our face, we will add a couple dashes of either aromatic or orange bitters.

> We adore bitters. Using them is one of the easiest and most subtle ways to change a cocktail's profile.

What's the difference? If there is a predominant style of bitters, it's the aromatic kind—think Angostura and Peychaud's—which builds its profile around bitter roots such as gentian, herbs, barks, and forward spice notes. In orange bitters we find pronounced bitter orange peel and Asian spices such as mace and cardamom, which give them a warm roundness that brighten up the cocktails in which they are used.

HOW TO USE BITTERS

Despite all sharing a bitter component, bitters vary by style and producer. It's worth taking some time to learn what you have, and we have just the man to guide you on the journey. While toiling away as a bartender in Edinburgh, Scotland, Adam Elmegirab made a name for himself by chronicling his journey through every recipe in Jerry Thomas's definitive 1862 tome, *How to Mix Drinks*. Thomas's recipes often call for products no longer available, such as various bitters. Adam (going by the name Dr. Adam Elmegirab) was one of the first enterprising bartenders to venture into producing his own bitters, starting with Boker's Bitters, moving on to Dandelion and Burdock Bitters (based on a British drink from the 1300s), and continually expanding his range.

Adam offers the following pointers:

1 SAMPLE BITTERS dashed into soda water, onto a sugar cube, or in a neutral long drink like a Vodka and Tonic to understand what flavors are present in your brand and style.

2 PICK OUT KEY FLAVORINGS or botanicals present in bitters and look to match them with flavors found in the spirit you're using or the ingredients you're mixing it with. Note the key flavorings in each (base spirit and bitters), then search the Web or use your own knowledge to pair flavors.

3 DON'T BE AFRAID to substitute different bitters in the same cocktail recipe, as each type will enhance and complement different flavors. The same drink, let's say a Whiskey Sour, will taste completely different depending on the bitters you use.

4 BE LIBERAL. Just because a recipe calls for 2 dashes doesn't mean you can't add 6 if that's your preference!

5 USE BITTERS IN FOOD to gain a better understanding of what they bring to the table. You essentially have a bottle of liquid spice (at the opposite end of the spectrum from soy sauce or Worcestershire sauce) and it can do wondrous things in dressings, marinades, sauces, or even dashed over ice cream, sorbet, and such.

THE BOTTLES TO BUY

Again, there's a panoply of flavors when it comes to bitters, but ours being, for the most part, a classically styled bar, we've opted for the big-time bitters players here: aromatic and orange. When it comes to aromatic bitters, we find that the original, Angostura, are still the best. Created by Dr. Johann Siegert as a medicinal aide to the Bolivian army, Angostura bitters found their way into cocktails through drinks like Pink Gin, originally drunk as a sort of alcohol-enhanced tonic.

Orange bitters have been around for just about as long as Angostura; the bitters-making Fee Brothers were in business in the 1860s. If you take a gander in a few cocktail books from the late 1800s, you will see references to orange bitters throughout. They were—and are— truly a workhorse.

Budget
($10 or less/
sizes vary)

AROMATIC

ANGOSTURA AROMATIC BITTERS As we mentioned, these were developed in 1824 by Dr. Siegert, who was based in the town of Angostura, Venezuela, as the surgeon general to Simon Bolivar's army. Siegert's bitters were originally used to treat scurvy and sea sickness. Today, they are the hallmark bitters in most cocktails, although artisanal bitters are making more and more customized appearances. The flavor of Angostura is what helps make an Old Fashioned an Old Fashioned and Pink Gin pink. It's herbal, slightly medicinal, a little spicy, and irreplaceable.

ORANGE

FEE BROTHERS WEST INDIAN ORANGE BITTERS If you like your orange bitters not too bitter at all, then you may like Fee's, which are almost Orange Crush–like in nature. (Compare them to Regan's, opposite, which seem to embody the term *bitter*.) The company has been making orange bitters since the nineteenth century.

Tip:
USING 50/50 ORANGE BITTERS

THIS "TRICK OF the trade" is a go-to combo for many bartenders. When a recipe calls for orange bitters, we often mix half Regan's and half Fee's. The resulting blend of flavors is balanced and complex, adding a bit of extra zing where needed.

Midrange
($13–20/
150–250 ml bottle)

ORANGE

REGAN'S

AROMATIC

DALE
DEGROFF'S

REGAN'S ORANGE BITTERS Before the cocktail resurgence, orange bitters were one of many long-lost ingredients. When drinks guru and bartender gaz regan couldn't find an orange bitters to use in cocktails, he made his own. If we can choose only one orange bitters, we feel that Regan's offer the best all-around flavor with a brightness all their own.

DALE DEGROFF'S PIMENTO AROMATIC BITTERS Like gaz regan, bartender Dale DeGroff has jumped into the ring with his own bitters and we love them. His concept for the flavor was inspired by pimento dram, an intensely flavored allspice liqueur. We find his bitters, while clearly in the aromatic camp, to be a cross between Angostura and Peychaud's, which has a dominant licorice element.

EVEN MORE BITTERS

BELOW IS A selection of alternative bitters companies to check out. No descriptions here. We'll let you do the legwork—it's half the fun.

Bar Keep Bitters	Bittermens Bitters	Dr. Adam Elmegirab's Bitters
Berg & Hauck	Bob's Bitters	
The Bitter End	Boudreau's Cocktail Bitters	Fee Brothers
Bitter Tears		Miracle Mile Bitters Co.
Bittered Sling	Brooklyn Hemispherical Bitters	
Bitters, Old Men		Peychaud's
Bittercube		Scrappy's Bitters

THE DRINKS

Frankly, there really isn't such a thing as a "bitters drink." After all, as we have stated, bitters are not the key ingredient. They are the extra something that makes many individual drinks unique. So what you'll see here is the Cocktail—capital "C," mind you—which is defined by only four ingredients, bitters being essential; and the Trinidad Sour, a sort of cocktail in reverse where the bitters purposely take center stage.

"Livy, my darling, I want you to be sure & remember to have, in the bath-room when I arrive, a bottle of Scotch whisky, a lemon, some crushed sugar, & a bottle of *Angostura bitters*. Ever since I have been in London I have taken in a wine-glass what is called a cocktail (made with those ingredients) before breakfast, before dinner, & just before going to bed. It was recommended by the surgeon of the 'City of Chester' & was a most happy thought."

—MARK TWAIN, IN A LETTER TO HIS WIFE, OLIVIA L. CLEMENS, JANUARY 2, 1874

COCKTAIL

GLASS: ROCKS | ICE: 1 LARGE CUBE (OPTIONAL) | MAKES: 1 DRINK

This is it, the big daddy of all mixed drinks, the one that lent its name to the whole kingdom—the Cocktail. The first printed mentions of the Cocktail appear in the early nineteenth century (or late eighteenth, if you're open for an argument), and the drink was a morning bracer. Some "medicinal" bitters, a good dose of alcohol (it kills bacteria, after all), and a spoonful of sugar to help it all go down. Now, that's a way to start the day.

If you've never compounded a proper Cocktail before, do it. In just one attempt you'll further your understanding of drink far more than by plunking down $70 for a bottle of South African elephant liqueur.

· ·

1 teaspoon light brown or raw sugar, such as Demerara

1 or 2 dashes aromatic bitters

1 teaspoon water

1½ ounces brandy, dry gin, genever, amber or white rum, or rye whiskey

· ·

1 Place the sugar in a rocks glass. Dash the bitters directly onto the sugar and muddle them together.

2 Add the water and stir to dissolve the sugar as much as possible.

3 Add a single large ice cube, if you like, then the spirit, and stir gently to combine.

TRINIDAD SOUR

GLASS: MARTINI | ICE: CUBED | MAKES: 1 DRINK

N ew York–based bartender Giuseppe Gonzalez's Trinidad Sour, which is a riff on the Trinidad Especial (bitters, almond-flavored syrup, lime, and the grape brandy–based Pisco Mistral), is a work of either modern genius or madness, depending on how much you like bitters. Continuing the "reverse" cocktail theme that's becoming more prevalent these days (see page 299), we've included the drink not only because it's tasty but also because it offers a brilliant example of thinking differently when it comes to crafting drinks. Don't be limited by what you see in a recipe, invent something new—well, delicious and new.

••

1 ounce aromatic bitters

1 ounce Orgeat Syrup, preferably homemade (page 379)

¾ ounce strained, freshly squeezed lemon juice

½ ounce rye whiskey

••

1 Combine all of the ingredients in a mixing glass, fill the glass three-quarters full with ice cubes, cover with a Boston shaker tin, and shake vigorously until thoroughly chilled, 15 seconds.

2 Strain into a martini glass.

DIGESTIVE BITTERS

WHILE SIMILAR TO aromatic bitters like Angostura, digestive bitters should not be confused with them in use or style. Where aromatic bitters add a subtle, often essential, flavor kick to cocktails, they must be used judiciously, in drops rather than ounces. Digestive bitters are consumed, logically, as a digestif at the end of a meal and, in some cases, as an aperitif before. They can be drunk solo, as they are essentially a liqueur, or mixed with something like club soda for an invigorating cooler. Made by macerating a proprietary mix of herbs, flowers, roots, bark, and sometimes citrus peel in alcohol, they include sugar syrup—which is never used in aromatics bitters—to take off the edge.

Most people are familiar with the German-made Jägermeister, which embodies the bold, bittersweet flavors of a classic digestif and has been appropriated by frat boys everywhere. In Italy, digestive bitters are legendary, and have a name of their own: *amari*. They range from the bitter orange Aperol to the more aggressive Cynar, the central component of which is artichoke (although it doesn't really taste like the spiky thistle at all).

And what of Campari with its famous bitter-orange-meets-cough-syrup flavor? Because it is usually drunk with a mixer, many people balk at the "digestif" classification, but it is surely a bitters of sorts.

All digestive bitters are an acquired taste, often more challenging for sugar-saturated American palates than for those of other nations, where bitter flavors are more readily embraced. Still, if you tend to overindulge at dinner, or want to tinker with your drinks in interesting ways, digestive bitters are worth exploring, as they each have a unique profile and are popping up more and more in cocktail recipes and bars around the country.

Some Other Digestive Bitters to Try

AMER PICON (FRANCE): The pronounced orange flavor makes this a natural addition to cocktails.

AVERNA (SICILY): Orange rind, herbs, and roots create a sweet, thick digestif with a bitter back note.

FERNET-BRANCA (ITALY): Brace yourself for this spirit's intense anise and cough syrup kick.

SUZE (FRANCE): This is uniquely flavored by gentian root, a wild, bitter herb.

PUTTING *it all* TOGETHER

CHAPTER 15

On Being a Good Host

You've learned how to make cocktails! Now what? Well, if you've come this far, you've read a bunch of drink recipes and hopefully made one or two of them in the solitude of your kitchen. Congratulations—you're halfway there.

Why only halfway? Because making drinks without sharing them is missing the point. Once you've learned the notes and practiced the melody, it's time for the recital. Cocktails are a social lubricant, and there's no better way to show off your skills than to throw a cocktail party. It's also a lot cheaper—and potentially less embarrassing—than spontaneously leaping behind the stick at your local faux speakeasy and screaming, "Who's ready for pousse-cafés?!" We don't judge; we've been there.

What follow are some key tips and sage advice on how to throw a cocktail party and guarantee its success.

HOW TO THROW A PARTY

Anyone can throw a party. Not everyone can do it well and live to tell the tale, but we're here to help you hedge your bets. You may consider what follows as a survival guide. We consider it just being a good host.

Luckily, throwing a party is a lot like riding a bike. Once you've learned how to do it, you never forget. Since you are reading this book, we can safely assume that you enjoy entertaining, whether it's for a few or for a multitude of guests. That said, there are some basic rules that make hosting any gathering a lot more enjoyable for everyone involved. Some of them we have learned from painful trial and error; some are simply the advice of trusted fellow party-throwing imbibers.

KNOW THE OCCASION

Is it summer or winter? Morning or evening? Girl's Night or Halloween? Elements like these are key to party planning because they determine the choice of food—and the choice of food (or lack thereof) determines the drink selection. Mother's Day brunch does not call for a

Manhattan; a French 75 would seem out of place at a Fourth of July BBQ (wait a week or so and break it out for Bastille Day).

Here are some basic pointers to keep in mind (and for some thematic drink suggestions, see pages 394 to 397).

IF DRINKS ARE THE FOCUS If you're throwing a traditional cocktail party—one without a full meal—you have a lot more flexibility and can create a cocktail menu with plenty of choices, both thematically and in terms of spirits. Sweet, dry, tart, strong—they all will work. Having said that, strong drinks present two key problems: Your guests are much more likely to get bombed (and much more quickly), and you'll burn through your stash much faster. Consider instead highballs or other drinks with a larger proportion of mixer. They take longer to drink, you can cut back on the booze, and your guests are less likely to wake up in your rosebushes.

> Consider highballs. They take longer to drink, you can cut back on the booze, and your guests are less likely to wake up in your rosebushes.

IF FOOD IS THE FOCUS Before eating, avoid sweeter drinks and focus on dry cocktails, which prime the palate for the meal ahead. Also, don't put too much focus on hard alcohol, as it offers the one-two punch of deadening the taste buds and getting you lit a bit too fast. We know, the steak-martini combo is a classic; we are just telling you what you don't want to hear. Prior to a meal, opt for drinks that are lighter and more tart, such as a collins or sour, which stimulate the taste buds and prime the stomach for food. Taking the extra step to pair the flavor profile of the drinks with the food to come—skip the Gin and Tonic before the spice-rubbed ribs and grab a Rye Buck—is also sound advice.

ON BEING A GOOD GUEST

"Contribute to the party or bar in one of three ways—
good looks, conversation, or cash."

—AIDAN DEMAREST, BAR OWNER AND CONSULTANT

BUT WHEN CAN I BREAK OUT THE HARD LIQUOR? Poker night, reading *Pale Fire* by the fire, before your first bungee jump, after your first bungee jump, and at any bar in Arizona.

CONSIDER YOUR GUESTS

For every cocktail lover, there is someone who is either scared of, doesn't like, or can't drink hard alcohol. Be mindful of that. A good host thinks of the guests first. Following is what you *must* have on hand at any party.

NONALCOHOLIC DRINKS Delicious drinking water is the greatest, cheapest gift this planet has to offer. It's essential not only to our survival but also to stave off the next day's hangover. Give your guests the ability to hydrate frequently and encourage them to do so by placing large pitchers of water, perhaps with citrus or cucumber floating in them for visual appeal, in strategic locations.

Offer something nonalcoholic that is as attractive as your handcrafted cocktails. Make it look like a cocktail and, if you're mixing, put as much care into its assembly. (We've given you a bunch of tempting virgin options—many of which can be spiked if you want them to do double duty—in chapter 17.) Try to encourage the diet soda-totalers to give it a try, but make sure to have diet soda on hand in case they pass.

LOW-ALCOHOL DRINKS Beer, wine, and hard cider pack less of a wallop (and make delicious cocktails of their own—see chapter 16). Keep them nearby. They also allow guests to self-serve, something you'll quickly come to appreciate after being trapped in the kitchen making drinks and missing your own party.

FOOD Even if it's a bag of chips, do not serve alcohol without food. You're not sixteen, and your parents aren't away for the weekend. Booze without food is not only irresponsible, but it breaks the number-one rule of being a good host: Take care of your guests.

COMMON SENSE Know when to cut a guest off and be prepared to do it. If they're truly a friend, they'll thank you in the morning (well, maybe not the next morning). When someone's had too much, steer them toward a nonalcoholic drink or engage them in conversation.

Have them sit down and let them rant. Not only will you be putting them in a place where they're more likely to stay put (inertia is your friend), you might gain a juicy bit of gossip or two (which you will never spread, of course).

KEEP IT SIMPLE

Preparation and control are two of the bywords of successful party planning. We never throw a party without thoughtful planning beforehand. This doesn't mean you have a lot of sleepless nights ahead of you, but it does mean that you need to be organized and insightful. With a food-based party, the key is balancing the workload with make-ahead dishes and on-the-spot preparations. Cocktail parties follow the same rules. Here are some ways to organize your beverage selection and preparation.

CREATE A LIMITED MENU Remember those college parties with the booze scattered across a countertop? That's a recipe for disaster. Choose the booze and you are in control of the party, your pocketbook, and, to some extent, your guests. Some options:

Feature a single spirit and ask your guests to bring bottles of that spirit, potluck style. Before the party choose four to six drinks featuring that spirit and let everyone try them with each of the bottles your guests brought (be sure to contribute one or more bottles of your own). This also allows you to select food that pairs well with the spirit.

> Choose the booze and you are in control of the party, your pocketbook, and, to some extent, your guests.

Choose ingredients that work in many drinks. For a sour, you need citrus and sugar. For a buck, you need citrus and ginger beer. Add in bottles of rye, sweet vermouth, and aromatic bitters, and you have a menu of Rye Bucks, Whiskey Sours, and Manhattans. Add gin, and you have Gin Bucks, Gin Sours, Fitzgeralds, and Pink Gin.

Best of all, a limited menu will keep the evening focused on the drinks you know, sidelining requests for "Screaming Vikings." Print out two versions of the menu. Put one on the bar for your guests. Put one behind the bar with recipes for you, or whoever is mixing the drinks. There is no shame in referring to a recipe. What is embarrassing is serving an improperly mixed drink.

CONSIDER BATCHED AND EASY-TO-ASSEMBLE DRINKS   This goes back to preparation. If you don't want to be stuck behind the bar—a mistake we have made more than once—then batched and easy-to-assemble drinks such as punches or even martinis are the way to go (see page 398).

If you're keen on showing off your mixological talents, consider dedicating part of your menu to batch-made drinks, which guests can serve for themselves. At worst, you'll need to ladle from a bowl into a glass—a bartending skill we're confident you can master. With one or two drinks premade, you can then shake or stir one more challenging specialty drink to your heart's content.

> Simply pour some booze into a glass, top it with a mixer, and let the drinks do most of the work for you.

Highball-type drinks, such as various bucks or Gin and Tonic, are another way to go. Any drink that doesn't require juicing citrus (though this can be done ahead of time, see page 65), shaking, or stirring is going to be much easier and quicker to make. If you're not confident in your skills, simply pour some booze into a glass, top it with a mixer, and let the drinks do most of the work for you.

BE PREPARED

When it comes to throwing a party, planning is everything. And planning includes a healthy dose of math. Luckily for you, making drinks is the easy addition, subtraction, and binomial distribution kind of math. Except for that last part. Once you know the math behind your bottles, drinks, and glassware, you can do extensive critical preparation well in advance of your party.

DOING THE DRINK MATH   A standard liquor bottle holds 25 ounces. The typical cocktail has roughly 1½ to 2 ounces of base spirit. This comes out to 12½ to 16½ drinks per bottle, meaning that for a party of thirty, you'll need two to four bottles of gin. Knowing how many drinks you'll get out of a bottle is key to buying booze for your party. It's always good to overbuy a little bit, especially if it's a bottle you don't mind having on hand.

How many will you need? A rough assumption is one drink per guest per hour, with a cap of 4 ounces per person. Four ounces isn't a hard cap, but it's a practical one—no one really needs (or should have) more than 4 ounces of booze in a night. The number of drinks per person is across all drinks offered, but some will be more popular than others. And of course, some guests won't imbibe, so you'll need to account for them. Ultimately, it's about knowing your crowd, and if you don't know your crowd, err on the side of generosity. It's also good to know in advance if your state or local retailer has a liquor return policy. If returns aren't an option and you have leftovers, then consider that an excuse for another party.

THE DRINKS MENU

As mentioned, a predesigned menu can be your best friend. With a menu before you, you can compute how much hard liquor, mixers, fruit, juice, and syrups you will need.

TAKE CONTROL OF YOUR COSTS If cost matters, choose spirits or brands accordingly. Further, the style of drink matters. Sours are a great party choice because half the drink is citrus juice and Simple Syrup. Likewise, bucks are mostly ginger beer. While we love a classic Cocktail (page 309), in a party situation, many people can be left feeling a little underwhelmed when they are handed 2 ounces of liquid in a 10-ounce glass.

HAVE EVERYTHING READY Premake your simple syrups, juice your citrus, lay out your equipment, and set out (clean!!) glassware about an hour before the party starts. Keep your bar space cozy with everything in arm's reach—too much room breeds chaos. Keep your guests in front of the bar—whether it's a real in-home bar or your dining room table—where they can watch you and chat with one another.

A note on garnishes: Garnishes dry out quickly, so don't slice citrus until you have to and keep garnishes simple for ease of preparation.

LOCATION, LOCATION, LOCATION

Why is it that guests tend to congregate in the kitchen at almost every party? The reason is simple—it's usually where the action is. The host is prepping, the food is cooking, the drinks are being mixed.

Think about traffic flow and choose your bar area accordingly to allow easy access to you and your guests. If a meal or complex

ON BEING A GOOD GUEST

A GOOD GUEST:

- will simply never drink to the point where he or she couldn't make a life-or-death decision.
- seeks to bring people together in meaningful discussion, without providing soapboxes and hobbyhorses for those debaters whose minds are already made up.
- would do her best to minimize jealousy and violence over mates, and stand up on the side of an underdog in the endless give-and-take of the rules of the community that are being written at any party.
- listens more than talks, and talks on the side of those who are shouted down.
- spends as she can afford to on ales and tips and cabs, but does not go into debt unless it's for a good reason.
- takes free offers (of drinks) reluctantly but graciously, and never mentions them again, except in her reciprocity.

A good guest in a drinking establishment never forgets just what bad things have happened unpunished in such establishments. He must never lose sight of his responsibilities as a man or woman to protect the weak from the mob and the bully. And to protect the Suicide from himself. The bartender is ultimately responsible, of course, but the guest in the bar is an able-bodied seaman on the Captain's ship. He will follow the bartender's lead as far as his conscience will allow, and if he can no longer, he will act unilaterally and deal with whatever consequences may arise. Fundamentally, no one hurts anyone in the bar without your passive participation.

**—SASHA PETRASKE,
BARTENDER AND BAR OWNER**

---

appetizers are being made, do not put the bar in the kitchen. If you have to, reorganize your furniture to encourage better flow. If you're doing hors d'oeuvres, serve them as far away from the bar as is practical—this will help spread out your traffic.

The "feng shui" of a party is essential. Clear away any little knickknacks. Put out coasters and napkins in easily accessible spots. Provide a centrally located trash can. And if you have a Tiffany lamp or a special vase from Auntie June, put it away—then you won't worry about it.

ABOVE ALL ELSE, BE A GREAT HOST

Throwing a party is enjoyable—but serious—business. While your guests are in your home, you are responsible for them, their enjoyment, and their well-being. For the duration of the party, you are not just their bestie, you are their host.

By the end of the evening, you should have your eye on each and every guest, sizing up their ability to get home safely. Call a taxi, offer a couch or bed if a guest clearly cannot travel, and call later that night or the next morning to follow up with your friends to be sure they arrived home safely (or ask them to call you). As a host, insisting on your guests' safety isn't rude or pushy, it's common sense.

Hopefully, as you look back on your party, you will feel the sense of satisfaction that comes from a job well done. And hopefully, your guests will appreciate your efforts. Remember your guests, and your guests will remember your party.

CHAPTER 16

Beer, Wine & Cider Drinks

You may be asking yourself—or anxious to ask us—why a book espousing a 12 bottle bar includes beer, wine, and cider drinks. Our rationale, which we hope you'll accept, is that most people interested in cocktails will typically have beer or wine on hand. Cider may not be as common, but it's too agreeable as a cocktail ingredient to leave out.

BEGINNING WITH BEER

Prehistoric tribes may have brewed beer before they learned bread making. Noah had it on the ark. George Washington made his own. Entire books have been written on the history of beer alone, and for good reason. It is likely to be the world's first fermented beverage and, as a starting point, it is an essential base, along with wine, for almost every spirit made.

Historically, beer drinks are far older than spirits. Harry Potter's favorite tipple, Buttered Beere (page 332), dates back to the 1580s. In modern culture, people don't often think of beer as a typical cocktail base, but the variety of flavor profiles and intensities makes it a very flexible ingredient, which explains why beer cocktails are enjoying a renaissance.

A WORD ON WINE

In this book, we call for three types of wine: white, red, and sparkling. The first two are chiefly employed in sangrias and glöggs (hot sangrias), with red also pinch-hitting as a float atop a couple of traditional cocktails. Sparkling wine, on the other hand, sees a good deal more use, and if you keep only one item in your fridge—food included—that item should be a bottle of decent Champagne or sparkling wine (see box, page 339).

CONSIDER CIDER

Y ou may see hard cider called for in old-school drink recipes. The term "hard" generally implies that alcohol is involved, at least on American and Canadian labels. Plain cider is the kid-friendly version.

Cider (without the *hard*), as it is labeled outside of North America, is immensely popular in Europe, particularly in France and Germany. Calvados is made from cider; American apple brandy and applejack (once as popular as rye) are as well. Similar in style is pear cider— perry in the UK, *poiré* in France.

Ciders vary from dry to sweet, can be cloudy or clear, and either sparkling (more common) or still. Taste a few to discover what flavor profile you prefer. And by all means, drink them straight, too; they work as a lovely, lower-alcohol stand-in for beer, fruity white wines, and Champagne.

Some of our recommendations are:

ANGRY ORCHARD APPLE CIDER (USA) Available in both sweet and dry versions, this is a good all-around choice, as it offers a pleasing middle ground in flavor.

ASPALL DRY ENGLISH DRAFT CIDER (ENGLAND) While we'll readily admit that this funky bottle comes rife with images of overripe (even spoiled) fruit, there's no denying that Aspall is one of the best cocktail mixing ciders.

CRISPIN "THE SAINT" (BELGIUM) With a touch of molasses, this cider is fruity and yeasty in flavor. You will love or hate this one, but it consistently ranks at the top of many people's list.

WANDERING AENGUS WANDERLUST (USA) Made from heirloom apple varieties, this Oregon cider is crisp, green-apple tart, and bears a vintage date.

WOODCHUCK AMBER DRAFT CIDER (USA) Just like the kids' stuff, but with a kick. Slightly sweet, with a bit of spice to it.

THE DRINKS

Beer

BLUE HARVEST

GLASS: ROCKS | ICE: CRUSHED | MAKES: 1 DRINK

We created the Blue Harvest chiefly out of necessity. Asked to host an event for a friend while keeping the budget low, we needed a drink with mass appeal, easy assembly, and as we said, a low cost. Eschewing hard liquor, we reached for a supermarket beer, inexpensive vermouth, and some quick-as-a-wink homemade spice syrup.

The resulting ersatz nineteenth-century "punch" brings out the best in all of its components—it's bitter and sweet, with lots of depth. It not only satisfies the cocktail drinker and the beer enthusiast alike, but also can be thrown together with little preparation. If you make a batch, and you should (scale as needed), don't worry about the beer going flat—you're after the flavor, not the bubbles, and the drink should be long gone before flatness sets in anyway.

• •

4 ounces Blue Moon Wheat Ale (or other wheat beer)

2 ounces sweet vermouth

1 ounce Harvest Spice Syrup (recipe follows)

Fresh whole nutmeg, for garnish (optional; see Note, page 70)

• •

1 Combine the ale, vermouth, and syrup in a rocks glass and stir gently.

2 Fill the glass with crushed ice. Garnish with a grating of nutmeg, if desired.

Harvest Spice Syrup

MAKES: ABOUT 2 CUPS

2 cups light brown or raw
sugar, such as Demerara

¼ teaspoon ground cinnamon

¼ teaspoon ground ginger

¼ teaspoon ground cloves

1 cup water

1 Combine all of the ingredients in a small saucepan over low heat and stir to dissolve the sugar. Remove from the heat.

2 Allow the syrup to cool to room temperature, transfer to an airtight container, and refrigerate. The syrup will keep, covered and refrigerated, for several weeks.

BROWN BETTY

GLASS: PUNCH | ICE: CUBED (OPTIONAL) | MAKES: 6 DRINKS

Should you have found yourself haunting the halls of the University of Oxford circa 1820, you likely would have enjoyed punting along the river Cherwell while drinking a bottle of Brown Betty. This perfect summer quaff is reputedly named for a university chambermaid of the era, who recommended it for just about any imaginable malady.

A good-quality Extra Special/Strong Bitter or similar style beer is in order here, lest the beer get lost in the brandy and lemon. Let the Betty rest for a day and it will go down even more smoothly—but be careful, the brandy will sneak up on you.

1 cup firmly packed light
brown sugar

2 cups water

1 lemon, sliced, plus extra
lemon slices for garnish

8 ounces Cognac-style brandy

16 ounces real ale, preferably
ESB (see page 333)

1 teaspoon ground cloves

1 teaspoon ground cinnamon

1 teaspoon ground ginger

Fresh whole nutmeg,
for garnish (see Note,
page 70)

1 Combine the sugar and water in a medium bowl and stir to dissolve the sugar.

2 Add the sliced lemon and let the mixture infuse, 15 minutes.

3 Add the brandy, ale, and spices and stir to combine.

Refrigerate until well chilled, 3 hours.

4 Serve in individual punch glasses with ice cubes, if you wish. Garnish each glass with a lemon slice and a grating of nutmeg.

Great Bars
THEN & NOW

THE GUINNESS BAR | CASHEL PALACE HOTEL |
MAIN STREET | CASHEL, COUNTY TIPPERARY, IRELAND |
+353/(0)-62-62707 | CASHEL-PALACE.IE/GUINNESS-BAR

IT WAS IN the town of Cashel, Ireland, that St. Patrick is said to have introduced Christianity to the country. Legend has it that wherever he stepped, a shamrock grew. A more tangible legend can be found in the Guinness Bar at the Cashel Palace Hotel. There, on August 17, 1740, Richard Guinness, the future father of Arthur (who founded the eponymous brewery) and overseer of the brewing for the local archbishop, is said to have created Guinness Stout. The original hops plant harvested by Richard Guinness still exists on the hotel grounds.

If you are lucky enough, as we were some years back, to find your way to the Cashel Palace's Guinness Bar, you will hear this story firsthand courtesy of longtime bartender Denis Heffernan. Not only will Denis regale you with tales of his forty-plus years bartending—he has served everyone from Richard Harris to Priscilla Presley, John Wayne to Ronald Reagan—but he will also pour you the most perfect pint of Guinness you have ever tasted, while noting its "health-giving" properties. If he is in top form, he may even break into a rendition of "Danny Boy."

BUTTERED BEERE

GLASS: HEATPROOF MUGS | MAKES: 9 DRINKS

When you need a break from studying for your O.W.L.s or a liquid respite from Mundania, here we offer real Buttered Beere. This isn't some theme-park confection, it's our adaptation—with the help of noted food historian and author Professor Ken Albala—of Thomas Dawson's recipe from *The Good Huswifes Handmaide for the Kitchin* (1588).

If five egg yolks and twelve tablespoons of butter don't give you an idea of how this tastes, we'll tell you that it's a rich, spicy time-trip back to the age of the Bard. (Make it with "real ale"—see opposite—for the most traditional expression.) As Will Shakespeare himself said of Buttered Beere, "O! she's warm. If this be magic, let it be an art. Lawful as eating." Or was that Harry Potter?

3 bottles (16.9 ounces each) real ale

½ teaspoon ground cloves

½ teaspoon ground cinnamon

¼ teaspoon ground ginger

Yolks from 5 large eggs

1 cup light brown or raw sugar, such as Demerara

¾ cup (1½ sticks) unsalted butter

1 Combine the ale and spices in a large saucepan over high heat. Bring to a boil, then immediately reduce the heat to the lowest setting to keep the mixture warm.

2 Combine the egg yolks and sugar in a medium bowl and beat until creamy, about 45 seconds.

3 Remove the saucepan from the heat and whisk in the egg mixture. Return the saucepan to low heat and whisk constantly until the mixture begins to thicken slightly, about 5 minutes.

4 Remove from the heat and quickly whisk in the butter until a nice foam forms. Serve warm in mugs.

REAL ALE

"REAL ALE" IS a British term coined by the Campaign for Real Ale (CAMRA) in 1971 to differentiate between artisan brews and the less unique, mass-marketed ones. The hallmark of real ale is that it is made the old-fashioned way, undergoing a secondary fermentation in a cask or bottle. Because of its handcrafted nature, real ale requires special care and trained staff to produce a perfect pint. When shopping for real ale in stores, look for the term "bottle-conditioned."

Recent CAMRA, Gold Medal winning, bottle-conditioned beers include the following:

- Embra (Stewart Brewing)
- Proper Job (St. Austell Brewery)
- Admiral's Ale (St. Austell Brewery)
- Titanic Stout (Titanic Brewery)
- Dorothy Goodbody's Wholesome Stout (Wye Valley Brewery)
- Original Port Stout (O'Hanlon's Brewing)
- Worthington White Shield Silver (Molson Coors)

CERVEZA PREPARADA

GLASS: COLLINS, CHILLED | ICE: CUBED | MAKES: 1 DRINK

Should you be up for a little extra zip in your *cerveza*, skip the artificial commercial brews and opt for this hot-weather stalwart from down Mexico way. The only thing that could make this most basic "prepared beer"—often called a Chelada—better is a pair of flip-flops and an ocean view.

Kosher salt, for rimming the glass

1 lime

1 bottle (12 ounces) cold lager

1 Cover a small plate with salt to a depth of ¼ inch. Cut a small wedge from the lime and halve it widthwise. Run a cut edge of the lime around the outer rim of a chilled collins glass to dampen it. Roll the glass in the salt to coat the outer rim.

2 Fill the prepared glass half full with ice cubes and juice the lime into the glass.

3 Pour the beer into the glass from high up, allowing the drink to mix naturally.

VARIATIONS

Add hot sauce, Worcestershire, or Maggi, a seasoning sauce popular in Mexico, to taste.

··

THAI CHELADA

GLASS: COLLINS, CHILLED | ICE: CUBED | MAKES: 1 DRINK

Maybe we're crazy, but something about the light beer–clam-tomato combination hawked at Los Angeles-area gas stations doesn't get our motors revving. The Thai Chelada takes that popular Michelada, returns it to its handmade roots, and adopts a wholly foreign culture—namely, the spicy and bright flavors of Thailand, which perfectly pair with a crisp Mexican-style lager such as Bohemia. This one is equally at home on game day or alongside a plate of garlic shrimp.

··

Kosher salt, for rimming the glass

Lime wedge

Handful of fresh basil leaves

1 recipe Thai Chelada Mix (recipe follows)

1 ounce strained, freshly squeezed lime juice

6 ounces lager, chilled

··

1 Cover a small plate with the salt to a depth of ¼ inch. Halve the lime widthwise and run a cut edge around the outer rim of a chilled collins glass and slide it around the rim, to dampen it. Roll the glass in the salt to coat the outer rim.

2 Place the basil in the prepared glass and muddle it.

3 Fill the glass three-quarters full with ice cubes, then add the chelada mix, lime juice, and lager and stir.

VARIATION: RED BEER

Combine just the bottle of beer and 2 ounces of tomato juice.

Thai Chelada Mix

MAKES: ABOUT 4 OUNCES

4 ounces tomato juice

1½ teaspoons Thai fish sauce

1 teaspoon Worcestershire sauce

¼ teaspoon Sriracha hot sauce

Combine all of the ingredients in an airtight container and stir. Taste for seasoning and adjust the sauces as desired. The mix will keep, covered and refrigerated, for up to 1 week.

DUTCH EAST INDIA DAISY

GLASS: ROCKS OR COLLINS | ICE: CUBED | MAKES: 1 DRINK

Edinburgh's Jason Scott, bartender and co-owner of the Bramble Bar, provided us with this refreshing spin on the classic sour. The layers of hoppy bitterness and genever funk are tempered by the always grounding orange and the sweetness of the grenadine.

2 ounces IPA (India Pale Ale)

1½ ounces genever

½ ounce strained, freshly squeezed lemon juice

½ ounce strained, freshly squeezed orange juice

½ ounce Grenadine, homemade (page 376) or store-bought

1 ounce club soda

½ orange wheel, for garnish

Fresh mint sprig, for garnish

1 Combine the IPA, genever, citrus juices, and Grenadine in a mixing glass, fill the glass three-quarters full with ice cubes, cover with a Boston shaker tin, and shake vigorously until thoroughly chilled, 15 seconds.

2 Strain into a rocks or collins glass and top with the club soda. Garnish with the orange and mint.

MAI TA-IPA

GLASS: COLLINS OR ROCKS | ICE: CUBED | MAKES: 1 DRINK

What to order on a sweltering day? A beer or a nice tiki drink? How about both in one? Bartender Jacob Grier shares our passion for beer cocktails, and after one sip of his Mai Ta-IPA, we're positive that you will, too.

1½ ounces IPA (India pale ale)

1 ounce white rum

1 ounce amber rum

1 ounce strained, freshly squeezed lime juice

¾ ounce Orgeat Syrup, preferably homemade (page 379)

½ ounce triple sec

Brandied Cherry (page 367) or high-quality maraschino cherry (we like Luxardo brand), for garnish

1 Combine all of the liquid ingredients in a mixing glass, fill the glass three-quarters full with ice cubes, cover with a Boston shaker tin, and shake vigorously until thoroughly chilled, 15 seconds.

2 Strain into a rocks or collins glass and garnish with the cherry.

Wine

RED SANGRIA

GLASS: ROCKS | ICE: CUBED | MAKES: 5 DRINKS

One of our go-to magazine sources for recipes and tips is *Cook's Illustrated*. The approach is no-nonsense and firmly entrenched in science—we have never made a bad dish from their recipe offerings.

This is our version of their red sangria. Smartly, it uses only oranges and lemons for the fruit component, making for the clean, citrus-forward flavor that typifies really good sangria.

The original recipe called for a bottle of cheap, fruity, medium-bodied red wine. We like mixing it up a bit. Sometimes we go for a full-on fruit bomb like Shiraz, and we once made a dynamite and very easy-drinking version with a fruit-forward rosé. We have also used tangerines (particularly clementines) to great effect. As for lemons, we prefer Meyers for their additional sweetness. To add some richness to the flavor, we use Cointreau instead of inexpensive triple sec (but if you have only the latter, that's fine).

---

2 large oranges

1 large Meyer lemon

¼ cup granulated sugar

2 ounces orange liqueur

1 bottle (750 ml) cheap, fruity red wine

---

1 Juice one of the oranges and strain it through a fine-mesh sieve to remove any solids. Set aside.

2 Slice the remaining orange and the lemon into ⅛-inch rounds.

3 Combine the orange and lemon slices with the sugar in a pitcher and muddle until the fruits release their juices and start to combine with the sugar.

4 Add the reserved orange juice, liqueur, and wine and stir to dissolve the sugar.

5 Refrigerate the mixture for at least 2 hours and up to 8 hours (we find that it lasts well into the next day). Serve over ice cubes in rocks glasses.

WHITE SANGRIA

GLASS: ROCKS | ICE: CUBED | MAKES: 5 DRINKS

Although not as common as the red variety, white sangria is sometimes more enjoyable on a hot summer day when red wine just seems a bit too heavy. If clementines are in season, we urge you to use them in place of the oranges (you'll need about five).

3 oranges, sliced

1 lemon, sliced

¼ cup granulated sugar, or to taste

2 to 4 ounces Cognac-style brandy, to taste

1 bottle (750 ml) y fruity white wine (such as a Spatlese-level riesling)

1 Combine the orange and lemon slices and the sugar in a pitcher and muddle until the fruits release their juices and start to combine with the sugar.

2 Add the brandy and wine and stir to dissolve the sugar.

3 Refrigerate the mixture for at least 2 hours and up to 8 hours (the mixture lasts well into the next day). Serve over ice cubes in rocks glasses.

CITY TAVERN CHAMPAGNE SHRUB

GLASS: FLUTE | MAKES: 1 DRINK

Pennsylvania is the epicenter of the shrub (see page 200), with Philadelphia's City Tavern, which dates back to the American Revolution, resting at the heart of the country's consumption of this tart-sweet summer quencher. Here is the Tavern's house variation, which combines a nice Champagne (provided the British blockades along the Eastern seaboard have ceased) with the traditional ginger beer. It's a

BETTER BUBBLES

REAL CHAMPAGNE isn't cheap—an average bottle starts around $40. If you have the money to spend, by all means, pop for Champagne. Still, don't let the inherent sexiness of Champagne's name and provenance keep you from exploring other sparkling wines. We tend to love anything sparkling, but for everyday drinking we don't often splurge. In fact, one of our favorite "let's have a glass of bubbly" bottles is a $5 German sparkler from Trader Joe's. Here are some other alternatives.

PROSECCO: Italian Prosecco is a dry sparkler but with less aggressive bubbles or dryness than Champagne.

CAVA: Hailing from Spain, cava is produced using the *méthode traditionelle* used to make Champagne, but, like Prosecco, is a fraction of the price, worth considering if you are using it as a mixer.

CRÉMANT: If you want to stick with something French, consider *crémant,* which is produced in Alsace (Crémant d'Alsace) and Burgundy (Crémant de Bourgogne), among other areas.

lovely way to class up any occasion, especially when entertaining delegates in town for the Continental Congress.

1 ounce Raspberry Shrub Syrup (page 202)

4 ounces Champagne or sparkling wine, chilled

4 ounces ginger beer, chilled

Pour the shrub syrup into a flute. Add the Champagne and ginger beer, stirring only if the Champagne fails to blend thoroughly with the other ingredients. Serve immediately.

RED GLÖGG

GLASS: PUNCH OR HEATPROOF MUG | MAKES: 7 DRINKS

Our—meaning David's—Swedish relatives would disown us if we didn't include glögg in this book. Unfortunately, nowadays, most of them opt for bottled preparations, believing them to be easier and just as tasty. They are wrong on both accounts. Not only is homemade glögg wonderfully scrumptious (think warm Christmas sangria), but if you can throw together ingredients in a pot and check it while it simmers, you have all the skills required to make it. Plus, you get to light a bunch of alcohol on fire. Nothing ushers in festive feelings quite like that.

15 blanched almonds, plus extra for serving

½ cup raisins, plus extra for serving

4 cups red wine (preferably Shiraz)

4 cardamom pods, gently crushed

3 whole cloves

1½-inch stick cinnamon

2 dried apricots

2 tablespoons chopped candied orange peel

Peel of ¼ orange

¾ cup light brown or raw sugar, such as Demerara

1 cup Cognac-style brandy

1 Combine the almonds, raisins, and wine in a large, nonreactive saucepan.

2 Combine the cardamom, cloves, cinnamon, apricots, and candied orange peel in a cheesecloth bag, tie it closed, and add it to the wine.

3 Place the fresh orange peel in a small bowl and cover it with the sugar. Let this mixture and the wine mixture stand overnight, at room temperature.

4 The next day, place the saucepan containing the wine mixture over medium heat and bring it slowly to a simmer. Do not allow it to boil. Add the fresh orange peel mixture and stir until the sugar is dissolved. Remove from the heat and stir in the brandy. Carefully remove and discard the cheesecloth bag.

5 Ignite the liquid with a lighter, allow it to burn for 1 to 2 seconds, then carefully extinguish it by covering the pot with a lid (you do not want to burn off the alcohol completely).

6 Return the pot to the lowest heat to keep warm. Remove the fresh orange peels if the glögg is going to sit for more than a few hours. Serve it warm, directly from the pot, with a few raisins and almonds in the bottom of each glass.

WHITE GLÖGG

GLASS: PUNCH | MAKES: 6 DRINKS

The Swedes have their strong, spicy red glögg (page 340); the Finnish folk prefer something a bit lighter, opting for a white wine as the base for their holiday punch (which, technically, they call *glögi*). Think of it as the difference between red and white sangrias. One is a bit more heady and rich, the other lighter and brighter. But, just as both sangrias are at home in the summer, you will find red or white glögg equally satisfying on a chilly, midwinter's eve.

We recommend a German riesling because of its fruity profile; look for one labeled "Spatlese," which will offer up an off-dry, light to medium sweetness, depending on the year of the bottling. Use the sweetness of the wine—and your own preferences—as a gauge for how much sugar to add to the final punch.

1 lemon

1 bottle (750 ml) fruity white wine

1 small (¼ inch) piece of peeled fresh ginger

1 bay leaf

10 whole cloves

½ cup Cognac-style brandy

4 cubes light brown or raw sugar, such as Demerara

1 Peel the lemon with a vegetable peeler, removing as little of the white pith as possible. Reserve the flesh.

2 Combine the lemon peel, wine, ginger, bay leaf, cloves, brandy, and sugar to taste in a medium saucepan over low heat and bring it to a simmer, stirring occasionally, until the sugar dissolves, 8 minutes.

3 Remove and discard the remaining pith from the lemon flesh and cut it into thin wheels.

4 Remove the glögg from the heat and strain it through a fine-mesh sieve into a large

heatproof bowl. Discard the solids; rinse and dry the saucepan.

5 Pour the warm glögg back into the saucepan and place over the lowest heat to keep warm. Serve in punch glasses garnished with a lemon wheel.

JERRY THOMAS' CHAMPAGNE PUNCH

GLASS: PUNCH OR MARTINI | MAKES: 6 DRINKS

Punch doesn't get much easier than this recipe adapted from the cocktail maestro himself. If you don't want to make Raspberry Syrup (page 372), homemade Grenadine (page 376)—or in an absolute pinch, good-quality store-bought—is a spot-on substitute. Either way, this punch is an easily scalable crowd-pleaser with pedigree.

2 ounces light brown or raw sugar, such as Demerara

Juice of 1 lemon

1 bottle (750 ml) Champagne or sparkling wine, chilled

2 ounces Raspberry Syrup (page 372), or Grenadine, homemade (page 376) or store-bought

1 orange, sliced into rounds

3 rounds (each ½-inch thick) fresh pineapple, skin removed

Fresh seasonal fruit, for garnish

1 Combine the sugar and lemon juice in a chilled punch bowl and stir until the sugar is dissolved.

2 Add the Champagne, syrup, orange slices, and pineapple rounds to the bowl and stir gently to combine. Serve in punch or martini glasses, garnished with fruit.

POPE

GLASS: PUNCH OR MARTINI | MAKES: 10 DRINKS

We first discovered Pope in Richard Cook's *Oxford Night Caps: A Collection of Receipts for Making Various Beverages Used in the University* (1827). The students, and professors surely, at Oxford, knew a thing or two about drinking, and *Oxford Night Caps* chronicles this admirably.

Pope is a fancy variation on Bishop, one of the great British holiday punches. Instead of mulled port, however, it opts for a lighter take on the spiced bowl, using Champagne. A word of warning—Pope is a lot of work, but it's not hard work, and the subtle but refined result is well worth the effort, especially if a punch is the centerpiece of your party.

• •

2 lemons

15 whole cloves

2 ounces light brown or raw sugar, such as Demerara

¼ stick cinnamon

3 to 4 whole allspice berries

¼ teaspoon roughly chopped whole mace

2 cups water

¾ cup boiling water

1 bottle (750 ml) Champagne or sparkling wine, chilled

Fresh whole nutmeg, for garnish (see Note, page 70)

• •

1 Preheat the oven to 300°F. Line a rimmed baking sheet with aluminum foil.

2 Stud one of the lemons with 12 of the cloves, place it on the baking sheet, and roast it in the oven until the lemon weeps juice, the peel turns golden, and the lemon feels inflated to the touch, 2 hours.

3 Meanwhile peel away the zest from the second lemon with a vegetable peeler,

removing as little of the white pith as possible; set aside the peeled fruit. Combine the peel with the sugar in a medium bowl and set it aside for 1 hour.

4 Combine the remaining spices with the 2 cups water in a small saucepan over high heat. Bring it to a boil, and boil until reduced by half, 10 to 15 minutes. Set aside.

5 Juice the peeled lemon and set the juice aside. Combine the flesh of the juiced lemon with the boiling water in a small heatproof bowl and let it steep, 5 minutes.

6 Add the reserved lemon juice to the sugar and peel, then add 1 ounce of the hot "lemon" water. Stir to dissolve the sugar. Remove and discard the lemon peel.

7 Strain the spiced water into the sugar syrup through a fine-mesh sieve; discard the solids. Add the hot roasted lemon. Allow the mixture to cool to room temperature, then remove and discard the roasted lemon and transfer the liquid to an airtight container; refrigerate until needed, up to 24 hours.

8 To serve, combine the spiced lemon mixture with the Champagne in a chilled punch bowl and garnish with a grating of nutmeg.

ONE PUNCH TO RULE THEM ALL

IN THE LEXICON of drink stories, the tale of Admiral Russell's Punch may be the most mind-bogglingly unbelievable, but utterly true. Meet Admiral of the Fleet Edward Russell, 1st Earl of Oxford. Given that Russell was a seafaring man who spent most of his life aboard a ship, it probably goes without saying that he was a mite perturbed when King James II told him that he would have to winter in Cadiz rather than return home for the holidays.

Not one to be scorned, Russell decided to bring Christmas to Cadiz, throwing a party to end all parties and then, cavalierly sending the bill to the Royal Navy. He commissioned a 700-gallon Delft fountain to be built as a punch bowl, hired a young boy to row about the fountain "stirring" the punch, and invited 6,000 guests to enjoy the spectacle.

In his book *Punch*, David Wondrich cites the *Edinburgh Advertiser* of 1772, which listed the proportions of the infamous punch as follows: "four hogsheads of brandy, eight of water, 25,000 lemons, 20 gallons of lime juice, 1300 weight of fine white Lisbon sugar, 5 pound of grated nutmegs, 300 toasted biscuits, and last a pipe of dry Mountain Malaga."

Unless you are aces with a kiln, we don't necessarily suggest you build a Delft fountain for serving purposes, but you can still enjoy a satisfying cup of Admiral Russell's Punch. And, perhaps, as Wondrich has done, you could float a little Playmobil rowboat and boy in it, as a bit of historical hyperbole.

Cider

MONTPECULIAR

GLASS: COLLINS, CHILLED | ICE: CUBED | MAKES: 1 DRINK

The motto at L.A.'s Spare Room in the Hollywood Roosevelt Hotel is "Every good story has a drink in it; bad ones require two." A good deal of the locale's success is due to beverage director Naomi Schimek, a ladies' lady and one helluva bartender. When we challenged her to create a hard cider drink, she didn't blink an eye, offering up this paean to Old New England (apples, rye fields, and all).

Despite the cider being the primary component, the spicy warmth of the rye shines through and melds seamlessly with the ginger and citrus. It's what a Fruit Cup (see page 103) might have been if it was made in the Northeast. As if this drink didn't already have enough going for it, it can be batched to scale exactly with ease, making it perfect party fare. And—yes, there is an "and"—you could swap out the rye for brandy or rum or even London dry gin to equally stunning effect. This is a classic—and sure to be favorite—summer long drink, but we wouldn't fault you for drinking it year-round. We certainly do.

• •

¾ ounce strained, freshly squeezed lemon juice

¾ ounce Ginger Syrup (page 374)

1 ounce rye whiskey

6 ounces hard cider

Rosemary sprig, for garnish (optional)

• •

1 Place the lemon juice, syrup, and rye in a mixing glass, fill with ice cubes, top with a Boston shaker tin, and shake briefly just to combine, 3 to 4 seconds.

2 Strain the mixture into a chilled collins glass (no ice needed).

3 Top with hard cider and add a rosemary sprig as an aromatic garnish, if you like.

SWEET CIDER

GLASS: MARTINI | ICE: CUBED | MAKES: 1 DRINK

P rohibition-era drinks, such as the Sweet Cider, typically used fruit juices to cover up the low quality of the bathtub gin being used. We've brought a little zip back to this one by replacing regular apple cider with hard (i.e., alcoholic) apple cider, which pairs beautifully with grenadine. The hard cider and the gin make this drink somewhat "dry," but the teaspoon of grenadine brings the brightness and richness of pomegranate—plus the sweetness that lends its name—to the fore.

1½ ounces dry gin

1½ ounces hard apple cider

1 teaspoon Grenadine, homemade (page 376) or store-bought

1 Combine all of the ingredients in a chilled cocktail shaker. Fill the shaker three-quarters full with ice cubes and shake vigorously until thoroughly chilled, 15 seconds.

2 Strain into a martini glass.

CHAPTER 17

Virgin Drinks

Rule Number One when serving someone an adult beverage is also to offer them food. Rule Number Two is to have an equally attractive nonalcoholic potion on hand, should your guests wish to forgo the hard stuff. Virgin drinks ultimately play two important roles in your bar: They provide an alternative to booze and they function as a convenient, ready-to-use base for traditional cocktails. Any of the recipes here will welcome a shot of spirit, allowing you to serve teetotalers and tipplers from a common well.

AGUA DE TAMARINDO

MAKES: 1 QUART

It's the exotic taste of tamarind that makes this drink worth the trouble. The best way to describe the flavor is as a combination of date (tamarind is often incorrectly referred to as the "Indian date") and citrus. Around the world, it is used in foods both savory and sweet, from *imli chatni* (an Indian chutney) and Worcestershire sauce to Mexican candies and *aguas frescas* (sweet fruit drinks). It's in this latter group—simple combinations of fruit, sugar, and water—that we find *agua de tamarindo*, which is often sold in taquerias and the like as a tart, refreshing cooler. Today, you can even buy it in bottled pop form from the Jarritos company.

We used a Rick Bayless recipe as the inspiration for ours, but unlike most folk drink recipes, this one seems to be pretty consistent wherever you look. Bayless recommends using traditional Mexican *piloncillo* (unrefined sugar), but any light brown or raw sugar, such as Demerara, will work. If you are using piloncillo, you may need to chop it up first in order to measure it.

If you have never used tamarind—which can be found at Asian food markets or on Amazon—be aware that it is one of the oddest ducks in the culinary world, hard on the outside and superglue sticky and bizarrely stringy on the inside. The piquant flavor that this jumble produces, though, is transcendent, so bear with the mess. Unless you're using this in the El Tamarindo (page 219), add 1½ ounces or more to a collins glass and top it off with club soda.

• •

8 large fresh tamarind pods

1 quart filtered or bottled water

½ cup piloncillo, light brown, or raw sugar, such as Demerara

• •

1 Use your fingers to remove as much of the shell and strings from the tamarind pods as possible, being sure to leave all the sticky flesh. If the pods break or some shell and string remain, that's fine.

2 Bring the water to a boil in a large saucepan and add the tamarind and sugar. Return to a boil for 1 minute.

3 Remove the mixture from the heat and transfer it to a nonreactive, heatproof bowl. Let it rest until the water is infused with the tamarind flavor, about 2 hours.

3 Scrape the tamarind flesh from the pods into the water using a spoon or your hands (hands are easier), discarding the seeds.

4 Strain the mixture through a fine-mesh sieve, pressing out as much liquid from the solids as possible.

5 Discard the solids, transfer the liquid to an airtight container, and refrigerate. The Agua de Tamarindo will keep, covered and refrigerated, for up to 1 week. Stir well before using.

• •

ARCTIC PUNCH

GLASS: PUNCH | ICE: RING (SEE PAGE 20) | MAKES: 6 DRINKS

Author Jacques Straub was a man of few words. Not only did he see fit to title his 1914 mixological compendium simply *Drinks,* but he offers no reason why the combination of lime, ginger ale, grenadine, and cold tea—forming the basis of Arctic Punch, which comes to us from

Straub's tome—conjures images of a snowy wonderland. Fortunately, the marriage of those same ingredients produces a sipper with all of the complexity and joy of a traditional sour with none of the sin. (If you wish to be sinful, however, most of the 12 Bottle Bar spirits work well in the mix. Simply add 8 ounces of whichever you like.)

¾ ounce Raspberry Syrup (page 372)

Juice of 1 lime, strained

2 cups ginger beer

1 cup unsweetened cold tea

Lime slices, for garnish

Combine the syrup, lime juice, ginger beer, and tea in a punch bowl. Place an ice ring in the bowl and garnish with the lime slices.

CONCLAVE

GLASS: ROCKS | ICE: CUBED | MAKES: 1 DRINK

Considering that one of the chief purposes of mixed drinks is to bring together friends and strangers alike, at some point someone was going to pull the appellation "Conclave" out of Old Mr. Thesaurus. We find no specific relation here between the drink and the name, but we will tell you that the Conclave tastes infinitely better than it reads on paper. Orange juice and milk may not conjure a winning combination, but for the little ones in your life—or just those wishing for something less powerful—this Strawberry Quik alternative will hit the spot.

Juice of 1 orange, strained

1 ounce Raspberry Syrup (page 372)

1 teaspoon granulated sugar

3 ounces whole milk, or your preference

1 Combine all of the ingredients in a mixing glass, fill the glass three-quarters full with ice cubes, cover with a Boston shaker tin, and shake vigorously until thoroughly chilled, 15 seconds.

2 Fill a rocks glass with ice cubes and strain the drink into the glass.

GINGER COOLER

GLASS: COLLINS | ICE: CUBED | MAKES: 1 DRINK

Los Angeles bartender Joseph Joaquin Valdovinos knows the value of the mocktail, noting that he wants all of his patrons to enjoy themselves, even if they can't or don't drink. The Ginger Cooler is a spicy-sweet nonalcoholic spin on a Pimm's Cup and for just that reason we'd recommend gin to spike it (if you must).

Orange wedge

4 cucumber wheels

4 fresh mint leaves

2 ounces ginger beer, such as Reed's Premium Ginger Brew

¾ ounce strained, freshly squeezed lime juice

¾ ounce Simple Syrup (page 369)

Brandied Cherry (page 367) or high-quality maraschino cherry (we like Luxardo brand), for garnish

1 Combine the orange wedge, cucumber, and mint in a mixing glass and muddle to express the juices.

2 Add the ginger beer, lime juice, and syrup, fill the mixing glass three-quarters full with ice cubes, cover with a Boston shaker tin, and shake vigorously until thoroughly chilled, 15 seconds.

3 Fill a collins glass with ice and strain the drink into the glass. Garnish with the cherry.

MINTY LIME COOLER

GLASS: COLLINS | ICE: CUBED | MAKES: 2 DRINKS

This nonalcoholic mojito comes from the Too Hot Tamales, who have served it for years at their popular Santa Monica restaurant, Border Grill. We've been drinking this for at least a decade—and now we finally have the recipe ourselves! Tart and refreshing, with just enough sweetness, this one will have your guests asking twice if you're certain there's no rum in it (if you wish to fortify it, add 1½ to 2 ounces of white rum per drink).

••

½ cup strained, freshly
   squeezed lime juice

⅓ cup granulated sugar

½ cup packed fresh mint
   leaves

12 ounces sparkling mineral
   water, chilled

Lime slices, for garnish

Fresh mint sprigs, for garnish

••

1 Combine the lime juice, sugar, and mint leaves in a blender and blend until pureed and smooth.

2 Fill two collins glasses with ice cubes and divide the lime juice mixture between them.

3 Top with the sparkling water and garnish with the lime slices and mint sprigs.

••

POISON APPLE PUNCH

GLASS: PUNCH | ICE: RING (SEE PAGE 20) | MAKES: 14 DRINKS

I t's possible that our website received more attention for this drink than for any other original recipe we created, which is ironic, of course, as it has no alcohol in it. Regardless, this is one tasty tipple. If you absolutely need to spike it, rum to scale—about 1 ounce per drink—wouldn't hurt one bit. Nor would vodka or brandy. And while we first made this for Halloween, it's a hit at any time of year.

This punch should be served right away, so make it just before you plan to enjoy it.

••

1 quart apple juice

1½ cinnamon sticks

½ teaspoon whole cloves

16 ounces ginger beer,
   such as Reed's Premium
   Ginger Brew

1 recipe Raspberry Syrup
   (page 372)

1 Combine the apple juice, cinnamon, and cloves in a large saucepan over high heat. Bring to a boil, then remove from the heat and allow to cool to room temperature.

2 Stir in the ginger beer and syrup.

3 Place an ice ring in a punch bowl and pour the punch over it. Ladle the punch into punch glasses to serve.

THE VIRGIN COBBLER

GLASS: ROCKS | ICE: CRUSHED | MAKES: 1 DRINK

Along with the Ginger Cooler (page 352), this is another mocktail from Joseph Joaquin Valdovinos. This ginger-raspberry combo is fruity, zesty, and has a bit of a kick thanks to the cracked pepper. James Bond used to drink vodka with black pepper in it, so we'll lean toward vodka should you want to fortify this one. Start with 1½ ounces and adjust to taste.

4 fresh mint leaves, plus 1 mint sprig, for garnish

2 ounces strained, freshly squeezed lime juice

1 ounce Simple Syrup (page 369)

2 ounces ginger beer (such as Reed's Premium Ginger Brew)

1 to 2 teaspoons raspberry preserves

Few dashes of cracked black pepper

1 Place the mint leaves in a mixing glass and muddle them.

2 Add the lime juice, syrup, ginger beer, and preserves, fill the mixing glass three-quarters full with ice cubes, cover with a Boston shaker tin, and shake vigorously until thoroughly chilled, 15 seconds.

3 Fill a rocks glass with crushed ice and strain the drink into the glass. Add the pepper and garnish with the mint sprig.

WASSAIL

GLASS: HEATPROOF MUG, WARMED | MAKES: ABOUT 8 DRINKS

Long ago, the ancient Greeks had a nasty habit of poisoning party guests they didn't like with the drinks they served. In the wake of this heartwarming "tradition," something known as "health-drinking" came about in nearby Rome, where hosts would be the first to sample their party punch, thus putting nervous revelers at ease. Flash forward to the twelfth century, when hosts would raise a glass saying *wacht heil*, wishing "good health," and guests would respond *drink heil*. This exchange eventually became the tradition of wassailing in Britain that is known to this day in wassailing songs and in the drink of the same name.

Nonstick cooking spray

6 small sweet-tart apples, washed and cored (we like Honeycrisp or Pink Lady)

1 teaspoon freshly grated whole nutmeg (see Note, page 70)

1 teaspoon ground ginger

1 cup light brown or raw sugar, such as Demerara, plus extra to taste

6 cups apple cider

1 Preheat the oven to 275°F. Spray a rimmed baking sheet with nonstick cooking spray.

2 Place the whole apples upright on the prepared baking sheet about two inches apart. Bake until tender, 1 hour.

3 Remove the apples from the oven and let them cool to the touch, about 10 minutes.

4 Peel the apples, discarding the peel, and place them in a medium bowl. Mash them with a potato masher into a fine puree. Add the nutmeg, ginger, and sugar to taste to the apple puree (it should not be overly sweet), stirring to combine. Set aside.

5 Place the 1 cup sugar in a large saucepan and pour just enough cider over the sugar to cover it. Heat the mixture over medium-low heat, stirring until all the sugar has dissolved. Slowly add the remaining cider and stir to combine. Cover the pot and bring the mixture to a low simmer.

6 Add the apple puree to the warm cider mixture on the stove and whisk until combined. Simmer, partially covered, until the flavors blend, about 30 minutes.

7 Meanwhile, heat the mugs by running them under very hot water. Dry the mugs and divide the drink among them.

CHAPTER 18

Garnishes, Syrups & Liqueurs

Whether it's a bottle of esoteric liqueur, a superpremium bitters, or the newest designer syrup (açai berry, anyone?), these are the sorts of indulgences that drive a drinks budget into the stratosphere. Furthermore, while they're certainly a lot of fun, they are simply not necessary to make a good majority of classic cocktails—certainly not those in this book—and, if you are eager to stay within a budget, they must be avoided. While we don't offer you a solution to that açai berry syrup, we do have a good number of recipes in our file folder that will help you count your pennies. As a bonus, you will find that house-made garnishes, syrups, liqueurs, and infusions taste far better than anything you can purchase. Fret not, if you just don't feel like making your own, we offer store-bought alternatives, too.

GARNISHES

Garnishes are great in a professional bar—take everything they will give you. After all, you are paying for them. At home, however, you are paying for someone, your guest, to throw them away. For this reason, we aren't very bullish on garnishing, unless it is necessary to the style or flavor of the drink.

CHOOSING FRUIT AND VEGGIES

The tastiest cocktails begin with the best-quality produce. It isn't worth cutting costs here; you truly do get what you pay for. If you can, shop at a local farmers' market, where quality and price are generally equally attractive. A few more rules to live by:

1 Buy organic when you can. Nonorganic fruits and vegetables are covered in pesticide residue and wax to keep them from rotting during transport. This is especially the case for oranges, which are at particular risk for exposure to pesticides. And since it is often the orange peel you drop into a drink, this is one fruit we always buy organic.

2 Buy the freshest produce you can find. As with fruits and veggies meant for eating, fresher is always better (there's nothing worse than a lime wedge that's too desiccated to squeeze).

3 Choose fruits and vegetables with unblemished skin.

4 Wash your fruit and vegetables with a solution of ¼ teaspoon dishwashing soap in a quart of water. You may need to scrub quite a bit to get nonorganic residue off the skin.

HERBS AND FLOWERS

WHILE HERBAL OR floral decorations aren't necessary when one is making drinks for oneself, they certainly make an impression when entertaining company. They offer bang for the buck and a little bit of fireworks, when used on the right drink. Remember, the character of the drink will dictate the herb or flower used. Below are some suggestions and the drinks on which we feel they are at home. As with fruit and vegetables, be sure they aren't sprayed with pesticides.

BASIL. Any tomato-based drink, such as the Bloody Mary (page 279) or the Caprese-tini (page 267), or the Cucumber Gimlet (page 272), Blushing Mary (page 278), Thai Chelada (page 334)

MINT. Any sort of julep or cup, mojito, shrub, Tea Time (page 174), Easter Sorbet Punch (page 111)

ROSE PETAL, GERANIUM, OR PANSY. Delicate, floral drinks, such as The "I Do" (page 173), Pink Lady (page 115), POM Gin Fizz (page 100)

ROSEMARY. Try it in the Fitzgerald (page 109) or Whiskey Sour (page 251)—especially if you change them up with Rosemary Syrup (page 252).

THYME. Most vegetable-themed drinks will work with a sprig of thyme, and also a Whiskey Sour if Thyme Syrup (page 252) is substituted.

CITRUS

There are three basic styles of citrus garnish: wedges, wheels, and twists. In order to ensure freshness and reduce waste, all three are best cut only as needed.

WEDGE Cut a ¼-inch wedge, end to end, from the fruit. Cut a little slit through the flesh and slip it onto the rim as garnish.

WHEEL Cut a ⅛-inch-thick round slice, widthwise, from the fruit. Cut a little nick through the peel in one spot and set the wheel onto the rim of the glass. (These can also be floated on a drink.)

TWIST With a vegetable peeler, peel a thin strip from the zest (leaving behind as much of the bitter white pith as possible)—usually either a 1-inch-long oval (ideal for flamed rinds, see page 8) or a longer, thinner strip. Twist the peel over the surface of the drink to express its oils and then rub it around the rim of the glass to lightly coat it with citrus oil. Finish by gently placing the twist on the rim of the glass or dropping it into the drink.

SYRUPS AND SUCH

Syrups, juices, tinctures, infusions: Many of these are crucial to the individuality of both modern and classic cocktails. Each of the recipes that follows in these pages corresponds to one or more of the drinks in the book. There are store-bought substitutions for many of these, but in the case of oft-used mixers like grenadine, which is employed in myriad drinks, we think it's very much worth your while to keep those at the top of your "make-at-home" list.

FLAVORED SYRUPS

Flavored syrups are where you can really have a field day. Simple syrup—sugar and water—is a perfect palette on which to experiment. Our standby flavorings, because of their ability to blend with so many ingredients while not detracting from them, are rosemary, mint, and lemon.

There are three methods of assembling your syrups, and each works best for certain ingredients.

HOT METHOD This works best for woody flavorings like rosemary, or for ginger.

Place 2 cups Rich Simple Syrup (page 369) in a small saucepan and add a handful of herbs or ginger with as much of the skin removed as possible. Bring to a boil over high heat, then cover the pan and remove it from the heat, leaving it at room temperature until it cools. Strain out the solids and store the syrup in the refrigerator in an airtight container.

WARM METHOD This is best for more fragile additives like fresh berries and those fruits that easily give up their juice, such as pineapple. Place 1 cup of the desired flavoring ingredient in a glass bowl. Add enough warm Rich Simple Syrup (page 369) to cover. Let the bowl stand at room temperature overnight, then strain out the solids and store the syrup in an airtight container in the refrigerator.

TEA METHOD For dried flowers (such as chamomile) or very delicate fresh herbs, like cilantro and parsley, brew a tea from the chosen ingredient first, then strain it and use the tea as the liquid portion of your Rich Simple Syrup (page 369). Brewing time and amounts will vary, but a good start is $1/4$ cup of herbs to 2 cups of boiling water, brewed for 7 minutes and then strained to remove the solids. Measure 2 cups sugar into a heatproof bowl and add 2 cups of the hot tea, stirring until all of the sugar has dissolved—this should yield about 3 cups of flavored syrup.

LIQUEURS AND INFUSIONS

L iqueurs and infusions are an easy way to add complexity to your drinks. Liqueurs will add sugar, while infusions will help concentrate flavor without additional sweetness.

A FEW NOTES ON INFUSIONS

Alcohol is a very forgiving medium and, as such, it is an infinitely malleable canvas with which to work. Still, there are a few ways to get the best out of your infusions. The basic "recipe" is quite general, so you can play with it as you will. This is an area where experimentation rules.

THE TOP FIVE EDIBLE PLANTS FOR COCKTAILS

AMY STEWART, author of *The Drunken Botanist,* has written an entire book on the links between plants, spirits, and cocktails, so we challenged her to list the five most useful, tasty, and versatile plants for cocktails. The ones that made the cut are relatively easy to grow at home and pack the biggest bang for the cocktail buck.

MINT: The type of mint to look for is spearmint, and there are several cultivars you can grow (the plants are not typically sold in stores) that lend themselves admirably to cocktails. As its name suggests, "Mojito mint" is ideal in mojitos, as the strain grown in Havana for Cuban mojitos. And "Kentucky Colonel mint" is a Southern type whose sweet profile blends expertly with juleps.

BASIL: In Amy's words, "basil adds a complex floral note to otherwise dull drinks." Basil and watermelon have a natural affinity for each other and basil works beautifully with light rum (as in our Watermelon Rum Shrub, page 199) and in vodka-based drinks because its vivid licorice flavor doesn't need to compete with any botanicals in the spirit.

CUCUMBER: Forget cucumber-flavored spirits. You can get the purest cuke flavor by muddling slices or chunks of cucumber right in the shaker.

STRAWBERRIES: The perennially popular fruit is easy to grow, even in confined spaces. Ever-bearing varieties produce more fruit over a longer season. All you need are a few berries to muddle in a No. 1 Fruit Cup Cocktail (page 103) or a Daiquiri (page 216) and you've taken your drink to another level entirely.

TOMATOES: These are the no-brainer of the plant kingdom when it comes to home gardening. Literally hundreds of varieties are there for the picking, including a slew of heirloom cultivars whose flavors can range from almost berrylike to almost citrusy. Pair them with gin or vodka, cucumbers or basil, and, presto, you have a salad in a glass.

Remember, infusions are meant to capture the freshness of your produce. They are seasonal and ephemeral. So make them, drink them within a month (if you want the flavors to remain bright), and enjoy them—don't expect to stock them away like a bottle of booze.

DIRECTIONS FOR A BASIC INFUSION

1 Fill a resealable glass jar—a quart-size Mason jar does nicely—halfway with your solid ingredients. Fruits, herbs, and vegetables are common, but other possible ingredients include tea, flowers, and spices (fresh, such as ginger or chiles, and dried, such as cloves or cardamom). Note: If you are combining flavors, such as jalapeño and garlic or strawberry and basil, infuse each one separately so you can tailor the infusion time for each ingredient, then combine the flavored liquids to blend.

2 Fill the jar about three-quarters full with good-quality, unflavored (of course) vodka, and let it infuse, tasting it frequently—every hour for short infusions and every day for longer ones (see below)—to achieve the flavor you want.

3 Once you like the flavor of the infusion, strain the liquid into a clean bottle, discarding the solids, then cover and store it in the refrigerator. (If you are combining infusions, do so when you bottle the liquid.) The infusion should last a few weeks to 1 month in the refrigerator.

INFUSION TIMES

- Delicate ingredients such as basil leaves and rose petals take only a few hours to release their perfume.

- Soft fruits and vegetables, such as raspberries, melons, and cucumber, need a few days.

- Citrus (usually only the peels) and spices can infuse for up to 1 month, but no longer or they will start getting bitter and funky.

When in doubt, start tasting the infusion a few hours after making it, and taste it again every hour (or every day for longer infusions) until you hit that sweet spot of flavor.

TOULOUSE-LAUTREC'S LEMON PIGS

MOST PEOPLE ARE familiar with Henri de Toulouse-Lautrec the painter, but few know that his artistic passion almost paled in comparison to his gastronomic obsessions. Not only did he adore drinking, he also loved to force drinks—mysterious concoctions of doubtful provenance—on his friends.

And along with his barroom bravura, he enjoyed little bits of whimsy, as with his "lemon pigs"—lemons with four toothpicks poked into their underside to resemble legs—which he enjoyed making and scattering around his bar.

Toulouse-Lautrec was born two years after Jerry Thomas published his *Bar-Tender's Guide*, so the golden age of cocktails was already in full swing and would continue to thrive until roughly around his death, in 1901. Lautrec performed his most famous mixological marvel at the home of Alexandre Natanson, one of the founders of the avant-garde magazine *La Rive Gauche*; it featured the dwarfish Lautrec, his head shaved for the occasion, holding court behind a makeshift mahogany bar. Over the course of the evening (February 16, 1895, to be exact) Lautrec mixed and stirred with abandon, racking up a grand total of two thousand cocktails served. By morning, the only things left standing were the lemon pigs.

THE RECIPES

Garnishes

COCKTAIL ONIONS

MAKES: ABOUT 35

Homemade cocktail onions rest head and shoulders above the store-bought variety. The lovely crunch, the delicate balance of sweet, spicy, and sour, not to mention the possibility of customizing the flavor profile to your liking, are all reasons that these beauties should be made at home. Drinks like the Gibson—a Martini (page 130) with an onion instead of a twist or olive—shine when garnished with a homemade onion.

12 ounces pearl onions, unpeeled (about 35 onions)

Boiling water

½ cup apple cider vinegar

½ cup rice wine vinegar

2 cups white wine vinegar

1 cup granulated sugar

1½ tablespoons kosher salt

1½ cups warm water

1½ teaspoons pickling spice

1 teaspoon dried rosemary

4 garlic cloves, peeled

1 Cut the root end off of each onion, being careful not to cut too much (just ⅟₁₆ of an inch or so). Place the onions in a large, heatproof bowl and pour boiling water over them to cover. Let them rest for 1 minute. Meanwhile, prepare an ice-water bath.

2 Drain the onions and submerge them in the ice bath until they are cool to the touch. Peel the onions with your fingers and set aside.

3 Combine the vinegars, sugar, and salt with the 1½ cups warm water in a large saucepan. Stir to dissolve the sugar and salt.

4 Tie the pickling spice in a piece of cheesecloth and add it to the vinegar mixture. Add the onions, ensuring that they are completely covered with liquid.

5 Bring to a boil over high heat and boil for 1 minute. (Any longer and the onions will lose their crunch.) Remove from the heat and transfer the onions and pickling liquid to a clean, dry jar.

6 Allow the mixture to cool overnight, loosely covered, at room temperature. Cover the jar with a tight-fitting lid, then refrigerate. The onions will keep for about 1 month in the refrigerator.

NOTE: Pickling spice can be found in the spice aisle of most supermarkets.

BRANDIED CHERRIES

MAKES: ABOUT 1½ QUARTS

Most of us grew up on imitation maraschino cherries—the day-glow beauties that tasted nothing like a cherry. Here's the real thing. And if you can't make the real thing at home, the best bottled brand is Luxardo, available online and from specialty food emporiums. If you live in an area where you can get sour Montmorency cherries, they are the ideal type. If not, we have used Bings and other dark, sweet types with great success.

6 cups water

3 tablespoons sea salt

2 pounds fresh cherries (see headnote), stemmed and pitted

4½ cups Cherry Syrup (recipe follows)

1 Bring the water to a boil in a large saucepan, then add the salt and stir until it dissolves.

2 Remove the pan from the heat and add the cherries.

Allow the cherry brine to cool to room temperature (if the cherries aren't completely covered, stir them occasionally), then refrigerate, covered, overnight.

3 Drain the cherries, discarding the brine. Rinse the cherries thoroughly under cold running water to remove as much of the brine as possible.

4 Place the cherries in a clean, lidded glass container and cover with the Cherry Syrup. Refrigerate for at least 2 weeks. The cherries are ready when all saltiness is gone. The cherries will keep, covered and refrigerated, for several months.

Cherry Syrup

MAKES: 3½ CUPS

3 cups granulated sugar

2 cups water

1 cup unsweetened, tart cherry juice (see Note)

Juice of 2 limes

1½ cups Cognac-style brandy

1 Combine the sugar and water in a medium saucepan over medium-high heat and stir to dissolve the sugar.

2 Add the cherry and lime juices and simmer until reduced to 3 cups, about 40 minutes. Skim any scum that appears on top of the liquid as it simmers.

3 Remove from the heat, stir in the brandy, and allow to cool to room temperature.

4 Transfer the syrup to an airtight container, and refrigerate. The syrup will keep, covered and refrigerated, for several weeks.

NOTE: Unsweetened cherry juice is available at Trader Joe's and most natural foods supermarkets.

Syrups et al.

SIMPLE SYRUP

MAKES: ABOUT 1½ CUPS

T he basic recipe for simple syrup is a 1:1 ratio of sugar to water, usually gently heated to help the sugar dissolve. In the old days, bartenders used something called gomme syrup, which had an extra ingredient, gum acacia, that gave the sugar water a silky texture. Since gum acacia runs well over $20 a pound, it's not a 12 Bottle Bar staple. Simple syrup will do just fine. Experiment with different types of sugar for different levels of richness.

Rich Simple Syrup (see Variation), at a 2:1 ratio, is right at home in any drink where you want to bump up the sweetness quotient. Alternatively, you can use less rich simple syrup to obtain the same sweetness level. Whether rich or standard simple syrup, the mixture can be scaled up and down as you need it without losing any flavor or texture in the translation.

· ·

| 1 cup water | 1 cup granulated sugar |

· ·

1 Heat the water in a saucepan over the lowest possible flame.

2 Add the sugar and stir to dissolve.

3 Remove the pan from the heat and allow the mixture to cool to room temperature. Transfer the syrup to a glass jar or bottle and refrigerate. The syrup will keep, covered and refrigerated, for 1 month.

VARIATION

RICH SIMPLE SYRUP Use 2 cups granulated sugar.

KEEPING IT FRESH

NOTE THAT SUGAR is a natural preservative, so syrups, with and without flavorings, will last quite awhile. Basic simple syrup can be stored in a glass jar or bottle in the fridge for up to 1 month; rich simple syrup, with its higher sugar content, will last that way for up to 6 months. If it takes you longer than that to use up your syrups (we think this unlikely), you can add 1 tablespoon of vodka to roughly double the storage time. In case you are wondering, it will not affect the alcoholic potency of your drinks.

If you aren't sure how "fresh" your syrup is, here is a good rule: If it's cloudy (or moldy!), throw it out.

MINT SIMPLE SYRUP

MAKES: 2½ CUPS

nfusing mint into simple syrup is a deceptively easy addition, but the intensity of the mint flavor is stunning. It is an essential component of our Crème de Menthe Liqueur (page 384).

2½ cups warm Simple Syrup (page 369)

1 cup fresh mint leaves, preferably spearmint

1 Combine the warm syrup and the mint in a small bowl and stir. Set aside at room temperature to infuse overnight.

2 Strain the syrup and discard the mint. Transfer to an airtight container and refrigerate. The syrup will keep, covered, in the refrigerator, for 1 month.

VARIATION

RICH MINT SIMPLE SYRUP Replace the Simple Syrup with Rich Simple Syrup (page 369) and proceed as directed. It will keep, covered and refrigerated, for up to 1 month.

HONEY SYRUP

MAKES: ABOUT 1 CUP

H oney syrup accomplishes two things: It dilutes thick and sticky honey, making it easier to work with, and it reduces the honey's tendency to be somewhat cloying. It has a far more pronounced flavor than sugar simple syrup, tasting quite distinctly of its honey base. When called for, in drinks like the Bee's Knees (page 106), Tea's Knees (page 124), or the Jamaica Honey Bee (page 189), it is an essential component of the flavor profile.

As honey comes in all different stripes, the variety you choose makes a big difference in the flavor of a drink. Although we adore orange flower honey on our biscuits, its pronounced orange qualities can actually compete with other elements in a drink. For cocktails, our favorites, for their subtlety, are wildflower and acacia—both gently sweet and aromatic, as well as less viscous as their orange flower cousin, which is best used in an orange-themed drink.

½ cup honey   ½ cup warm water

Combine the honey and warm water in a small mixing bowl and stir until blended. Allow the syrup to cool to room temperature, then transfer it to an airtight container and refrigerate. The syrup will keep, covered, in the refrigerator, for several weeks.

HONEY MINT SYRUP

MAKES: ABOUT 1 CUP

T his is essentially a simple honey syrup, but the addition of the mint creates a subtle herbal tinge that sets it apart.

Handful of fresh mint leaves   ½ cup water
½ cup honey (preferably
   wildflower)

1 Place the mint in a heatproof bowl.

2 Combine the honey and water in a small saucepan over medium-low heat and stir until the honey has dissolved and the mixture is hot but not simmering, about 10 minutes.

3 Pour the warm honey syrup over the mint and let it steep at room temperature for about 3 hours.

4 Once the syrup has fully cooled, remove the mint. The syrup will keep, covered, in the refrigerator, for up to 1 month.

RASPBERRY SYRUP

MAKES: ABOUT 1 CUP

Fresh raspberries can have an almost ephemeral flavor, but when used in a syrup, their true berry loveliness shines through. This is an incredibly flexible syrup that can be used in many cocktails, but also as a base much like Shrub for nonalcoholic drinks.

1 cup Rich Simple Syrup (page 369)

1 cup fresh raspberries, washed and dried

1 teaspoon strained, freshly squeezed lemon juice

1 Place the syrup in a small saucepan over the very lowest heat and warm through, about 1 minute.

2 Meanwhile place the raspberries in a bowl and gently muddle them with a wooden spoon.

3 Add the lemon juice to the berries and stir to combine, then add the warm simple syrup and again stir to combine. Allow the mixture to sit overnight at room temperature.

4 Strain the syrup through a fine-mesh sieve or multiple layers of cheesecloth and discard the solids. Transfer the syrup to an airtight container and refrigerate. The syrup will keep, covered, in the refrigerator, for up to 2 weeks.

BLACKBERRY SYRUP

MAKES: ABOUT 1¼ CUPS

¾ cup fresh blackberries,
washed and dried

1 teaspoon strained, freshly
squeezed lemon juice

¾ cup water

¾ cup granulated sugar

1 Combine all of the ingredients in a medium saucepan over low heat and cook, stirring several times, until the sugar has dissolved and berries have broken down, 20 to 25 minutes.

2 Raise the heat slightly, keeping the syrup below a simmer, and cook, uncovered, stirring occasionally, until the syrup has reduced and thickened to the consistency of pancake syrup, about 20 minutes.

3 Strain the syrup through a fine-mesh sieve or several layers of cheesecloth into a heatproof, nonreactive container and let cool. Store, covered, in the refrigerator, for up to 2 weeks.

CARAMELIZED PINEAPPLE SYRUP

MAKES: ABOUT 2 CUPS

This syrup tastes just as it sounds—it's a caramel apple with pineapple instead. Food grade citric acid can often be found in small bottles in a supermarket's canning section or labeled "sour salt" in the kosher food section, as well as online (see Resources, page 393).

2 cups cubed fresh pineapple

2 tablespoons light brown or
raw sugar, such as Demerara

Pineapple juice (optional)

1 cup of water

2 cups granulated sugar

¼ teaspoon citric acid

2 ounces amber rum

1 Combine the pineapple and brown sugar in a large sauté pan and toss the pineapple in the sugar to coat it evenly.

2 Cook, stirring, over medium-high heat until the sugar caramelizes and the fruit is browned and fragrant, adding a tablespoon of pineapple juice (or water) as needed to keep the pineapple from sticking to the pan, about 10 minutes.

Remove from the heat and transfer to a large, heatproof bowl.

3 In a 2-quart saucepan, combine the water, granulated sugar, and citric acid. Cook over the lowest possible heat,

stirring occasionally, until the sugar dissolves completely, about 20 minutes.

4 Remove the syrup from the heat and pour it over the caramelized pineapple. Allow the pineapple to cool to room temperature, then cover the bowl with plastic wrap and let it sit at room temperature for 8 hours or overnight.

5 Strain the syrup into a bowl, reserving the liquid an discarding the solids. Strain the liquid again to remove any foam, then stir in the rum. Transfer the syrup to an airtight container and refrigerate. The syrup will keep, covered, in the refrigerator, for up to 1 month.

GINGER SYRUP

MAKES: ABOUT 1 CUP

Ginger syrup is an intensely sweet-spicy addition to any drink. This recipe comes from English Gins Brand Ambassador Trevor Easter, who uses it in his Tea's Knees (page 124), a gin version of the celebrated Scotch-based Penicillin (see page 1).

Our version of the recipe calls for making fresh ginger juice with a blender and a fine-mesh sieve; if you have an electric juicer, by all means use it.

8 pieces peeled fresh ginger (about 1½ inch each)

4 ounces water

⅔ cup granulated sugar

• •

1   Place the ginger in a food processor fitted with a steel blade, and pulse for a few seconds. Add the water and puree to make a paste. (Alternatively, use a blender and do this in thirds, adding enough water to make a paste.)

2   Transfer the paste to a fine-mesh sieve, set it over a small bowl or a measuring cup, and press hard on the paste with the back of a wooden spoon to extract as much of the juice as possible. You will have about ⅔ cup of juice.

3   Combine the ginger juice and sugar in a small saucepan over low heat and cook, stirring to dissolve the sugar, about 5 minutes. Remove from the heat.

4   Allow the syrup to cool to room temperature and transfer to an airtight container. The syrup will keep, covered, in the refrigerator, for about 3 days.

VARIATION

SWEETENED GINGER JUICE   This sweetened juice is similar to the Ginger Syrup above, but it is not heated, producing a brighter flavor with more fresh ginger bite. Combine 4 ounces ginger juice with 3 ounces granulated sugar in a mixing bowl and stir until combined. Store in an airtight container, refrigerated, for up to 3 days.

GRENADINE

MAKES: 3 CUPS

P lease, please, please, if you make only one of the syrups in this section, choose grenadine. Nowhere is homemade more superior to store-bought than with this pomegranate-based mixer. Everything from the depth of the color to the intensity of the sweetness (to your own taste) is controlled in a home-cooked batch. Further, it's used in too many cocktails to even list them. To find the flower waters called for, see Resources (page 393).

2 cups unsweetened pomegranate juice, such as POM

4 Cups granulated sugar

Food-grade French orange flower water (see Note, page 100)

Food-grade rose water

1 Heat the pomegranate juice in a medium saucepan over very low heat until just warm, 2 minutes. Add the sugar in batches, stirring until it is dissolved and the syrup is clear.

2 Pour about three-quarters of the syrup into a heatproof container, and heat the remaining one-fourth over medium heat until it is reduced by half. Add the reduced syrup to the reserved syrup.

3 Add about 6 drops each of the orange flower water and rose water—just enough to accent the syrup subtly. Allow the grenadine to cool to room temperature, transfer it to an airtight container, and refrigerate. The grenadine will keep, covered, for several months.

OFF-THE-SHELF SUBSTITUTE: Fee's American Beauty Grenadine

LEMONGRASS SYRUP

MAKES: 3 CUPS

T his syrup from Charlotte Voisey, the William Grant & Sons portfolio ambassador, imparts a distinct ginger/herbal lemon quality to her Lemongrass Is Always Greener (page 275). We use it in Amy Stewart's Lemongrass Mojito (page 220) as well.

3 cups Simple Syrup
(page 369)

12 fresh lemongrass stalks,
coarsely chopped
(see page 220)

1 Combine the syrup and lemongrass in a blender and blend to as smooth a consistency as possible. There will still be some very small pieces of lemongrass remaining.

2 Transfer the mixture to an airtight container and allow it to sit at room temperature for 8 hours.

3 Strain the syrup through a fine-mesh sieve or multiple layers of cheesecloth and discard the solids. Return the syrup to the airtight container and refrigerate. The syrup will keep, covered, in the refrigerator, for several weeks.

LIME CORDIAL

MAKES: 9 OUNCES

While this recipe may seem daunting at first, it is not difficult at all and produces such a nuanced cordial that you'd be doing yourself and your guests a disservice were you not to make the effort at least once. The cordial will continue to improve as it sits, producing a dry, subtly spiced, lime-centric cordial.

1 heaping teaspoon coriander seeds, crushed

10 cardamom pods, crushed

½ cup boiling water

¾ cup plus 3 tablespoons baker's sugar

3 limes, cubed

Peels from 3 large oranges

1 rounded teaspoon food-grade citric acid (see Note)

2 ounces water

1 Place the coriander seeds and cardamom pods in a heatproof measuring cup or

mug, add the boiling water, and brew, stirring occasionally, for 15 minutes. Strain the infusion through a fine-mesh sieve into a heatproof container, and set aside (it can be stored, covered, in the refrigerator until needed).

2 Combine 3 ounces of the coriander-cardamom infusion with ¾ cup of the baker's sugar in a small saucepan over low heat and warm, stirring, to dissolve the sugar. Set the syrup aside (it, too, can be stored, covered, in the refrigerator until needed).

3 In a medium nonreactive bowl, combine the remaining 3 tablespoons baker's sugar, the cubed limes, and the orange peels, and muddle to extract the juices. Strain through a fine-mesh sieve, pressing down on the solids to extract the liquid into a nonreactive airtight container. Set aside.

4 Stir together the citric acid and water in a small bowl until the citric acid has dissolved completely.

5 In a nonreactive airtight container or glass bottle, combine 3 ounces of the citric acid mixture with 3 ounces of the coriander-cardamom syrup and 3 ounces of the citrus juice. Taste and adjust the sweetness; if you prefer something a little sweeter, add more of the syrup to suit.

6 Refrigerate the cordial, covered, for at least 5 hours to let the flavors develop (they will continue to develop as it sits). The cordial will keep, refrigerated, for up to 1 month.

NOTE: Citric acid can be found in the canning or kosher food sections of a supermarket, and also online (see Resources, page 393); it is sometimes labeled "sour salt."

TEA SYRUP

MAKES: ¼ CUP

This syrup calls for a "strong" black tea, such as Lapsang souchong or English Breakfast, but you can easily make Tea Syrup from any tea you choose, including green, jasmine, and chamomile.

½ cup hot black tea, brewed for 3 minutes

½ cup granulated sugar

1 Combine the hot tea and sugar in a small saucepan over very low heat and stir to dissolve the sugar. Remove from the heat.

2 Allow the syrup to cool to room temperature, transfer it to an airtight container, and refrigerate. The syrup will keep, covered, in the refrigerator, for up to 1 month.

ORGEAT SYRUP

MAKES: 6 CUPS

M odern orgeat syrup is made from almonds and tastes very much of the nut itself, with the perfumey addition of orange flower water and, in our case, rose water (see Resources, page 393, to find both). It is said that the origins of orgeat trace back to sweetened barley water, but for the past two hundred years, the recipe has been an almond-infused syrup. Making it at home is a simple process, with the results far outshining coffee-shop perennials such as Monin or Torani (though you can use those in a pinch).

Homemade orgeat may settle in the bottle, forming a white film of almond powder on top. This is normal. Simply pierce the layer with a toothpick or other clean, sharp kitchen tool and shake the syrup to recombine.

8 ounces raw almonds (preferably marconas, see Resources)

1 quart filtered or bottled water

8 cups granulated sugar

¼ to ½ teaspoon food-grade orange flower water

¼ to ½ teaspoon food-grade rose water

1 Toast the almonds in a large skillet over medium-low heat, tossing regularly, until just beginning to turn golden, 6 to 8

minutes. Transfer the almonds to a bowl and let cool to room temperature.

2 Using a chef's knife, coarsely chop enough of the almonds to produce 1 cup. Set them aside.

3 Place the remaining almonds in a food processor fitted with a steel blade and grind into a fine meal.

4 Combine the filtered water, sugar, chopped almonds, and ½ cup of the ground almonds in a large saucepan and heat over high heat until the mixture reaches a boil, 8 to 10 minutes.

5 Remove the mixture from the heat, stir, and cover, leaving the lid ajar to allow any steam to escape. Let sit for 12 hours.

6 Strain the almond mixture through a fine-mesh sieve into an airtight storage container using a wooden spoon to press out as much liquid as possible. Discard the solids.

7 Add the orange flower water and rose water, beginning with the lesser amounts and increasing to taste (the almond flavor should remain dominant). Store, covered, in the refrigerator, for up to 1 month.

PINEAPPLE FOAM

MAKES: ENOUGH TO TOP ABOUT 6 DRINKS

his foam is light and airy, just as you'd expect. We use it as a layer on our Laughing Zombie (page 214), but you could certainly try it on any other tiki-style drink you fancy. We make ours in an iSi creamer (see Resources, page 393), but any rechargeable whipped-cream maker will work.

Whites of 2 large eggs

1 ounce white rum

2 ounces strained pineapple juice

1 ounce Simple Syrup (page 369)

Dash orange bitters

1 Combine all of the ingredients in a cocktail shaker and shake without ice to combine, 15 seconds.

2 Pour into a chilled creamer. Charge the creamer according to the manufacturer's directions, shake, and refrigerate until needed. The foam mixture will keep, inside the creamer and refrigerated, for 1 hour.

COCONUT MILK SYRUP

MAKES: 1 CUP

This is essentially a homemade version of store-bought Cream of Coconut. For clarification, coconut water is the liquid found inside the coconut itself, while coconut milk is made from fresh coconut simmered in water; it has the consistency of cow's milk. Cream of Coconut, which is much thicker, is generally sweetened; in canned or bottled versions, it often has a number of chemical additives, which is why we opt to make our own.

½ cup coconut milk
(we like Thai Kitchen)

1 cup granulated sugar

1 Heat the coconut milk in a small saucepan over low heat until warmed through, 3 to 5 minutes.

2 With the pot still on the heat, add the sugar in two batches, stirring to dissolve completely between each batch. Remove the syrup from the heat.

3 Strain the syrup through a fine-mesh sieve into a small bowl, discarding any solids. Allow the syrup to cool.

4 Pour the syrup into an airtight container and store in the refrigerator for up to 1 week.

Liqueurs & Infusions

ADVOCAAT

MAKES: ABOUT 3 CUPS

This egg custard liqueur, originally from Holland (some histories claim it was originally a Caribbean beverage made with avocados, but we'll skip that version), is so thick, you can literally eat it with a spoon. As it is also very boozy—that's what advocaat is supposed to be—feel free to scale back the brandy.

10 large egg yolks

½ teaspoon salt

1⅓ cups granulated sugar

1½ cups Cognac-style brandy

2 teaspoons pure vanilla extract

1 Combine the egg yolks, salt, and sugar in a medium bowl and beat with an electric mixer until glossy and thickened to the consistency of custard, about 90 seconds.

2 Slowly trickle in the brandy, beating constantly. (The mixture will become thin again.)

3 Pour the mixture into a medium saucepan over low heat, or the top of a double boiler set over simmering water. Warm the mixture, whisking constantly to prevent scorching, until the Advocaat thickens and coats the back of a spoon, 5 minutes.

4 Remove from the heat and whisk in the vanilla extract. Allow to cool, then transfer to an airtight glass container and refrigerate. The Advocaat will keep for up to 1 week.

OFF-THE-SHELF SUBSTITUTE: Bols Advocaat

BLACKBERRY LIQUEUR

MAKES: ABOUT 24 OUNCES

n France, this is known as *crème de mure, mure* being the word for blackberry. This is surprisingly easy to make, especially given the juicy berry payoff it produces.

••

3 cups granulated sugar

1 cup water

3 cups 80-proof vodka

3 cups ripe blackberries

••

1 Combine the sugar and water in an airtight container and shake to dissolve the sugar. Add the vodka and stir to combine. Gently stir in the blackberries, taking care not to cut or crush them.

2 Let the mixture infuse, covered, at room temperature until the berries have lost most of their color, 10 to 12 days.

3 Strain the liqueur through a fine-mesh sieve or multiple layers of cheesecloth and discard the solids. Pour into an airtight glass container and refrigerate. The liqueur will keep for 3 to 6 months.

OFF-THE-SHELF SUBSTITUTE: Crème de Mure

STORING HOMEMADE LIQUEURS

ALCOHOL IS NATURE'S great preservative. As such, you will often read that homemade liqueurs can be stored on the shelf for up to a year or more. Call us overly cautious, but we put them in the fridge (we like them chilled for drinks anyway) and keep them for three to six months, sometimes less. And, as with syrups, we always test our liqueurs for funky smells or flavors and look for mold—when in doubt, throw it out.

"COCONUTTY" VODKA

MAKES: ABOUT 1 CUP

This infused vodka, courtesy of Los Angeles bartender Dan Long, has an intense coconut flavor, making it a natural complement to a tropical drink.

1 cup vodka

½ cup sweetened, shredded coconut

1 Combine the vodka and coconut in a glass container and allow them to infuse at room temperature for 1 day.

2 Strain the vodka and discard the solids. Transfer to another airtight glass container. The vodka will keep, refrigerated, for up to 1 week. It may separate; shake it to blend.

CRÈME DE MENTHE LIQUEUR

MAKES: ABOUT 5 CUPS

Back in the '70s, almost everyone had a bottle of vivid dark-green crème de menthe in their home. It was the fashionable thing to do. Well, we say that, along with bell bottoms and psychedelic butterflies, green crème de menthe should be confined to the past (unfortunately, it is still available in stores). Our homemade Crème de Menthe has neither the grotesque color nor the medicinal mouthwash flavor. Instead, it is full of invigorating, clean mint flavor and, in a Stinger (page 67), it makes a killer after-dinner drink. It ain't so bad over vanilla ice cream either.

1 recipe Mint Simple Syrup (page 370)

2½ cups vodka

Combine the syrup and vodka in an airtight container, shake to combine, and refrigerate. The liqueur will keep for 1 month.

OFF-THE-SHELF SUBSTITUTE: Crème de Menthe (the clear variety, please)

CUCUMBER-INFUSED VODKA

MAKES: 1 BOTTLE (750 ML)

Like the "Coconutty" Vodka (opposite), this cucumber-infused version packs in the fresh, crisp flavor of cucumber. Use the freshest cuke you can find and enjoy a sip of summer.

1 large English cucumber, peeled, seeded, and coarsely chopped

1 bottle (750 ml) vodka

1 Combine the cucumber and vodka in a large, wide-necked glass container with a tight-fitting lid. Seal and set aside at room temperature to infuse for up to 2 weeks (no longer).

2 Strain the vodka through a sieve and discard the solids. Transfer to another airtight glass container and store at room temperture (or chilled) for up to 1 week.

GUNPOWDER LIQUEUR

MAKES: ABOUT 12 OUNCES

We were blown away when we first tasted this intense liqueur, which Seattle bartender Jamie Boudreau created for his Gunpowder and Smoke cocktail (page 121). The inclusion of a teaspoon of smoky black tea is what gives this liqueur its distinct flavor.

1 teabag or 1 heaping teaspoon
    smoky black tea leaves
    (such as Gunpowder or
    Lapsang souchong)

1 cup boiling water

2 cups granulated sugar

½ cup Cognac-style brandy

1 If the tea is not already in a bag, place it in a tea strainer. Place the tea bag or strainer in a heatproof bowl and pour the boiling water over it. Allow to steep for 3 minutes, then remove and discard the tea bag or loose tea.

2 Add the sugar ½ cup at a time, stirring each addition until fully dissolved. Let

the tea syrup cool to room temperature.

3 Place 1½ cups of the tea syrup in an airtight container, add the brandy, and stir to combine. (Any leftover syrup can be stored, refrigerated in an airtight container, for up to 1 month.) The liqueur will keep in the refrigerator for 3 to 6 months.

LIMONCELLO

MAKES: 2 BOTTLES OF LIQUEUR (ABOUT 750 ML EACH)

Along with breathtaking scenery and decadent food, the Amalfi Coast is famous for Limoncello, served as a digestif, after meals. Despite the time it takes, this is a relatively simple liqueur to make, especially given the mouthwatering payoff. Limoncello can be used in many ways, including in drinks that require a citrus vodka or need a lemony boost, such as the Limoncello Drop (page 266). Or serve it ice cold on its own. It's also lovely with sparkling wine, much like a Mimosa or Bellini. The recipe can easily be doubled.

8 medium lemons (preferably
    organic) with bright yellow,
    strongly scented skins

1 bottle (750 ml) 100-proof
    vodka

1 recipe Simple Syrup
    (page 369)

1 cup water

1 Gently remove the zest from the lemons with a Microplane grater (see Tools of the Trade, page 16), taking care to remove only the very top yellow layer. Alternatively, peel the zest from the lemons with a vegetable peeler, leaving behind as much of the bitter white pith as possible. Place the zest in a glass jar (a large Mason jar works well) and add the vodka.

2 Seal the jar tightly and let the mixture infuse at room temperature, shaking it daily, until the lemon zest loses its color, turning the vodka a vibrant yellow, 7 to 10 days.

3 Moisten a double layer of cheesecloth with water and strain the vodka through it into a clean glass jar or bowl, squeezing the zest through the cloth to release all the liquid; discard the solids. Add the simple syrup and the water and stir to combine thoroughly.

4 Using a funnel, transfer the mixture to 2 clean, dry 750-ml glass bottles.

5 Place the bottles away from direct light and let them rest 3 to 4 days. The Limoncello will keep, covered, in the refrigerator, for up to 6 months. Store it in the freezer for the iciest service.

OFF-THE-SHELF SUBSTITUTE: Limoncello (we like Pallini, which uses Sfusato lemons, a variety grown on the Amalfi Coast, or Ventura Limoncello Company).

LAPSANG SOUCHONG– INFUSED GIN

MAKES: ABOUT ½ CUP

Any dry gin will work in this infusion, but some, like the Beefeater 24, which uses tea as a central botanical component, work better than others. English Gins Brand Ambassador Trevor Easter created this to top off his Tea's Knees cocktail (page 124); the recipe will make enough for eight drinks. You can easily double it, and if you just can't get enough of that smoky flavor, you can even make a liter bottle using ½ cup of tea leaves. We also like it in a Gin and Tonic (page 115). As Lapsang souchong tea has a distinctly smoky flavor, so does the infusion. Be extra vigilant about the time on this infusion, as oversteeping the tea will lead to an unpleasant, bitter taste.

½ cup dry gin

1 tablespoon Lapsang souchong tea leaves

1 Put the gin in a small nonreactive container and add the tea leaves. Let the mixture steep, tasting it periodically, until the tea's flavor has been fully absorbed into the gin, 20 minutes.

2 Strain the gin through a fine-mesh sieve) into an airtight container discarding the solids. It will keep at room temperature for up to 1 month.

SPICED SWEET VERMOUTH

MAKES: ABOUT 2 CUPS

How do you make sweet vermouth even yummier? It's simple: add spices.

2 cinnamon sticks

Small handful cardamom pods

2 cups sweet vermouth

1 Combine the cinnamon and cardamom in a small sauté pan over low heat and toast until fragrant, about 2 minutes (watch them carefully so they don't burn).

2 Transfer the still-warm toasted spices to a glass jar and add the vermouth. Set aside at room temperature to infuse for 1 day.

3 Strain the liquid through a fine-mesh sieve into an airtight glass container, discarding the solids. It will keep at room temperature for up to 1 month.

CHEATER'S CUP

MAKES: 1 BOTTLE (750 ML); ENOUGH FOR 25 DRINKS

The most traditional and popular bottled "cup" comes from Pimm's, whose founder, James Pimm, originally made bottled versions using gin, rum, brandy, and other spirits. The one below is a standard "cheat" for making a bottled cup at home—and it's a very solid imitation of the classic.

10 ounces dry gin (40% ABV, or 80 proof, works best)

10 ounces sweet vermouth (we use Punt e Mes)

5 ounces orange liqueur (a darker style, like Grand Marnier)

Combine all of the ingredients in a glass bottle or airtight container and shake to combine.

The fruit cup will keep, sealed, at room temperature for several months.

TINCTURE OF CLOVE

MAKES: 2 OUNCES

The simplicity of this mixture belies the complex payoff. Created by bartender Justin Darnes to top off his Gambler's Fix (page 152), it imparts a whiff of spice to an already intriguing drink.

2 ounces dry gin

12 whole cloves

1 Combine the gin and cloves in a small glass container and set aside to infuse, at least 6 hours.

2 Strain the tincture through a sieve into a spouted measuring cup (for easy pouring) and discard the solids. Transfer to a cocktail mister and store in the refrigerator for up to 1 month.

TWO BLIND PIGS
QUICK & EASY COLA BITTERS

MAKES: ABOUT 2 CUPS

Fancy making your own bitters? This recipe, courtesy of bartender Justin Darnes and his Two Blind Pigs bar consultancy, can be made in as little as a day (if you go outside of the 12 Bottles and use a dark overproof rum). Even better, they're made from and taste like cola. We're fond of them in Whiskey Sours, but they work well in most drinks calling for aromatic bitters.

Some of the ingredients here may be unfamiliar to you (the kola nut and licorice root, for instance) but they are traditional in the making of bitters or soda. By their very nature, bitters are intended to be nonpotable and are used sparingly in drinks. If you are taking medication or have concerns about any of the ingredients, please consult a medical professional before consuming them.

Galangal is a rhizome, similar to ginger, and is available at Asian markets or online. Kola nut is a flavoring agent derived from a species of evergreen tree native to Africa; we purchase it in dried, powdered form. Quassia chips come from a tropical shrub and are used as a bittering agent in cocktail bitters. To source all of the above, we frequent the Monterey Bay Spice Company (see Resources, page 393).

- -

24 ounces cola, preferably sugar-based

1 teaspoon chopped dried galangal

½ vanilla pod, split lengthwise

Zest of ½ lime

Zest of ½ lemon

Zest of ½ orange

½ teaspoon powdered kola nut

½ teaspoon mace

½ teaspoon chopped dried licorice root

½ cinnamon stick

1-inch piece fresh ginger, peeled

8 whole cloves

About 1 cup amber rum (preferably navy-strength)

1 penny-size quassia chip

- -

1 Combine all of the ingredients except for the rum and the quassia in a 1-quart saucepan.

2 Bring the mixture to a simmer over medium-high heat and reduce the liquid to 1 cup.

3 Remove the saucepan from the heat and pour the contents into a 2-cup (or larger) measuring glass. Add to the syrup an equal volume of amber rum. Drop in the quassia chip.

4 Cover the mixture with plastic wrap and let sit at room temperature until the desired degree of bitterness has been reached, 3 to 4 days (if using navy-strength rum, let the mixture stand 24 hours).

5 Strain the mixture into an airtight container through a fine-mesh sieve, discarding the solids. The bitters will keep in the refrigerator, for 1 month or more.

RESOURCES

AMAZON.COM: Our first-stop shop for pretty much anything we need—both in terms of ingredients and equipment—especially because most other vendors sell through the site. If we fail at Amazon, then we branch out. This is definitely a good place to find cocktail books, both modern and historical, and also where we purchase sugar-based colas like Mexican Coke and Boylan, plus other esoteric ingredients and mixers, like Demerara sugar, food-grade citric acid, orange flower water, and rose water. They also have all sizes and shapes of glassware (including the syringes we use for the Corpse Reviver Shots on page 82), and pretty much all of the bar equipment we recommend.

COCKTAILKINGDOM.COM: Any barware you need, from mixing glasses to strainers to ice molds, can be found at this site. You can buy the Lewis Bag (see page 21) directly from them as well.

K & L WINE MERCHANTS (KLWINES.COM): We are lucky enough to have one of the best-curated fine liquor and wine shops around, right in Los Angeles. K & L sells every spirit we use here and can get you everything else you desire. And yes, they will ship to you (depending on the shipping laws of your state).

MONTEREY SPICE COMPANY (HERBCO.COM): If you start to become a bitters-making addict or decide to start creating numerous esoteric, old-time infusions and tinctures, this is the place to look for exotic herbs and spices. We bought our spices for Two Blind Pigs Quick & Easy Cola Bitters (page 390) here.

DRINKS BY THEME

Poker Night

Girls' Night

Brunch

Summer Barbecue/Pool Party

Halloween

Christmas / New Year's

DIY COCKTAIL BARS

These do-it-yourself bars allow you to sit back and let your friends be their own bartenders. And don't forget to let them practice their skills by mixing drinks for their host.

THE BUCK BAR

Few drinks are easier to self-serve than a Buck. Put out a card instructing guests to add ice to a collins glass, followed by their choice of spirit and ginger beer to fill the glass. Add a squeeze of half a lemon or lime (drop the shell into the glass), *et voilà!*

Setting up a Buck bar is simplicity itself:

- Lay out your spirits. (Any spirits. Really.) Plus 1½- and 2-ounce jiggers for measuring the liquor.
- Add a bowl each of limes and lemons with a sharp knife and hand-held citrus juicer (see Tools of the Trade, page 16) alongside.
- Keep the ginger beer nearby but chilled.
- If you're feeling fancy, include some sprigs of fresh mint.

THE BLOODY MARY BAR

Given the sociable nature of brunch, a Bloody Mary bar is a good way to encourage conviviality and break the ice. Depending on how comfortable you are with your guests mixing their own drinks—which means doling out their own alcohol—you can set up a user-friendly scenario with the juice bases, alcohol (vodka, gin, tequila, or others—see page 120), hot sauces from Tabasco to Sriracha, and toppings ready to mix (see below for suggestions). If you want to be in control of the booze, let guests add their own spices and toppings.

To set up a Bloody Mary bar:

- Offer various "Bloody" and one to two booze options: vodka or tequila in the Mary, or variations like a pineapple-mint

Green Snapper (page 118) or beet and carrot Montford Snapper (page 119).

- Offer a variety of toppings (feel free to use one or more!):

Bacon	Hard-boiled eggs
Beef jerky	Olives
Celery stalks (of course)	Pickle spears
Cherry tomatoes	Pickled veggies
Crab's claw	Radishes

THE CHAMPAGNE COCKTAIL BAR

Like a Bloody Mary bar (opposite), a Champagne bar encourages conversation and makes your guests feel special. Guests can easily mix up their own cocktails to taste using this basic rule of thumb: When adding juice or liqueur to a Champagne drink, aim for a ratio of 1 part juice or liqueur to 2 parts bubbly.

- For a budget-friendly Champagne cocktail bar, put out bottles of sparkling wine—don't invest in expensive Champagne in this instance, but grab a handful of sparkling wines (Prosecco, Cremant, Riesling). Avoid rosé, as the additional flavors will muddy the character of the cocktail.

- Set out orange juice, cranberry juice, even pineapple juice, or provide nectars like peach and passion fruit. Or let guests squeeze their own citrus like tangelos and tangerines (a handheld juicer is essential for this).

- Put out a bottle of homemade Blackberry Liqueur (page 383) for modified Kir Royales, or Limoncello (page 386) for an extra spike of citrus.

- For a classic Champagne Cocktail, set out a bowl of sugar cubes and bottles of aromatic and orange bitters. Add a little instruction card that says to add a sugar cube to the glass and douse the sugar in bitters, then top with bubbly.

RECIPE INDEX

T

V

W

Z

GARNISHES, SYRUPS & LIQUEURS

CONVERSION TABLES

Approximate Equivalents

1 cup granulated sugar = 8 oz = 220 g

1 cup (firmly packed) brown sugar =
   6 oz = 220 g to 230 g

1 cup confectioners' sugar =
   4½ oz = 115 g

1 cup honey or syrup = 12 oz

1 large egg = about 2 oz or about 3 tbs

1 egg yolk = about 1 tbs

1 egg white = about 2 tbs

Liquid Conversions

U.S.	IMPERIAL	METRIC
1 teaspoon	⅛ fluid ounce	4 ml
1 tablespoon or bar spoon	½ fluid ounce	15 ml
2 tablespoons	1 fluid ounce	30 ml
3 tablespoons	1½ fluid ounces	45 ml
¼ cup	2 fluid ounces	60 ml
⅓ cup	2½ fluid ounces	75 ml
½ cup	4 fluid ounces	125 ml
⅔ cup	5 fluid ounces	150 ml
¾ cup	6 fluid ounces	175 ml
1 cup	8 fluid ounces	250 ml
2 cups (1 pint)	16 fluid ounces	500 ml
1 quart	32 fluid ounces	0.95 liter

Weight Conversions

U.S./U.K.	METRIC
½ oz	15 g
1 oz	30 g
3½ oz	100 g

Number of Shots in a Bottle

SHOT SIZE	BOTTLE SIZE	NUMBER of SHOTS
1 oz	750 ml	25
1¼ oz	750 ml	20
1½ oz (U.S. standard)	750 ml	17
2 oz	750 ml	13
2½ oz	750 ml	10
1 oz	1 liter	34
1¼ oz	1 liter	27
1½ oz	1 liter	23
2 oz	1 liter	17
2½ oz	1 liter	14

Drink Calculator per Number of Guests at a Party

6 people	9–18 drinks
8 people	12–24 drinks
10 people	15–36 drinks
20 people	30–60 drinks
30 people	45–90 drinks

ABOUT THE AUTHORS

Dᴀᴠɪᴅ Sᴏʟᴍᴏɴsᴏɴ and Lᴇsʟᴇʏ Jᴀᴄᴏʙs Sᴏʟᴍᴏɴsᴏɴ are the husband-and-wife publishers of the popular blog 12bottlebar.com. Mr. Solmonson has written for both film and television, while Ms. Solmonson, spirits and wine writer for *L.A. Weekly*, is also the author of *Gin: A Global History* and the forthcoming *Liqueur: A Global History*. The Solmonsons live in Los Angeles.

ACKNOWLEDGMENTS

In writing this book, we turned again and again to countless food and drink professionals, all of whom—to a single man and woman—welcomed our questions and offered everything from tips and tales to recipes. We've said it many times, but we can't say it enough: This community is an incredibly generous lot and we are proud to be a part of it, in whatever small way.

When we considered the acknowledgments, we realized that the people we had reached out to were folks with whom we would want to have a drink. So herewith, as a gesture of our gratitude, we offer our contributors' responses to the question, "If you could share a drink with anyone at any time, who would it be, where, and what would you drink?"

• •

"The drink would be a big glass of absinthe with Oscar Wilde. No more, no less than that, though."—*Professor Ken Albala*

• •

"The drinking world is full of so many colorful characters. Vincent van Gogh painted a haunting portrait of a glass of absinthe, and on some level I'd relish the chance to share a well-louched glass of Delaware Phoenix's Meadows of Love with the painter. But I think Ernest Hemingway would have much better stories to tell, and I would love to have a daiquiri—a proper Papa Doble—with him at El Floridita."—*Daniel Berman*

• •

"It probably would be with Donn, at the original Don the Beachcomber in Hollywood in 1934. Why? Because that's like seeing the Big Bang in person."—*Martin Cate*

"Hunter S. Thompson. An incredible journalist, freethinker, and social commentator, but with an unbelievably chaotic side. I would love to meet him at his 7:05 p.m. slot for his only meal of the day and a couple of margaritas . . . as his brain gears up to try to understand journalism, the American dream, the world of politics, and life itself."—*John Clay*

"It would have to be Einstein, for a highly witty and educational chat over a cold, dry gin martini. In his lab, of course, where I could covet his equipment!"—*Tony Conigliaro*

"Stirling Moss. Champagne. May 1, 1955 (having won the Milie Miglia and setting the unbeaten, even to this day, time of ten hours, seven minutes, forty-eight seconds to complete one thousand miles on standard Italian roads). As a motorsport fanatic and a proud Englishman, this would be my dream drinking moment from history without a doubt."—*Justin Darnes*

"I'd like to be sitting with Samuel Clemens, Groucho Marx, Mae West, and W. C. Fields drinking Manhattans and listening to Louis Armstrong live while we place our bets on the Kentucky Derby." —*Dale DeGroff*

"I would have a Negroni with my son at my bar Neat, 100 years from today. [It] is a perfect long conversation starter and I could come back and check up on my work on both the bar and my son."—*Aidan Demarest*

"An El Presidente with Charles H. Baker Jr. at the Hotel Nacional in Havana, anytime in the late 1930s, because he was a man, and that is a country, with endlessly fascinating stories."—*Philip Duff*

"Sam Malone on September 30, 1982, at Cheers drinking a Gibson, so I could be a part of yelling 'NORM!!' for the first time. . . . And also to be a part of my first exposure to the bar world."
—*Trevor Easter*

• •

"As it's just one drink, it's got to be Monica Bellucci. Anytime in the last thirty years, please. I don't think I need to give my reasoning."—*Adam Elmegirab*

• •

"I'd like to make my father an Old Fashioned and sit at my bar with him to fill him in on my life as a bartender. He passed away in 1999, so he missed my transformation into taking this job seriously as a career."—*H. Joseph Erhmann*

• •

"Nelson Mandela at sunset somewhere outside . . . sipping a glass of Angelica Cellars—slowly. Because when Mandela was released from prison, it moved me in a way that I can't describe."—*Susan Feniger*

• •

"A dram of his favorite Johnnie Walker Black with Christopher Hitchens sometime before he died too soon in 2011. He's one of the writers I admire most and I missed the opportunity to have a conversation with him the one time we crossed paths at a bar in DC."—*Jacob Grier*

• •

"Charles Bukowski. Growing up in the bar business (Grandpa, Dad, now me), I think his relationship with alcohol was complex but probably the closest I ever saw to real life. We would most likely drink some cheap whiskey and port wine."—*Giuseppe Gonzalez*

• •

"I'll say Chas Baker Jr.—solo. We'll talk and drink. We'll discuss cocktails, the world, art, and women. Then we'll go partying with Errol Flynn, Ernest Gantt, and Papa. We'll use some liberal largesse and lure FDR to join us. We'll all be living large and, trust me, a 12 bottle bar will suit us just fine!"—*Ted Haigh*

"A bender with Raymond Chandler would be something to write home about."—*Daniel Handler*

• •

"[I'd] spend my time drinking my favorite tipple (Beefeater or Plymouth Martinis, mixed to how my mood at the time suits), with good friends from the present who I get precious little time to see but who are always there. And in comfortable familiar surroundings, whether that be at home or in any of a number of bars that I feel very at home in."—*Sebastian Hamilton-Mudge*

• •

"The great hero in Irish history, Michael Collins. He had the thinking of goodness and kindness for the poor and the underprivileged, and established our Republic of Ireland."
—*Denis Heffernan*

• •

"I'd have to choose a shot of Jack Daniels with '80s-era David Lee Roth. That guy was an animal."—*Dan Long*

• •

"As a bartender, the drink I would like to have is a Ramos Gin Fizz with Henry Ramos. No one has ever tasted a real Ramos Gin Fizz in modern times. I don't think any of us have managed to replicate it. I'd like to talk the fine points of the Ramos Gin Fizz."—*Chris McMillian*

• •

"I would love to have a Sazerac with Henry Miller in Paris during his heyday writing years."—*David Myers*

• •

"I'd like to bend elbows with Jesus, I think. We'd probably drink high-end Rob Roys or some other sophisticated cocktail that wasn't around when he was here last. I'd love to get his take on what went down with his message after he returned to spirit. We'd be drinking in some dive bar on the Bowery, no doubt. He'd insist on picking up the tab. I'm pretty sure about that."—*gaz regan*

"I would totally hang out with Willy Wonka, drinking beer at Woodstock."—*Naomi Schimek*

••

"Hunter S. Thompson, my good mate Craig Harper, Kevin Smith, and the original lineup of The Runaways drinking beer and whiskey (Scotch) at a bar that's a mix of Kadie's Club Pecos (*Sin City*), Bob's Country Bunker (*The Blues Brothers*), and Moe's Tavern (*The Simpsons*). Why? Because drinking should be fun!"—*Jason Scott*

••

"I'd love to go back in time and hoist a glass of Jane Austen's spruce beer with her. Why? It's Jane Austen, and she made beer from spruce trees! Who wouldn't want to get in on that?"—*Amy Stewart*

••

"A Ramos Gin Fizz, with Henry C. Ramos himself, in 1888, when the drink was invented at the Imperial Cabinet saloon in New Orleans. It would be amazing just to sit down with him and talk to him about what his feelings were on cocktails."—*Joseph Joaquin Valdovinos*

••

"Ernesto Che Guevara. I have long been fascinated with his level of conviction. It would be interesting to bring him up to speed on world affairs over an aged-rum mojito—the flavors would pair well with the cigar he would inevitably be enjoying."—*Charlotte Voisey*

••

"I would have a drink with Ovid, the Roman poet, because he was about the wittiest so-and-so who ever spit an olive pit. He could call the place, the time, and the drinks. I'd rather drink ditchwater with him at the dreary village on the Black Sea where he spent his exile than any exquisite in gilded surroundings with just about anyone else."—*David Wondrich*

And to those of you whose sentiments we never managed to collect, we must also raise a glass: Jamie Boudreau, Adam Carolla, Lydia Chao, the City Tavern, Mike Gabriel, Marcy and Megan Gonzalez, Tim Kilcoyne, Alex Kratena, Michael Lomonaco, Jacco Maccacco, Dre Masso, Mary Sue Milliken, Mike Nelson, Amanda Palmer, F. Paul

Pacult, Sasha Petraske, Anna Post, Todd Robbins, Deanna Sydney, and Tait Family Farms. Apologies if for some unforgiveable reason, we forgot anyone.

To our tireless team at Workman, for believing in what we believe in, and making it a reality.

To our friends and family, whose arms we never twisted to taste drink after drink.

And to our little guy, because this book has taken up more than half of his life. We look forward to his proposed sequel *The 100 Bottle Bar*—and we hope we're allowed to contribute.

To conclude with Bear-Fighting.